2/5/17

When Sleeping Women Awake, Mountains Will Move

by Barbara de Souza

To my Dear "Best" Friend with all my Love and gratitude for our wonderful time together – helping me reintegrate to the U.S.A., For helping me learn the Southern way of living. I am so Grateful

I Love you

B

LUCAS PARK BOOKS

ST. LOUIS, MISSOURI

ISBN: 9781603500630

Published by Lucas Park books
www.lucasparkbooks.com

Printed in the United States of America

Contents

Dedications

In the many times that I returned to the U.S. during my 40 years in Brazil to visit or on itineration, I was told over and over that I should write a book of all the many stories I told or preached.

"Wait till I retire," I would say. Then at eighty-one, my husband and I returned to the States, but my heart was not here; it remained in Brazil. And so the return was painful.

I thought perhaps I could relive it by putting it down on paper, starting with the year I arrived in Brazil, 1967. And I also thought it would be a way for my children, grandchildren and even great-grandchildren to know why I was so far away from them for so long. So it was for them that I was putting down my memories, as well as for myself, so that as time went on I would never forget my wonderful experiences with these magnificent women.

So amidst tears and smiles, I began. Then my daughter Judy gave me the name of an editor, Taylor Sisk, she had read about in the newspaper. So Taylor and I began emailing, discussing the theme of the book reflected in the title. After several weeks of this, he wrote me that he was beginning to suspect that I thought he was a woman – the name "Taylor" being both a man's and a woman's name – but that, in fact, he was a man. I immediately said that this arrangement wouldn't work, that my book was about women. But he said that having learned more about the book, he was very interested and would like to meet in person. So I told him to come visit and that if I felt it wouldn't work, I would tell him. Well, it did work. We hit it off right away. I owe much to his patience, for I am not a writer, just a storyteller.

As I wrote, I was flooded with memories – memories of the wonderful women I'd had the privilege of knowing and whose empowerment I'd witnessed. Their victories became my victories, and I only wish there were pages enough to tell all their stories, each one adding to my story. I watched them change, and with their changes I too changed. I too was empowered.

I dedicate this book first to my children and grandchildren, from whom I was absent for so many years: my daughters, Carol Ackley, Susan Lukens and Judy Brown; and my grandchildren, Jamie and Tyler Brown; and Clinton, Ashley and Walker Lukens. Though my parents, Ruth and George Mosley, died while I was still in Brazil, they did visit me there, and I always knew that they understood my work and were proud of me, and they were always encouraging.

And, of course, there is my husband, Agostinho (Gus) de Souza, my partner, co-worker, the shoulder on which I cried and with whom I jumped with joy in our victories, who was at my side watching tragedies and conquests, births and deaths. We celebrated together at victories and cried together at losses, such as funerals, even of our many pets.

I dedicate it to my mission partner, Sue Christopher, my dearest friend, supporter and work partner all these years, helping to make our ministry possible. Without her, we would never have accomplished all we did.

I also dedicate this book to the Rev. Richard Hoblin, pastor of the First Congregational Church in River Falls during my time there, 1981 to 1985, who is responsible for so many of my victories in my work in Brazil, as well as for leading me to my ordination. Without his presence in my life, I might never have succeeded in the work I went back to Brazil to finish.

I dedicate it to the late Rev. Mitchell Whiterabbit, the seminary professor who was with me all the way as I pastored the Winnebago United Church of Christ in Black River Falls, Wisconsin, as a summer internship for my seminary studies; and the Rev. David Savides, the association minister of the Northwest Association of the United Church of Christ, who led me through the ordination process and encouraged me to turn in my ordination paper even though it was so different from the others.

I dedicate this book to the Revs. Delbert Permann, United Church of Christ, and Donald Stannard, United Methodist, who were my advisors while in United Theological Seminary, listening to me, encouraging me and advising me, which I so often needed.

I dedicate it to the Rev. Chris Myers, present pastor of the First Congregational Church, United Church of Christ, the church where I was ordained. He, after becoming pastor of my home church in River Falls, Wisconsin, came to visit us in 2007, his church's missionaries, in Brazil and has been very supportive of our ministry and our donor account, the Brazilian Fund.

Also to the Revs. David Vargas and Felix Ortiz, former executive directors of the Latin American and Caribbean regions of the Global Ministries, the Disciples of Christ and the United Church of Christ, who guided me and supported me through good times and difficult times. Rev. Vargas met me in Brazil in the late eighties and fully embraced my mission and was responsible for my becoming a missionary for the Global Ministries. He became my friend and advisor. And it was appropriate that he accepted for me my United Church of Christ, Women in Ministry, Antoinette Brown Award in 1997, as I couldn't leave the mission field at that time.

I dedicate it to Prof. William Romoser, who welcomed me into my campus ministry job and supported me as I tried to live up to this position, which I knew nothing about. He became a cherished fan, always boosting my morale.

I also dedicate this book to Sabino and Teresa Camargo and Ana Maria and Letacio Jansen, my close Brazilian friends and English students, who, listening to my experiences, always told me I should write a book.

I dedicate this book to the hundreds of church donors and others to our mission clinic and education ministry. Without them we could not have built the clinic and supported it.

And last, but far from least, I dedicate this book to all the women with whom I have lived and worked, as well as the many others I've had the privilege of knowing, so very many of them not in this book, as it was impossible to tell all their stories. They all have enriched my life over these forty years and were my teachers, teaching me about love, dedication, determination and persistence.

In Honor

I write this book in honor of Dom Helder Camara, Catholic Archbishop of Recife, bishop of the poor, an advocate of liberation theology, nominated four times for the Noble Peace Prize and in 1975 awarded the Pacem im Terris, whose quotes I carry with me in my heart:

"Like my brother Martin Luther King, I have a dream.... When one person dreams alone, it is only a dream. When we dream together, it is the beginning of reality."

"When I give food to the poor, they call me a saint. When I ask why they are poor, they call me a communist."

In Milwaukee, when he spoke at an ecumenical conference in 1984: "As long as one child goes to bed hungry, there will be no peace."

At that conference, when a Protestant minister pointed out that she was among many Protestant women in the audience who had been ordained and yet the Catholic Church denied women that position, he answered, smiling, that his grandmother taught him that though men might be the head of the house, the women were the neck. And with that, he put his hands around his neck and moved it around, bringing the women to their feet.

To this tiny giant who held my hand and blessed me, I offer this book in memory. He is no longer among us, but he too said I should put my experiences in a book. Yes, we two liberation theologians had much in common.

And I write this book in honor of all the magnificent women portrayed in it, as well as the so very many whose names and stories are not mentioned. There are so many women not mentioned in this book, remarkable women who walked into my life: nuns, pastors, visitors, plus so many students and co-workers, the women who became leaders of their communities as they moved about their simple but difficult lives, all of them leaving their marks on my heart, my life, my theology and who I am today. There would be no way to include them all, but I can see them, can hear them. Surely they awakened me so that I could move some mountains. They truly embody the title, an ancient Chinese proverb, "When sleeping women awake, mountains will move."

Resurrection Poem

A seed planted that continues to give life,
contagious to those bodies which are thirsty for
    justice.
The resurrection of bodies ...
The resurrection of the bodies of women
who can begin to speak the things they could not;
and turn into words what they should not;
and walk where they were once prohibited;
to scream when they are told to be quiet;
to get up when they should remain seated;
to organize themselves when they should be
    submissive;
to hope for the new things when they are taught to
    repeat the old.

The Resurrection of women's bodies
is for all a sign of liberty,
breaking forth in all places
and giving birth to the divine in humanity.

        – Sister Ivone Gebara, Catholic theologian and
                author and my dear friend

Prologue

In 1967, at the age of thirty-seven, I left my happy small-town life and went with my three daughters to Brazil, where my husband, Jim Ackley, was hired for an executive job with a multinational company. And my life was forever changed.

I came from a very comfortable middle-class family. My father was an advertising executive; my mother, a stay-at-home mom. My parents were very liberal and open in their opinions and thoughts, especially, as I look back, for that period in time. My mother was a Southerner and my father a Northerner. My father was a people person, my mother more of a homebody, perhaps because she didn't drive and we lived some distance from town.

One thing that stands out in my memory was their concern for equality and justice for people. My parents' friends and my own were from all types of ethnic and religious groups, and our home was always open. They were also supportive of our lives when we became adults and went out on our own.

I met my second husband, Agostinho de Souza, known as Gus, in Brazil, and it is with and through him that I began to learn about Brazil's poor, life in the favelas and the injustice that this class system produced.

As you'll hear me say several times in the course of this book, I never imagined that this simple health educator course would have the impact it did. Thinking back now, it's hard to describe what I was seeing with these women. When a course would begin, 90 percent of the women knew nothing about health, disease prevention or causes. Some were so shy, I could hardly get a word out of them. Few had the self-esteem to imagine what they could do.

As time went on, and TV became more accessible to the poor, the world was opened up and women saw more. But still their hands were often tied, and only in church programs did they have the freedom to learn and discuss. That's why most of the courses were conducted through church groups, within churches, as this made it acceptable to their husbands.

As the courses proceeded, it was amazing to me to see the creativeness the women used in displaying what they were learning, their self-esteem growing to the point that a previously shy woman could get up and show a poster she'd made or act out a scene about a health issue. I watched as the women came to know one another, working in group assignments and sharing their lives, comparing and comforting.

What they learned was, to my mind, almost theological – that their bodies are their own, and that they too are allowed to enjoy sex.

Naturally, this would have an effect on their marriages, some for the better; in some cases, it meant a rethinking of the marriage.

By way of introduction, I would like to tell you a story that's a compilation of stories that I heard from the many women I came in contact with throughout my life in Brazil.

****

My name is Rosiete Maria Silva, and I'm now 28 years of age. I want to tell you something of my life as a representation of all the poor and oppressed women of my country, Brazil. Perhaps knowing my story will help the world to understand the injustice that women suffer; perhaps my story will touch hearts and my daughters and all the little ones like them will be freed from slavery of female oppression. It is a painful story; be thankful that is not yours or your daughter's or your granddaughter's. It's a painful story, but it's true.

I was born in a mud hut in the rural part of the northeast of Brazil, Alagoas. I was the ninth child, only four of which had survived the first few years of life. My father was a dirt farmer. An absent landlord owned our land; my father had seen him but once in his 18 years on the land. This landlord sent a representative out to the farm monthly to collect payment for the use of the land. My father had probably only seen cash in the hands of others in the closest city to us when he went to trade some of our crops, or handmade articles, for the things we needed for survival. We had no money. All rent was paid in crops, food from our mouths.

Mother made all our clothes and we struggled to produce the foods we needed: pork, chickens, eggs and vegetables. We rarely ate meat; it was our most valuable item for trade in the city. We had a cow, and thus milk, a very precious commodity.

But there had been the bad years, when that was all we had. There had been the years of floods or droughts when if it hadn't been for that cow fewer of us would have survived. Those years, there was little for us to eat, let alone to make payments for the land. How I remember those days. While my mother wailed, the man took away the few chickens or a pig. She knew then that perhaps there would now be no meat or eggs for perhaps a year. We had only beans and one cow.

But then there was that terrible year. It hadn't rained for more than six months and my father had lost all his crops. Then that man had come and taken away what little we had left. We were down to nothing, really nothing!

When the man came that fateful day – oh, I'll never forget that day. He told my father that he would have to take the cow. Mother screamed and wept and we children, seeing all this and sensing the drama, began to cry as well. It was a wailing! Mother threw herself upon the man, crying for the life of her children; there were now seven of us. The man pushed her aside, and when it looked like my father would attack, he pulled a gun and shot at my father's feet.

What crying went on that day. But then there was always sadness about us. Even in our moments of laughter, tears were just under the surface.

I remember the day we packed up and went to the next farm, about an hour away. It was the first time some of us had been that far away from home. We girls could never be taken into town; that would be too risky. Some might want us for servants, my mother said, or worse.

When we arrived at the next farm after the hot dusty trip, at first no one even came out to meet us. Then a man came out of the hut, his head bowed, and called my father, who then beckoned to my mother. She went into the house, and when she came out two other women came out with her. Then children followed, all crying.

There followed a lot of bustling and scurrying; fires were started and water taken from the rain barrels behind the house. The way they were throwing the water around, I knew it was serious, for water was too precious to be wasted like that.

I heard my mother say, "She'll never make it; she's lost too much blood." Then she shook her head, "Ah, if only there were someone to help."

Well, I was to learn later in life that what she was talking about was a doctor or a hospital or some medicine, things we all knew little of.

Soon we heard a baby cry and then wailing and screaming, voices singing in the most painful way. We knew. We were used to that sound. Another life had come quickly into the world and just as quickly had left it. Or so we believed. It had happened many times in our own house. We knew the routine. In an hour or two, everything would be back to normal and the family would scatter, each to his or her own chore for the burial. People within a short distance would be told and food – what little could be spared – would be prepared for the funeral, and, well, it was almost exciting in a way. We would see other people. We girls would be kept busy and, if not, hidden. But at least from a distance we could watch.

Mama said there were some families who just went out and buried their babies without all that fuss, but that it was a sin. "God has given and God has taken away," she said, "and this needs to be acknowledged."

I used to wonder why God would do that – I mean, allow a woman to have all that pain, like I'd seen Mama have, and then take the cause of that pain away. If God were going to take the baby, why should the mother go through all that?

But Mama told me that was sinful thinking. I should not question God. Then I thought of all that food that the other families brought with them – families who, like us, had just barely enough to feed their own, perhaps only one meal a day. Why was it important to make this sacrifice for a dead baby?

But suddenly, my thoughts were interrupted; things seemed different. No one came wailing out of the house and no one was setting off on horseback or in an ox cart to warn others of the coming funeral. In fact, I heard a baby crying again. It couldn't be. No, it couldn't! Then my mother and another woman came out of the house crying and throwing up their arms. "She's dead! My God, she's dead! What will Senhor Pedro do now. And the other children! And the baby! Oh! God!" The wailing went on.

The worst had happened. I knew that now. The mother had died. And so the baby was probably lost too, as there would be no milk unless one of these other women had milk to spare, and even this would be denied if the nursing mother's baby was too thin.

But then I was told that this family had two cows, so maybe this baby could live, if the milk sickness didn't kill it or all those other things, like weed death, vomiting, diarrhea or the pig sickness. We lost babies from all to these causes.

But I could still hear that baby crying, and no one had even mentioned what sex it was. If it were a girl, it would be better off dead, for herself and the family. Girls were more of a problem, a burden, especially if there were more than two already in the family. If it were a boy, well, he would be another hand on the farm one day, if he survived childhood, and that in itself was a trick. Without the mother, it would nearly take a miracle.

Well, now my story may seem unbelievable to you, but it's the truth. The baby survived, but each day was more and more of a struggle. Life for this family, for all of us, was day-to-day survival. Then the fever hit the area and even adults were dying. Someone called in a priest, and this was surely a sign that it was a real disaster. Priests never came out to us, except maybe every two or three years to marry and baptize when they'd heard that many of us were living in a sinful state. If the priest was being called, somebody knew we were in trouble.

But, I wondered, was it we as people whom the priest came to save, or our souls? Medicine, which we needed, was nonexistent. We had no money anyway, just our crops for trade by the sweat of our brows.

****

Then it happened. Senhor Pedro walked into our hut one day and took our mother away, and I was thrust into womanhood. I became the mother for my family – my sister and I did. Childhood ended for us that day – if you could call what we'd had childhood.

Now you're wondering what could have happened. I hesitate to tell you for fear that you won't believe me: My mother was traded for a cow!

Let me explain. The family of Senhor Pedro was dying without a mother; the oldest girl had been taken with the fever and the next oldest were boys. The baby was weakening every day and there were farm chores to be done if any of the family were to survive. Senhor

Pedro knew that we'd lost our cow and that we had too many children and a new baby too, and not enough to feed them. Having no milk was taking a toll on all of us and might mean death to the younger ones. So my father needed a cow more than he needed a woman and more children. Senhor Pedro's family needed a mother. It was a matter of survival, my mother told me, as she bid us goodbye.

"And it's not as if I will never see you again," she told us. "It may only be temporary, and you can come to visit me when you're not busy. Your brothers can bring you."

Yes, believe it or not, in minutes we'd lost our mother, and had become women, my younger sister and me. In additional to our regular chores, we had become cooks, seamstresses, weavers and more for a house of eight.

I was only eight or nine years old.

****

I'm going to skip the next few years of my life. They were too sad and painful. We did see our mother, but only two or three times a year. We were all too busy; there was no end to the day. I was glad Mama had taken the baby with her.

We had a year of drought. My youngest brother died and my sister, my helper, fell out of a tree and broke her arm. It took months to mend, and during that time the burden of the work fell completely on me. Her arm mended, but in spite of all my father did to avoid deformation, it was crooked. She was then limited in what she could do to help with chores. There was no laughter, only hunger and work, work, work.

Then, suddenly, just as our mother had left us, I too was taken away. It all happened like this.

One day we saw a lot of dust in the distance and heard the sound of horses. This was rare in our area because almost all our neighbors had sold most of their valuable stock and few had horses or oxen anymore. But it was an ox cart, coming right to our front door. It was a big one, and my father was in it.

I wiped my hands and forehead and went to the front of the house. I was alarmed. What did this mean? How did my father get into this cart? I thought he was out in the fields or had gone to the city, walking many hours, to see what he could trade.

A tall man, a gentleman my father's age, I guessed, climbed out of the cart, looking hot and uncomfortable, as if he were not in the right place. My father gruffly called me to him. I heard him say, "She's strong, a good worker and never complains. I'm sorry that she doesn't know how to read and write, but, well, you know, sir, there are no schools around here, and," he paused, bowed his head and shuffled his feet, "what is a poor farmer like me to do with too many girls?"

The man looked me over from head to toe, touched my arms and said, "Well, she's quite small and she's a bit too pretty. But what I would really like to know is, is she clean? You know, I mean about her body. My wife will see that she learns how to work around the house but will expect her to take care of herself, to be neat and clean in appearance. If she works well and fast, she might even teach her to read and write a little. Though, in my estimation, that would do nothing but get a girl like her into trouble."

My father nodded his head. "All I want is to know that she is no trouble to you, sir. And whatever you can do for her, I hope she will be deserving. I mean, I know she won't be deserving, but I hope her work will be to your liking."

Then my father bowed his head and mumbled, "And how will the money get to us?"

I couldn't believe it. I felt like I was being sold! I was to hear of other stories like mine in the years to come. I later learned that other families had been forced to sell their young girls as maids to the rich families in the nearest cities so that they might feed the rest at home. Baby girls were sold. Sometimes it was to pay the rent for the land and sometimes cash was exchanged. Then there were others, like me, who would work and each month the poor family would receive cash in return for this endless child labor, twelve and fourteen hours of work a day.

But I didn't know any of this yet. In the next dazed minutes, I collected all I had: two old dresses and a kerchief. Then I was bouncing my way in an ox cart – to where, I didn't know. I didn't know if I would ever see my family again. I don't know for sure how old I was. We were never able to keep track. But I know that I hadn't become a woman yet; I hadn't seen the blood of womanhood yet.

Yes, I worked, and I earned my money, which I never saw. I never learned to read and write. I lived in a cubbyhole, smaller than most bathrooms, with no window. When it was hot, I felt that death might be better. It was worse than sharing that hammock with my sisters in our hot mud-and-wood hut. I lived in an apartment building, so I seldom

xvii

felt the earth under my feet. I no longer felt the comfort of my swaying hammock; I slept on a board. I was seldom spoken to except to be given orders.

In the beginning, I was allowed to make mistakes. But after a while, I was just yelled at and sometimes pushed around or slapped. I overheard the man tell his wife not to let me on the streets to shop or to walk with their children because I was too dumb and too pretty. Me, pretty? I had never seen myself in a full-length mirror, so how could I know what this meant? And dumb? How could they know if I was dumb; they'd never really spoken to me, let alone listened to me.

****

I became a woman. I sensed my body filling out and one day I stopped to look secretly in the mirror in the wife's room, for now I was tall enough. No, I wasn't ugly, at least not like I'd thought I must be, even after what I'd heard the man say to my father. I wasn't beautiful, at least not like the wife in all her lovely clothes. But I was not ugly!

More years passed, nothing new, just more work. After a time, I didn't know if my father got his money or if he'd lost tract of me, for it seemed like we moved so often. If he had continued to come, I'll never know, because I never saw him again and I was too shy to ask.

When I was about fourteen or fifteen, we moved days and days away to the big city of Rio de Janeiro. There I found freedom and captivity. I found freedom from one form of slavery and became captive to another, captive to another form of oppression. I became more of a nothing than I had been. I joined the life of the living dead.

As I was older now and the family for whom I worked was new to the city, I was given responsibility for the children while they trained another maid, who they paid, to do the household chores. As they became more involved in the life of the city, I was more frequently left on my own. The new maid cared little about what I did as long as I kept the children out of her hair.

So I would take them to the city square. I sat on the benches day after day while the children played. At first I talked to no one; I was too afraid. But after a while, I met other maids – babas, as I learned they were called. I also learned a lot about life from these other young women. And I met a young man. He was working in the gardens in the square. He tried to talk to me, but I was too shy. The other maids encouraged me and joked with me about this man's attraction to me.

xviii

After a few weeks, I got over my shyness and we began to talk. He listened when I shared a bit about myself and my life; he told me that I was a slave, that I should run away, that I had a right to make my own decisions and have a life of my own. But where could I go? He soon had an answer for that too. He said he would take care of me. He said I was beautiful and that he wanted me to stay with him; he planned it all. He held my hand and told me not to worry, that now I would be free.

So one night, I snuck out of the apartment and he was waiting for me. He took me to a small room – a kitchenette, he called it. It was not much bigger than my room had been. It was to be our living room, kitchen and bedroom, all in one, almost like back on the family farm. He kept me there for weeks. He brought food, and at first he was so nice to me; he even sometimes brought me clothes and favors. But he had his pleasures with me too. He used me and abused me.

Soon I knew that something was wrong with me. Though I knew nothing about my body functions, I knew that I was going to have a baby, this man's baby. I didn't say anything to him; I was too afraid. But he noticed it too after a while and began staying away for days and days. At my insistence, he gave me the key to the apartment, and for the first time in my life I was truly free.

As I got heavier and heavier, he disappeared for weeks, saying he had a job elsewhere. Finally, he stopped coming at all. I was glad that he was gone, but the food was running out and the lady down the hall who collected the rent kept asking me when he was coming back to pay. She soon knew, as I did, that he was never coming back. But she was a kind woman, a mother and grandmother, and she felt sorry for me in my condition. She would ask how I was and if I needed anything. She brought me fruits and scraps from her table.

Then the time came. I felt the pain coming on. I was scared, but I had seen Mama do what needed to be done many times, so I knew what to expect. But no one can explain the pain of another, the agony of being alone in pain. I had gathered cloth out of garbage heaps. I had even begged for money. What a disgrace that had been, but it had allowed me to buy some of the things I thought I might need when the hour of the birth came; the things I'd seen my mother use.

The hour was coming. The pain was getting worse and worse and I could hardly hold my breath, but I was afraid to scream out. The water was boiling, the pieces of cloth folded into diapers were ready, the cloth for the delivery was sterilized. I was so scared and so alone. I knew about women bleeding to death. What if I died like the other mothers of my childhood? What if I died and the baby lived? What if the baby wasn't "quite right," as Mama used to call those sick and weakling ones? Could I let it die, as so many had?

"Oh, my God," I cried out. "Where are you, God? I can't stand it! Mother; oh, Mother! Oh, God!"

Then, suddenly, it was all over, and a little wiggly thing was at my side. I wanted to hold it, but I was too weak and there was more pain. It seemed like so long before I could tend to it. I cleaned it up, washed all around me and lay down exhausted to finally look at this new being at my side that I had brought into the world.

Another girl, like me. How sad! A wave of pity overtook me, a pain and anguish that I haven't the words to explain. A girl! Why was I so sad? What had women done to deserve what I had known of life? I was so tired. Where was I going to find clothes for this little thing and food for myself, and, "Oh, God, if you exist, help me!" Then blessed forgetfulness came to me in sleep.

****

I'll spare you the details of sleeping in alleys and under bridges; of the horror and humiliation of begging for a crust of bread, washing one's few clothes in sewer pipes in the streets, bathing in rain water; of abdominal pains, cramping and weakness, the pain of hunger and abandonment; and of death.

One morning when I woke up under a bridge where I had spent several days, my baby was dead. She was about eight weeks old. There were no tears, only a sense of relief. Do you think that is a sin? What could I give her? How long could I have watched her cry with hunger and exposure, with the pain of diarrhea and the heat, the terrible heat, and no water to relieve it?

What did life have in store for her? To be like me? No! A worthless, miserable creature like myself, to raise another like me? God forbid! Or is there any God to forbid, to love or care?

Now I was free, free to find work. Without a baby, I was free to get a job. I could find a way to earn money and go back home. But where was that? I didn't even know the name of the city I'd come from. I had left there before I was educated in the names of things and places. I didn't even know how to read bus signs. And worst of all, I didn't know my father's full name or our address. I was a grown woman, a mother; I had given birth and buried my dead by the age of sixteen or seventeen, but I didn't know where I'd come from. I know it seems strange, but that's the way it was.

I found a job. In the next three years or so, I had several. I was underpaid and mistreated in all of them. But that first money that I earned was the most precious. I thought it was my ticket to independence. I thought so for about three or four days, and then it was gone for necessities. I never saved one cent, and except for the uniforms that some of my employers gave me, I never had anything to show for my work. I worked sometimes twelve hours a day too. I was often not well, weak and hungry. And when I fainted or couldn't get all the work done, I was fired.

I had several boyfriends; really, too many. They told me I was beautiful. I would look in my tiny mirror and ask, as I had asked before, what does beautiful mean? But I needed those men in my life. They gave me some respite from my otherwise dull and overworked life. They took me on rides to places I'd never seen. They taught me how to get around the city, to read bus signs and a few other words. All of this made me feel that I had found freedom. I could now come and go as I pleased. I could take bus rids on my day off and sit for hours on the beaches and dream about life. These days became my days of freedom and brought some happiness to my life.

These men also brought me food and sometimes gifts and nice clothes. I'm not going to try to fool you: These things weren't free. I paid for them. I learned that being pretty wasn't such a good thing; that these expressions of beauty, these gifts, came with a cost. I learned that one paid for all good things, and the payment was not always pleasant. I had to give myself in what they called "love." I thought I knew what this word meant, though I had never heard my mother speak about it this way. In fact, Mama hadn't had a whole lot of time to speak about anything.

But if this was love, I didn't understand it. I got pregnant several times. But as soon as I began to show, the men disappeared. I lost two babies in the very early stages. I was more than relieved because

I knew I would be fired as soon as the pregnancy showed. I was fired from one job when I showed my condition. That baby was born dead in an abandoned shack; a boy.

But then there was little Paulo. When I became pregnant with him, I was sure I would be fired. But no; in fact, to my surprise, the family I worked for even treated me better. I got better food and clothing. For the first time, I was taken to a doctor. After several visits, I was told that when the time came a woman would come to assist me with the birth. I couldn't believe it!

My beautiful baby boy was born comfortably and with warm clothes to greet him. He was washed clean. For the first time, there was cleanliness all around me. I felt so good. My baby was so beautiful and fat – and a boy! Oh, how I thanked God. The next months were such joyous ones. I worked little. I spent my time with Paulo, happily nursing him. My life was a luxury, even the cracker-box room I lived in now was clean and full of lovely things. This was beyond my wildest dreams.

As that first year ended, I was encouraged to wean Paulo, and he began to spend more and more time with my employer's family, in the part of the house that even in my favored days I wasn't invited to enter unless it was time to clean or serve.

****

Then one day, as I was singing in the kitchen, doing my chores, my world came crashing down. As had so often been the case, it was the result of the decisions of others that I was powerless to change. Once again, in seconds, I lost everything. The lady of the house told me that she would no longer need my services, that her old maid from years before had returned and wanted her job back. There wasn't enough room for me, she told me.

"But where can I go to work with a small child" I asked. All feeling had gone out of me and I had to hold onto the counter to keep from falling.

"No one hires a maid with a child, and I have no money. I'll be on the streets again. I can't do that to Paulo after all he's had here."

I was crying now. I was imploring. I knew I should never be doing this in front of a woman who was worlds away from me. What could she understand of an insignificant life like mine?

"Oh, I know," she said, "but we'll keep little Paulo until your life gets better. We love him and we'll treat him just like our own, and you can come and see him whenever you like."

When I walked out the door that next day with kerchief and bag in hand to look for a job, I knew in my heart I had lost my son. It was more horrible than I can describe; in this small child, lay all the happiness I had ever known. In him, lay the meaning of the word "love." Through him, I learned what love was.

I visited him on my days off, twice a month. At first, he recognized me, held out his little hands to me crying and then laughing in joy. But as time went on, he was less and less happy to see me, until it finally came to the point of his indifference.

When he was sick, they nursed him through it. They gave him so much. Then he became very ill. They called and told me that he was so sick he would have to be hospitalized, and that to check him in they needed a birth certificate. I didn't have the money for a late birth registration, nor did I have a birth certificate of my own. I realized that day that I didn't even exist.

They registered little Paulo in their name and my nonexistence was confirmed on his birth certificate; my non-importance was validated. I had been born, lived – or, rather, survived – given birth, lost and given birth again and again until finally I had a son, my own living flesh, yet I was not alive; I did not exist.

But I should be grateful to these people. They had taken my child; my burden had become their joy. They had given him a better life and a chance. They had made a child exist from a nonexistent mother. They had freed him from oppression, the oppression of nonexistence. They had given him life; they had given him his birth. I should be grateful for their kindness, shouldn't I? And they freed me, freed me to captivity again, the captivity of oppression, slavery, of nonexistence. I, Rosiete Maria da Silva, a non-being at almost twenty, am, I believe, a captive.

Why do I write this story? How does this story concern you? How can you free me? How can you bring freedom to me and other women like me?

I can't answer that. It's too difficult and complicated. I don't want readers to feel guilty. I don't tell this story to make you cry. But I want you to remember. Only by our remembering that I do exist, I and others like me, can I really exist, can I move from nonexistence to existence, from captivity to freedom. Be aware that my story is not so different from that of thousands of other women in the world, maybe some even closer to you than you think, but most especially in what is called the third world. You can be aware of the fact that the way you live, spend your money, choose your priorities and vote affects me and others like me, affects our future, our education, our value and opportunities. We can't do it alone. We need to be helped to understand our value; we need to acquire the self-esteem to move forward. We need education, and only you can give us this ticket to self-esteem and freedom from oppression.

First, just love me, and not judge me, especially by your standards, by your rules, by your way of life. Just accept me the way I am and reach out to those like me. You can release me from captivity and from nonexistence. You can help to bring freedom to oppressed women like me in the world. You can make it possible for us to have the education needed to rise above all that I have suffered. Just by reading this, you have made me exist!

Our Introduction to the Favela

It was 1967, I was living in Rio de Janeiro and, being a very active person, I wanted something to do. I had a maid – something I wasn't used to. Her name was Rosa, a good Catholic woman, and she would see me crying and being generally unhappy. One day, she said, "Why don't you go see the priest at my church? He might be able to help you."

Rose said that the priest spoke English, but he didn't; not at all. He spoke Italian. But somehow, with my little Portuguese, we communicated, and he said, "Oh, we have a lady from the church here that visits in the favela, the one right here above your house." He said I should go with this woman, Dona Clotilde, and meet some of the people up there. Little did I know that these visits would change my life and mark my future in Brazil.

For two or three weeks, usually about twice a week, I went with Dona Clotilde on her visits, and she began to

The favela of Tavares Bastos

1

introduce me to the people of this favela – which is the Portuguese word for shantytown – called Tavares Bastos.

One day while visiting, I heard a scream, and in a nearby hut I found a child, a two-year-old boy, who was having difficulty breathing. With my first aid training and Girl Scout knowledge, I jumped right in and performed artificial respiration on him. Having been asthmatic as a child, I knew what he was feeling. And I became an overnight hero.

The next thing I knew, every time I visited the favela people would come running up to me, "Would you look at my child?"

So I began to go regularly to Tavares Bastos, and it was like going back a hundred years. At that time, there was no TV in Brazil and phones only for the well-to-do. There were no sewers, electricity or running water. These people were truly isolated in their poverty.

Dona Clotilde usually took food and clothes to some of the very poorest community members. One of the first people I came to know was Dona Maria do Portuguese.

Dona Maria was a tiny, tiny black lady, probably in her late sixties, who lived in a very tiny hut, perhaps the size of a large bathroom. She had no bed, just a large mattress laid on cardboard and a curtain, behind which was a can she used for a toilet.

In the front of the hut, by a small wooden window shutter, was a table with a large basin filled with water that she used to wash her dishes and that was then carried behind the curtain where she would give herself a bath. On another small table were a burner with room for two pots for cooking and a small gas tank.

As far as I could tell, Dona Maria had no source of income other than an elderly man who came to see her on weekends and who supported her, or so we heard. The neighbors told us that he had a wife and family in Portugal, but had left them some years before to make a living in Brazil.

Dona Maria was not well; she'd had several attacks of high blood pressure, so I took her to a health clinic. I knew little yet of how the public health system worked, but I knew from some of my wealthier acquaintances that there was a clinic that treated a certain number of poor each month free of charge. So Gus and I took her there.

She had numerous tests done, and was found to have quite high blood pressure and anemia. She couldn't read or write, but we were told that her Portuguese partner could. So we left a message for him at her home, and, returning a few days later, found that he had brought food but only enough to last while he was there and there was no medication. So we bought the medication for her until we took her back to the doctor, told him her story, and the doctor then supplied the medication.

But this approach to health care couldn't continue, and as Gus and I became more and more familiar with the favela and the people we began to take patients to the public health center on the other side of town. The doctors there became interested in what I, an American, was doing in the favela and the orientation we were giving to their patients, and so they began to give us samples of medications they received from the pharmaceutical labs. Thus were we able to supply Dona Maria and others the medications they needed, along with explanations on how to take them correctly.

Dona Maria, alone in the world, other than this Portuguese man, was our primary worry. As time went on, she became more and more dependent on us. She had no refrigerator; few in the favela did at the time. We later bought her a toilet and asked some of the men to install it where it would drain under the house and into the side alley. But for this to happen, it had to be placed beside the front door, and she had to move her "kitchen area" to behind the curtain.

We only met the mysterious Portuguese about two years later when he collapsed in her hut with a mild stroke. He was in bad shape. We took him to the doctor and medicine was prescribed along with rehab and rest. Dona Maria cooked for him, bathed him and medicated him.

We then got to know him, and, though his accent in Portuguese was very difficult for me to understand, we discovered that he received a pension from Portugal and that all his property was in his children's possession. He said he wasn't legally married, but one of his documents said to the contrary.

His condition grew worse, and he had another stroke and was hospitalized. In those days, the public hospitals were not at all what they are today; everything was in poor condition. The doctor told us there was nothing that could be done for him, that he was dying.

This put us into a panic. If he died, his Brazilian pension would be gone, and Dona Maria would have nothing. The only way she could collect was to be his wife. The solution was to find a priest to marry them, and fast!

We explained this to the dying man – who I'm not certain understood it all – and, when he was fully conscious, he agreed to marry Dona Maria.

Now the objective was to find a priest and the documents necessary to prove he was single and could marry, plus his pension documents. We discovered he was much brighter than we thought and knew exactly where the document was that declared he was single. When he had had his first stroke and had come to stay with Dona Maria, he had brought a briefcase with him. We found a church marriage license in it, but his passport said he was single. We took this document to the priest.

The next issue was that Dona Maria had no birth certificate, no documents to prove that she existed. At that time, money could buy anything. But given that we needed the document almost immediately, we paid dearly for it.

It was also true in those days, the early seventies, that a marriage by a priest was as good as a civil marriage, so having the priest come to the hospital and marry them would make it legal: Gus and I as witnesses, and tiny Dona Maria, silent with her head bent down at all times. Her new husband had to be prompted when it was time for him to speak, and when the ceremony of five to ten minutes was over Dona Maria took out a clean handkerchief and shed a few tears. She signed her name with a fingerprint and her new husband was propped up to sign his.

It was all done just in time, for the man died two days later, and Dona Maria soon had the money she needed to keep her alive.

She lived for some years after. We took her regularly to her doctors' appointments and saw that she took her medicines.

But a surprise was to come to us. Dona Maria went to the president of the favela (yes, there was even a board of directors of this community) and told him that since she had no family to inherit her hut, when she died she wanted it given to us, Gus and me. She signed the papers with her thumbprint and registered her wishes.

She somehow, it seemed, had known her time was coming. One day soon after she'd signed the papers, she didn't come out all day to get water from the public faucet. Neighbors banged on her door, but there was no answer. The door was broken down, and there she was lying beside the toilet we'd had installed for her. She was dead of a stroke.

It was only then that we learned she had willed the hut to us. It became our first community free pharmacy and a sort of office for our health education ministry – a gift given in love and gratitude. She'd known we loved her, and her love for us was shown in this gift. She was a remarkable woman.

****

Now that the hut was ours, we had to clean it out and make some alterations and reinforcements. The day this was done is one I will never forget. Bricks had to be put under the foundation to make it stronger because it was sagging. So the president of the favela said, "We're going to take a day, and everybody's going to put bricks under it."

We bought the bricks and had them deposited at the entrance to the favela because it was impossible for a vehicle to drive in on the community's narrow roads. So the bricks would be brought in by hand. The adults could carry quite a few at a time. But for children who wanted to help – and there were quite a few – it was one at a time. They weren't discouraged in the least.

5

It touched my heart and made me smile to see the little ones, some still in diapers, which they clutched tight (the wet ones hanging especially low) as they worked, toting one brick at a time, undiscouraged, laughing all the way. What a sight!

We built shelves for our sample medicines and pictorial educational materials for the little health education groups we were forming. We put a sign out front: "Dona Maria do Portuguese's Community Pharmacy." And then there was a big celebration. A Portuguese priest came, and I didn't understand a word he was saying, but all the women had made food. It was a great party.

This was just the beginning. A few years later, we'd acquire the hut next door. But that's another story.

Extraordinary Women

When I met Dona Sebastiana, she was already in her late sixties or early seventies. Her hut was right across from our pharmacy. She was a midwife, or was so called because she had delivered more than half of the infants in the favela. She could predict the sex of the baby you were carrying by looking at your stomach. This was Dona Sebastiana, who with her kerchiefed head and worn-out sack was always ready for the call.

Her son had two women at the same time. In fact, the three of them slept in the same bed. When the son wanted to have his way with one, he'd just ask the other one to turn her face to the wall.

Both of these women worked, so Dona Sebastiana took care of all their children. It was amazing to watch what this very tiny woman could do. To retrieve water from down the long hill, she would fill up large cans and balance them on her head. The plot beside her hut was vacant, and you would see her out there bathing all those children. Then someone would call her, and she would run to their house and deliver a baby, do whatever had to be done after and then hurry back to those children. This was her daily life – day after day after day.

What a privilege it was to come to know women such as Dona Sebastiana. There's a saying in Brazil: "Your mother is your mother for all your life, while your father could be anyone." That may seem a harsh judgment, but I saw its truth borne out time and again. The female figure is constant; the male figure, not as much. Most of the women I'm writing about raised their children by themselves and regarded men as necessary for the money they could earn and for procreation.

Such was the case with Dona Sebastiana.

Dona Sebastiana was like no woman I had ever known. She was born in the interior of the country, and didn't know her exact age. Her mother was a midwife and Dona Sebastiana learned the tricks of the trade from her. She never talked about her former life, and it never occurred to me at the time to ask for details. She came to Rio following a man (a husband?) I never met.

Dona Sebastiana

Her head was always wrapped in a kerchief and her housedress, though worn, was always clean. She usually had diaper pins stuck to her dress and maybe a pacifier in her hand as she stepped up out of her hut, which was a few steps below the level of the road. Her hut was on the corner next to the stairs that led to the lower part of the community, and she had a small plot where she could hang her clothes and the children could play. She had an outside kitchen, which later had a roof placed over it.

Dona Sebastiana never went down the hill to shop; others did this for her. In fact, she never left the favela except when we accompanied her to see the doctor.

One of her daughters-in-law, Suely, had a child who was so undernourished that Gus and I took him in for a while. Luizinho was a handsome young boy, and Dona Sebastiana's favorite at the time. She was always so grateful for whatever we did for her grandchildren, as she was the sole caretaker when Suely would fight with her husband and leave him, only to return, get pregnant again, and then there would be one more child for Dona Sebastiana to care for.

Some years later, her son brought home yet another woman, with two children he said were his. Dona Sebastiana cared for them all. She was, to me, a heroine, the first of many I would come to know.

****

8

As I said, Dona Sebastiana was a midwife, but she never charged a fee; after all, this was her community; her neighbors needed her.

She was very matter-of-fact about it all, but you could tell she enjoyed her role in the birth of a new life. Many pregnant women came to our little hut, and as I would talk with them, take their blood pressure and so forth, Dona Sebastiana would join in with her own advice. When the baby was born, she would be there to cut the umbilical chord, then would say a prayer, and would then briefly take the baby away. She never told me why or what she did with it, but most probably was adhering to a superstition, a cultural belief – many of which would become familiar to me.

She would visit the new mother daily for at least ten days, bathing her and the infant and giving instructions. This was this extraordinary woman's life, day after day.

As we became friendlier, I would try to outguess her as to the sex of the not-yet-born infant. In all my years there, she was always right. I would ask her how she knew and she would tell me that it was by the size of the stomach, the way it was shaped, etc. I never understood, but she did guess right.

****

One day when I was there in our little hut clinic, a neighbor woman came running in and asked me to come with her. As we hurried down the crude road to the woman's home, she told me that her neighbor's daughter had come with her two children to visit and had begun to feel labor pains. When we arrived, I could see that the baby was about to be born. This woman's mother had left to go down the hill to buy food.

The job fell to me. The neighbor went to call an ambulance, and so my helpers would be these two children: a girl of about seven and a boy of five or so. I sent the girl to boil water and the little boy to find someone to call Dona Sebastiana. The girl and I put towels under her mother and prepared the bed, and then, as the water boiled, we sterilized the scissors and whatever rags I could find. As the pains got worse, I realized I might have to do this alone. Though I had delivered two babies, I had done so with the help of women more experienced than I. But I had only this little girl to assist me, and that would have to do.

Then, just as I could see the baby was crowning, in walked my savior, Dona Sebastiana, with her own equipment.

This was the first time I'd seen her at work. She was tidy, efficient and calm, and, to my surprise, she began to sing. She hummed and sung the whole time, as she calmly went about bringing this new life into the world, cutting the chord, bathing the little girl, soothing the mother as we cleaned her up – her assistants, myself and the two children, all obeying her orders.

I just watched her and wondered: Does she have any idea of her value? She can't read or write. She uses herbs and all sorts of things as her treatments. She raises other women's children in her home, and manages it all with seeming ease. It was her life, and she accepted it. Her value was incalculable.

Observing this woman's life was beginning to mold my ideas about women. As I watched her grandchildren grow, finish high school and get jobs, I knew that whatever happened to them was because of this humble and illiterate woman. All of these children finished high school, and the two girls were a part of the first group of teenagers to whom I gave sexuality classes and explained birth control. As I watched them observe the lives of their father's two wives, I knew they would be different. They went out into the workforce. Dona Sebastiana delivered one of the granddaughters' first baby, but the others were delivered in hospitals, and I watched Dona Sebastiana's face as they came home with the infants. She was by now certainly in her late seventies, aged beyond her years. She examined them from head to toe, carried through with her routine as always, and said her prayer.

Though the grandsons didn't do quite so well as the girls, they finished high school, got jobs and were good fathers when their time came.

But there was one who broke her heart and mine too: Luizinho, who had lived with us while we treated his malnutrition. He got mixed up with the wrong crowd. He was such a handsome teenager, smart and polite, and I believe he could have been saved. He was my friend, but never told me what he was into. He was shot before he reached twenty in a police action involving suspected drugs. I cried at his funeral. Dona Sebastiana didn't cry, but her old, wrinkled face showed her pain. She had been unable to save this one.

****

One of the few things Dona Sebastiana feared was dying without a birth certificate. This woman with at least five children that we knew of – plus who knows how many grandchildren beyond the ones who lived in the favela – did not exist in the eyes of the law and would be buried as an indigent, which to her would be terrible, and was unthinkable to us as well.

We took her to the cartorio, the public registry, one where we were known for our work, and told her story. The registrar asked her a few questions. Did she know where she was born, her birth date? Did she remember her parents' names? She didn't know the year of her birth or her father's name, but was able to answer enough. We would serve as witnesses and she would sign with her fingerprint. We waited for the document to be prepared, and as it was handed to us, those waiting in the registry, who had been watching this elderly woman receive her first document, applauded.

Dona Sebastiana clutched her precious document: her proof that she existed and her guarantee that she would be buried with a name. It brought tears to her eyes, and ours too, and still does today.

****

Dona Leopoldina and Senhor Antonio were an older couple, probably in their late sixties or early seventies, though they looked much older. They had three grown sons – or survivors, as you will see – in their late thirties or early

11

forties, who no longer lived with them. They were from the impoverished northeast region.

As the story goes, Dona Leopoldina had had at least a dozen children, many dying in early infancy of dehydration, diarrhea, measles and more – there were no treatments where they lived for these illnesses and infant mortality was high. But one of her sons claimed that some of these infant deaths were because of the syrups and teas Dona Leopoldina made from the leaves and branches she found in the woods, many of which we know today are poisonous.

Both of the old folks were illiterate, and Dona Leopoldina still cooked over a woodstove in her tiny two-room favela hut. The water at the bottom of the hill ran out of open pipes, and people would go down the hill with large empty paint cans, collect it and carry it back up the steep hill. And I can remember seeing Senhor Antonio walking up the hill empty handed, while behind him, plodding along, came little Dona Leopoldina, carrying a large pail of water in each hand and sometimes a smaller one on her head.

One day as I was working, I was called to come quickly to Dona Leopoldina's hut; she had died, I was told. I rushed to the hut, and there she was, laid out on the kitchen table, her hands folded on her chest, a candle in each, weeping neighbors standing around, many praying. What a scene!

The women who had prepared her, drew away for me to get closer. As I looked at her, I noticed a pulse in her neck and immediately felt for the pulse in her wrist. It was beating just fine.

Before I could shout that Dona Leopoldina was alive, she groaned and tried to sit up. She looked at the mourners at her side. "What are you all doing here?" she asked, as the candles dropped from her hands to the floor.

"A miracle," some said. Others began to pray louder, even wail, and I had to smile. Dona Leopoldina had fainted and, in ignorance, her neighbors had prepared her for her burial. Sudden death was not uncommon to these people, isolated in their poverty.

I looked over and saw Senhor Antonio, who up until now hadn't moved. The look of relief on his face said, "Well, things will go on as before." And, probably, "Get up senhora, it's dinnertime."

****

I was sitting in my little hut in the favela one day when Dona Joaquina walked up to the waist-high wall in front and announced that she was going to clean my pots and pans.

"You rich ladies need maids; you don't know how these pans should be cleaned," she said. "You can tell a lazy woman by the condition of her pans."

And so she stepped in with her scrubbing brush, took my pans and scrubbed until, honestly, you could see your face in the aluminum. She then set them out on top of that wall for all to see that Dona Barbara knew how to care for her pans, and walked off.

This elderly, small, skinny, light-skinned black lady, hunched over, her head bound day and night in a kerchief, a pipe perched in her mouth, was my protector. She growled at me, scowled at me, but would walk in with a broom and sweep the floor, or just sit on the old couch while I talked with patients, my dog jumping into her lap, listening, showing by her body language or the expression on her face if she approved of or believed what the person was telling me. She was extremely alert if a strange man who might be armed came into my hut. She could be out washing her clothes in the tank in front of her house but would drop everything to "protect" Dona Barbara. And if my dog should growl, she would pick up the long, heavy wooden cane that she used when she begged on the streets and arrive with it, armed.

Dona Joaquina begged on the crowded streets of the square below the favela. She would walk between the cars, risking her life to approach the car windows, usually at a stoplight; but if the light turned green, she just stayed where she was. Given her age, most cars would wait to move forward until she gave up. She was always so embarrassed when she saw us, and would disappear. We never mentioned to her that we'd seen her, that we were afraid for her, for this would have humiliated her or she would have said it wasn't her.

13

Dona Joaquina lived in a ramshackle hut a few down from ours. No one knew her age, but she must have been in her seventies. She lived with her daughter and her daughter's two boys. The boys' mother worked and Dona Joaquina would walk them down the hill to school every day, beg till midday, then pick them up and bring them home. You could hear her coming, complaining to the boys about their appearance, their schoolwork and so on. I never heard her show any signs of affection for them, though I knew, as did everyone else, that she loved them – it was to meet their needs that she begged. It was just her way; she was gruff with everyone.

But this woman would show what she was made of, the love she had for these grandchildren. The boys were some eight years apart in age. The younger boy always helped his grandmother, and often she took him to beg with her, not because she didn't want to leave him alone, but because begging with a child is always more lucrative. The older boy, as he reached his teens, began to go around with a bad group of boys, often skipped school and was constantly under the rod his grandmother wielded. As he got bigger though, she could no longer get through to him, and though she would cover up for him when he got into trouble, and lectured him, it had little effect on him.

The only thing this old woman could do was try to protect the younger boy. She was rough with him too, but he seemed to weather it better. She could neither read nor write, but she wanted the best for this boy. She would lay down her life for either of them, as was to be proven.

The older boy was soon into drugs and the police came looking for him often. We all saw them coming and saw her quick action to warn him if he was home, so he could run to the woods behind the house, or lie to the police that he didn't live there. And the police, recognizing the old beggar, would go away. Then we would hear her ranting and raving at him or see her running after him in the streets with her heavy cane, trying to hit him, and he would laugh, let her catch him, and then he would hug her so tight that she couldn't hit him.

One day after lunch, when Dona Joaquina was taking her afternoon nap on the floor, the police came and knocked on her door, calling for her grandson who was napping beside her. We can imagine that she got him up so he could flee to the woods, but he was so slow, and the police were determined to break this drug dealer and began kicking the door with their boots. The door was weak and cracked, and would have been easy to break in.

What the police had not counted on was that Dona Joaquina was not going to let them in till her grandson got upstairs and out to the woods. She put her tiny old body against the door. Of course, it finally did give in; but when it did, it tossed the old lady across the room and fell on her, knocking her unconscious. The policemen ignored her and searched the house. In the meantime, I was called to tend to her. I saw that she was breathing and there was no blood, so I decided not to wake her. The police were still there and I was afraid she would wake and say or do things to make them violent with her.

They asked who I was, made their threats and left. Dona Joaquina came to. And though stunned at first, she had the sense to only groan and say nothing, for fear the police were still there.

Some months later, this grandson was shot in a drug raid. He was wounded, but hid, and in the night came home to be nursed and protected by his grandmother.

The following year though, he was murdered, his body found in the woods where he so often had hidden from the police, most probably killed by a man as much in trouble as he was. Dona Joaquina was never the same, perhaps, folk would say, because her head had been hit so hard when the door fell on it. But I knew better. She had lost someone she had loved, and whom she had failed to be able to save.

She became more protective of her other grandson, who turned out fine, finished high school, got a job, married and became a father. His mother, who was generally oblivious of the family dynamics, died shortly after her son was killed.

But Dona Joaquina lasted till the other boy married, an old and bitter lady, but an example for me of a woman's love and sacrifice.

****

I became well acquainted with many doctors and nurses at the public health clinic as I accompanied the favela dwellers to their consultations. I heard many stories, but this one is just unforgettable. I will call this woman Dona Maria, as it's so common for women to have "Maria" in their names.

Dona Maria had been coming to see an obstetrician every eighteen months or so for years. After at least eight pregnancies, her prenatal care had become routine. As she would leave the doctor's office after each consultation, the nurse would say, "See you next year." And Dona Maria would answer, "No, this is my last."

But, sure enough, she'd be back in a year and a half or so.

But then one year, as she was receiving her customary "See you in a year or so," Dona Maria was emphatic in her response.

"No, she said, "this time I won't be back for sure."

"We've heard that before," the nurse said with a smile.

"No", Dona Maria repeated, "this time it's true; I won't be back. My husband and I are separated. He left home."

And for a while it looked to be true. Time passed, and she didn't return. Then one day, several years later, there she was again.

"Oh, my, what are you doing here?" the nurse asked. "You're not pregnant again, are you, Dona Maria?"

"Guess so," Dona Maria said, with a sigh of resignation.

"How come?" the nurse asked. "You said your husband had left home."

"He did," Dona Maria replied, shrugging her shoulders.

"Then how could you be pregnant again?"

"Well," she said, "he does come to visit the kids every once in a while!"

16

The Status of Women Who Don't Have Children

In the Brazil of this time, as in much of the world, women's value was determined by their ability to have children, and this was especially true for poor women. The country's culture was, and is, one of close family relationships. Children are cared for by their parents, especially the mother, and then when the parents grow old the children become their caregivers. Thus, especially among the poor, the more children, the better to divide that care. But until such time, women were the glue of the family. Men were largely free to do as they pleased. Such were the roles when I arrived in Brazil in 1967.

I began to meet women who came from the poor northeastern states in search of work and to send money back to their families. These women worked mostly as maids and could rarely object to sexual advances by the sons of the family. If they became pregnant, at least this child was guarantied a good life. The risk was always that the employers would take the baby for their own. Often, the employers would coerce the woman to give up her rights to the child but allow her to remain working in the home – but maybe they would dismiss her. So, often, the maid would accept these terms; she had nowhere to go.

Rio and, even more so, São Paulo were havens for people from the rural impoverished northeast in search of jobs and a better life. The man would usually come first, sending his wages back home to his family, trying to save enough to bring them to the city. This, of course, wasn't easy, and often took years, during which time men often found other women companions and started another family.

****

17

I want to tell you about a man who came to Rio for another reason: to find a doctor who could help him and his wife have a living child, since his wife's three previous pregnancies had ended in stillbirth or death in infancy, and she was pregnant once again.

The man had relatives who had migrated and would give them a place to stay until they found their own. These relatives lived in the favela where Gus and I operated our pharmacy/clinic. Knowing that we gave out sample medications and took people to a public clinic, they brought the young woman to me. After hearing her story, we knew what must be done: find an OB and tell that story. This we did, and for the next six months or so we took her to the doctor every month and saw that she had all the medications and exams she needed.

Everything went just fine; she was young and though a bit malnourished when she came, she quickly recovered and gave birth easily to a beautiful girl. The smile and sparkle in her eyes when we went to bring her home was a joy for all of us. The little one, named Victoria, developed into a seemingly healthy infant.

Then one day when Victoria was about nine months old, a neighbor came rushing to our little clinic. She was breathless, saying, "Come quickly; Maria needs you."

The panic in her voice alarmed me, so I dropped everything and walked the narrow uneven path to her hut. As I walked into the hut, Maria jumped up and thrust a bundle into my arms.

"Dona Barbara, do something, she isn't breathing."

I looked at the little face wrapped in a pink blanket, put that face to mine, and there was no breath; her chest was still. She was dead. By the touch of her skin, I surmised that she must have died some time ago, perhaps during the night.

I can't explain how I felt. My heart was broken and I ached beyond description for this mother. While so many of the women in the favela had more children than they could handle, this woman just wanted this one.

What does one say at a time like this? I was at a loss for words. I put the baby down and said to the sobbing Maria the only think I knew would comfort her, "God knows best. She is with God."

This blaming of God was not something that I believe, but it was a common reaction in tragedy for these people, and the only comfort I could find for her. What needed to happen was to get an autopsy to find out why the infant had died, and maybe a clue as to why the others before had as well.

But, no, that wasn't culturally acceptable. The baby was buried, and a woman had lost hope. She was, in her own estimation, and that of many others, a failed woman. She knew her destiny.

And, sure enough, within a month or so, her husband put her on the bus and back to her family. Within a few months, he had found another partner.

A Mother's Sacrifice

Knowing the importance of children in a woman's life, this next story may surprise you.

I had been working in the favela for some time and was involved in a charity effort run by nuns from one of the large churches in the area. One day, one of the nuns called me and asked me to go to a corticio with her to visit a woman who had just had a baby.

Corticios are large homes that many years ago were inhabited by wealthy families but during recessionary times were abandoned. Poor families moved into them, dividing up the rooms and even putting in makeshift curtains or partitions to divide the larger rooms into smaller ones. Each family had a room to live in, a home. And some of these families consisted of seven or eight people.

It was into one of these homes that the nun took me. Behind a curtain was a bed, a camp-type stove and clothes hung and piled everywhere. Three children who sat on the bed playing a game looked up and smiled expectantly, anticipating the sweets the nun always brought with her. A woman was sitting on a large box that served as a chair, nursing an infant. Her hair was disheveled, her housedress torn and ragged like the children's clothes. Only the infant was well dressed.

The woman stood up and said to the nun, in a completely emotionless voice, "Have you told her why you brought her here, sister?"

I looked from the woman to the nun.

"No", the nun said, "I think you should tell her yourself."

The woman turned to me; her eyes were dull, as was her voice.

"I need someone to take my baby," she said. "I cannot keep him"

She looked around her, and continued.

"As you can see, we don't even have enough for us, and I must go back to work. When I am at work, my daughter," she said, nodding to a girl of perhaps six or seven, "cares for the other two, but she can't care for a baby."

I swallowed hard, and said, "This is your son; he came from your body, and you must know that if you give him up you will never see him again – your own flesh and blood."

She looked at me as if she didn't understand what I was saying. "It is my son's life I am thinking of," she said. "If he stays here, he will die like the one born last year, right sister?"

I took the infant in my arms. There was no father in the picture. Did each one of these children have a different father? I felt no condemnation or judgment, only sadness, deep sadness. I too am a mother. She was giving up her son to save him, to give him life!

Yes, I took this baby, took him home, took him to a doctor, a friend of mine – for without a birth certificate, no other doctor in the city would have looked at him. My daughter and I and a woman who was living with us at the time cared for the infant, but it just wasn't possible for us to keep him.

What could I do? I felt the weight of my responsibility.

****

One of my English students was a well-to-do Argentine whose husband worked for a multinational corporation. She had lived in several countries, including the U.S., and was to return there, and wanted to brush up on her English. When our conversational class was over, I told her I needed to get home to the baby.

"A baby?" she asked. "Whose baby?"

I told her the story, and as I was finishing it, her maid, who had overheard the conversation, asked to speak to her in another room.

The woman was away quite a while. When she returned, she told me that the maid, also an Argentine, who had been with her for some years, was unable to have children because of a childhood illness, and that she and her husband, a Brazilian who worked in a bakery, wanted children so badly.

21

Before the woman could go on, the maid entered the room, crying. "Please, dona," she said, "you would make us the happiest couple in the world. We don't have much; we are not rich, but we are rich in love."

Her patroa looked at me and said, "I can vouch for this couple, and I will buy them everything they need for this baby. They are a good couple."

Before I go on, I need to explain that giving babies away, or selling them, was not uncommon among the poor of Brazil at the time. There was a public maternity hospital, and often well-to-do women would wait at the door where the new mothers came out and claim babies already promised or ask a mother if she wanted her child, if she could care for it.

I went home and thought and thought. Was this right? I felt almost like I was playing the role of God. But, I thought, this woman wanted this baby sight unseen. She hadn't even asked the sex of the child. The man had a good job – bakeries never go out of business in Brazil – and they had the help of a family she had been employed with for ages.

So a few days later, I called and said I would bring the baby boy for her to look at, to be sure she still wanted to be responsible for this life. The maid answered the phone.

"Oh, I'm sure," she said excitedly. "I haven't slept since you came, just thinking about the baby, and my husband and I have been praying all this time for this baby to come to us. My patroa has bought clothes, a crib and everything we need. Please come soon."

****

It was on an especially hot day that we drove to the apartment building in this very elegant area of Rio to turn the baby over to his new mother. The sun was blaring in my eyes as I looked down on the infant whose fate was in our hands, and I too, silently, said a prayer.

With the sun in our eyes, I couldn't see the maid and her patroa on the sidewalk at the entrance of the building till we stopped the car. The maid rushed to me and took the infant, crying and praying. Sight unseen, she loved him – just as a woman who's given birth immediately loves her child, sight unseen. She handed the baby to her husband, who had waited quietly in the background, and dropped to her knees in front of me, taking my hand and kissing it. Love abounds! An emotional moment for us all.

About five years later, the father, who was visiting his family in Rio and had his son with him, called me. He said he was at the bus station and would be leaving soon, and would I like to come down and see them. I was giving a class at the time and couldn't, so he put the little boy on the phone.

"Hi," the boy said. And that was enough.

A Woman's 'Choice'

There was a young woman from the rural northeast who would come to our pharmacy hut to get vitamins for her four small boys, one of whom was quite undernourished. The family lived in a very tiny hut, the size of a small bedroom, on top of another hut. You could see through the floorboards to the family living below. There was room only for the one double bed where they all slept, two chairs, a stove, a basin for washing and a toilet can. It was very crowded. Her husband worked in construction and just barely made enough to get by.

The young woman told me she needed help; she was pregnant again. I told her not to worry, that we would take her to the public health clinic to see an OB.

"But Dona Barbara, you don't understand; I can't have this child," she said. "You can see how we live; we cannot, cannot have another." And she began crying. "I've tried everything to lose it, but nothing has worked, and now it's probably too late. Women have suggested going to a woman who can do something, but I'm afraid."

I comforted her as best I could, and said, no, it was far too dangerous to go to this woman, and that she had four boys who needed her.

She did well during the pregnancy, never missing her doctor's appointments, but she kept reminding me that she couldn't keep this baby. "Please," she would say, "find someone to take my baby."

Time went on, and I worried and worried.

"What if it's a girl," I said.

"Oh, Dona Barbara," she cried, "that would make it worse; four boys and a tiny girl and no privacy."

****

One day, a nurse I knew well at the public clinic came up to me and asked if I knew of a woman who was unable to keep her baby. Her priest had asked her if she knew of anyone. This nurse knew that I worked in a favela and, as I said, this type of transaction was not unusual among the poor.

My head began to spin. I said that I would like to talk to this priest. He called me, and by his heavy accent I knew he was not Brazilian. He told me that his sister, who was a nun and was working in Argentina, was returning to their country, Spain, and wanted to find a baby to take to their sister, who was unable to have children. I told him there was a slight possibility that there was a baby, but that I wasn't certain because the mother might change her mind upon seeing her infant.

He said he understood, and told me his sister would call me as soon as she arrived in Rio on her way home to Spain.

Soon this baby would be born, and the mother had told me that she would not bring it home, that she would tell everyone, including her husband, that the baby had died. She said that if I couldn't find someone to take it, she would just abandon it in the hospital.

I said nothing, but prayed that what I was thinking to do would be right.

The nun, who had a thick Spanish accent, called me when she arrived in Rio, and I told her of this mother's situation and that if she didn't change her mind upon seeing her baby, I would take it and call her. I also told this to the mother, and she said she would call me from the hospital to come and get the baby. I relayed this to the nun, and she said that she wanted to be there regardless of whether the mother changed her mind or not.

****

The day came, and the young mother went off to the hospital alone. In those days, women in public maternity hospitals who had normal births stayed but twenty-four hours. When I arrived in the favela later that morning, I

25

was told that she had gone to the hospital. When I was able to reach her on the phone, she told me to come the next morning and she would turn the baby over to me. No one was to know that this baby existed, she said.

My heart was heavy, but I called the nun as promised and she said she would meet me at the hospital entrance the next morning. Gus went with me, and we arrived at the entrance just as the mother was coming out with a nurse, who held the baby in her arms. The nurse handed her over to me and left us.

I looked at the pretty new one, absorbed by her blue, blue eyes, not at all common in this part of Brazil. I then looked up at her mother, noting her blue eyes as well.

I asked, "Are you sure you want to do this? It's a girl, and you have four boys. Are you sure you know what this decision means?"

Without any show of emotion, she said, "Yes. Particularly because it's a girl, I have to do this. It will give her a life we can't."

As we were speaking, a car drove up, and out stepped two nuns, both in dark habits, which even then was uncommon in Brazil. One of them approached us quickly and introduced herself, all the while staring at the infant.

The mother looked up at her, smiled for the first time, and handed her the baby. I choked up.

The nun looked at the infant lovingly, then handed her to the other woman. She then reached out for the mother, drew her in and held her, saying that God understood that she was unselfishly giving her baby a chance for a better life, and that this she was guarantying her – that she was taking the little girl to her sister in Spain, who was unable to have children but was well able financially to give her daughter a wonderful life. She said that God would bless the baby as well as the mother.

It was an emotional moment. There were no tears in the young mother's eyes, but her face showed her pain. The nun then blessed us all and walked away with the precious bundle, whose fate we had just determined.

The mother turned to me and said, "Remember, we're to tell my husband and others that the baby died, and I don't want you to mention her to me again."

Then she got in our car and we drove her to her favela hut. I watched through the mirror as we drove; the tears flowed down her cheeks, but she made no sound.

I thought to myself: the ultimate sacrifice. Heartbreaking as it must have been, she did what she felt she had to do.

****

But the story didn't end there.

Six months later, the phone rang; it was the nun. I was so surprised to hear from her, thinking that she would want to sever all communication.

Her voice was softer than I remembered it. "I'm sorry to bother you; really, I am," she said. "But I forgot a detail, a very important one." She hesitated. "I will need a birth certificate to get a passport for her, and I can't do that without registering her birth."

Oh, my; I'd never even thought of that. I had assumed that she and her brother would solve that, and said as much.

"But," and she again hesitated, "how can I register her as my child if I'm a nun? I've asked my order to release me from my vows, but this will take time." She sighed, and there was a long pause. "Barbara, I'm still a nun; I can't say I've given birth to a child."

I told her we'd find a solution. When Gus came home, he said he knew a man in one of the public registries and would speak to him. He called the man and made an appointment.

When we went to pick the nun up, the door opened and, to my surprise, there she stood in civilian clothes; she had shed her habit for this important day. And now for the first time, I noticed her eyes. I remembered how blue the little girl's eyes were, and now this woman stood before me with the child in her arms – their eyes the same blue!

My heart skipped a beat.

And not only the eyes: This ex-nun had the curly hair so typical of the mixed-racial Brazilian people. The little girl would have the same hair. I remember thinking, "This baby could easily be hers."

So off we all went to the registry. The story my husband had told the registrar was that the nun had been a governess in the home of a wealthy family and the son had invaded her bedroom several times and left her pregnant, for which she had been dismissed without references. This was not an unusual story, and it passed easily. And though the woman kept her face down, shyly, the whole time, she knew this was the only way. Now the infant girl was hers. She could get the passport and leave for Spain, taking this precious bundle to her sister.

But the story is still not over – and perhaps you've guessed by now. A year passed, and we received a letter from Spain from the woman with a picture of the child sitting on her lap. And this, as I recall, is what it said:

"Here we are, my daughter and I in the yard. Yes, she *is* truly my daughter, and only God can repay you for what you did to bring us to this happiness."

Her brother told me later that she had every intention of giving the baby to her sister but had grown to love her so that she couldn't imagine giving her up. We never heard from her again.

Dona da Guia and the Pill

After we were given Dona Maria's hut, I began to give talks about sexuality and birth control. Given that Brazil is a dominantly Catholic country, pills were not available for purchase, but I had many friends who sent them to me, as did some doctors at the public health clinic where we took people to be treated. We would take women to these doctors and they would give them samples and some extras to me for our pharmacy. These doctors knew of our work, and some of them even visited us.

Dona da Guia had come from the rural interior northeast with her six children, some born within ten to twelve months of each other. She was very thin, illiterate and, to put it mildly, a bit scatterbrained. She was a good woman, a loving mother, but her kids were just plain lucky not to be sicker than they were. Prior to coming to our favela, she had lost several children to various diseases to which they were prone because of poor nutrition and living conditions. Dona da Guia knew nothing of preventative health care and always assumed that God took her children because it was their time.

She had been pregnant most of her married life and was overworked, tired but cheerful, totally unaware of the possibilities for a better, healthier life.

Her children wore ragged clothes. The older two went to school, but not the others, as there wasn't enough money to dress them all in school clothes. It seemed as if Dona da Guia came to me every month fearing she was pregnant and begging me to do something so she wouldn't be. I talked to her, explained the cycle so she could be aware of her ovulation period, but I knew she just wasn't understanding. Plus, women like her were hesitant to look at their bodies, and certainly never touched the intimate parts. It had to be the pill. But was she capable of understanding?

I took her to a gynecologist at the public clinic, and after an examination the doctor gave her a six-month supply of birth control pills and told me to explain to her how to take them. But as I said, Dona da Guia understood very little of her body, couldn't read or write, and was most certainly unable to take this medication on her own. I would have to hand them out to her.

There were twenty-eight pills, seven of which were placebos, but they all had to be taken on the day prescribed. We started out with me giving them to her a week at a time, until after the third month, at which point she was able, I hoped, to do it on her own. Her husband, of course, couldn't know what they were, and we invented the story that they were vitamins.

Dona da Guia was thrilled. Two years passed without her being pregnant, which had never happened before. About this time, her husband's construction company sent him to Teresópolis, a tourist city an hour or so away. Dona da Guia was in a panic, for how would she get her birth control pills? With fear and trepidation, I gave her a six-month supply and told her to take one a day and when she had only fifteen left to come see me or not have sexual relations.

****

So off she went to Teresópolis. My life was so busy, I hardly kept track of time, and the days flew by without me realizing those six months had long since passed. When I did, I thought to myself, "Oh, she's certainly pregnant by now, and that's why she hasn't returned." About a year and a half had passed when I heard that Dona da Guia and her family were returning to the favela.

One day I looked out my window, and here she came, with her younger children in tow. She wasn't pregnant, or at least wasn't showing, and I saw no new faces. She was smiling, and came up and gave me a big hug, saying how glad she was to be back, for it had been difficult living in Teresópolis.

"How wonderful you look," I said, though she seemed thinner than when she had left. "We missed you. How are the children?"

"Fine," she said.

My curiosity was getting the best of me.

"Why didn't you come back for more pills when yours were gone?" I asked. "I only gave you enough for six months."

"No," she laughed. "I still have a few left!"

"Impossible," I said. "How did you manage that?"

She smiled, and proudly replied: "I was very careful, and rationed them, for I knew how important they were."

"You rationed them?" I exclaimed. "How?"

"Well, my husband was only home every other weekend, so I only had to take them when he was home." She said this with such pride, certain that her good judgment would please me.

Why she didn't get pregnant – who knows? We'll leave that one to the gods!

Dona Dejanira and Her Daughter

Dona Dejanira was a woman to be reckoned with. She was a large mulatto woman who dressed in torn clothes, smoked a pipe and walked the streets, two dogs in tow – and the dogs wore earrings – carrying a big sack that she filled with anything she found that she could sell or use. The sack might contain food, old clothes, rags, pots and pans or cans. She was a street beggar. She had a scar on her face, an old knife wound, and she scared the children with her size and sneers.

This is how I knew her, but the favela dwellers told me that years before, before she had acquired syphilis, she dressed well and worked. The disease had affected her mind, I was told. She climbed the hill to her hut wedged under the shack of another family and loaded her tiny home with junk. She ranted and raved, and had been jailed a few times, but they never wanted to keep her long; she was too hard to control. She would go into bars, harass people for money and have a few drinks, sometimes tossing men aside.

But she really loved Gus – perhaps because he always treated her with respect and kindness. Often when he saw her on the streets scaring people into giving her some spare change, he would take her to the nearest bar that would serve her and buy food to fill the big can she always carried.

One day, she walked into a bar in the favela, pushed some men around and demanded a drink. Everyone knew that if she drank too much she could become violent, fighting anyone, and she was, as I said, a big woman. Gus was walking by the bar and saw Dona Dejanira inside. He marched up to her, took her by the hand, sat her down at a table and began to talk to her, telling her she shouldn't drink, that it was no good for her health. Everyone looked on, stunned, as Dona Dejanira smiled, arose, and the two walked out together, hand in hand.

She had decided some time before this that she was expecting a baby, and would tell people this as she begged. Up in the favela community, when she told of her pregnancy she said that Gus was the father. So whenever he reminded her that drinking wasn't good for her health, he would add that, after all, she was going to be the mother of his baby. Of course, folks laughed, but Dona Dejanira took it all quite seriously.

****

One day, near her home, Dona Dejanira got into a fight with Dona Rosa, a neighbor whose cat Dona Dejanira had supposedly killed. The woman was verbally abusing her, calling her all kinds of ugly names. Dona Dejanira sneered and took it for a while, then went into her hut, grabbed a bottle, broke it against her table and went after Dona Rosa, throwing her to the ground, fully intending to cut her up.

A crowd gathered and someone called the police station at the bottom of the hill. Gus was called, and just as Dona Dejanira was about to stick the broken bottle into Dona Rosa's throat he arrived and screamed, "Dejanira, put that bottle down right now. Do you hear me? Now!"

And she did. She dropped the bottle. Dona Rosa sprang from her clutches and began running up the path to meet the police, who were just arriving, yelling that this woman was going to kill her.

Upon seeing the police, Dona Dejanira went back into her shack. One of the policemen started toward her door, but my husband advised him against it – too dangerous, he said – telling him that he would deal with her. The crowd agreed.

The policeman, not about to let some crazy woman show him up, paid no heed, stepped into the open door and, within a few seconds, came sailing right back out, past us expectant onlookers and a pretty fair distance down the hill. He came to rest in a vacant lot.

The other two policemen now unholstered their guns. But again Gus intervened, promising to take her to a nearby public mental health clinic. He called to Dona Dejanira to come out, which she did, reluctantly, and told her to put on

33

some decent clothes, that he was taking her to the doctor to have their baby.

The policemen gaped as Dona Dejanira went into her shack, put on one of her raged dresses and a kerchief, re-emerged, closed her door and joined my husband for a stroll to our car, smiling at the crowd as she passed.

With great sadness, Gus took Dona Dejanira to the mental hospital and admitted her. Though he may have saved her life, he nonetheless felt like a traitor.

But, as had been the case every other time she had been committed or incarcerated, she was soon let out for being a nuisance.

There were other incidents over the many years we were there in the favela. And then Dona Dejanira disappeared into the streets. One day, years later, we saw her, and she immediately came to us. She was dirty and much thinner, and much calmer. We sat on the curb of the street and she told us she had found a new home and asked us to feed her. We did, she went off, and we never saw her again.

****

But the story I'd like to tell you now is of her daughter, Elizete. Yes, Dona Dejanira had a daughter, who led a most precarious life, as you can imagine.

Elizete was a thin girl who often spoke out with foul language, but in the next instant would be smiling and cuddling up to one of the neighbor women. Life would have been even more difficult for her were it not for these women, who took her in when her mother went back out to the streets or hit her too many times. They saw that she ate, and she even attended school for a few years.

But with no immediate, consistent adult supervision, Elizete was free to live as she wished, and while still very young she broke away entirely from her mother.

By then, she'd grown into a rather tall and very thin teenager. She often came to our little clinic hut and asked for a bandage or vitamin. She was fourteen or so when I noticed that there was a swelling in her abdomen; that she was suddenly getting plumper. I called her in and asked

34

her some questions in a language she could understand, attempting to discern what the neighborhood women had told her about menstruation, or pregnancy or sex in general.

As I questioned her, I wondered if she even knew what was happening to her. She didn't want to talk about any of it though, and neither did any of the neighbors. I'd never seen her with a male, but I was sure she was pregnant.

Time passed, and I didn't see Elizete for several months. Then one afternoon, one of her neighbors came running in, saying that Elizete was sick and that Dona Dejanira was throwing things around in their shack. I ran over. Dona Dejanira was ranting and raving, throwing bottles and cans all over the place. Elizete was lying on the bed, moaning and frightened; she was in labor.

Was I prepared to deliver this child-mother's baby? As I weighed my limited options, Dona Rosa, the same neighbor with whom Dona Dejanira had fought, arrived, very quickly assessing the situation. She opened Elizete's legs, and as Elizete screamed, the baby crowned.

Dona Rosa began shouting orders: "Get some cloth, boil water and bring string and scissors! And fast!"

Suddenly, it was over, and Dona Rosa and I had brought this little girl into the world. Amidst the din of Dona Dejanira's rant, the cries of this child-mother and the bloody mess on this rotten mattress, a new life came to be.

And despite the misery of it all, the absence of any hopeful future, a new life gives all a sense of miracle, the miracle of creation, of love incarnate.

Dona Rosa brought a diaper and a few things for the baby. I lifted the little one and took her to a nearby bar and weighed her. I don't remember the weight, but it was fine.

As I started back to the shack, where Dona Rosa was cleaning Elizete up, an ambulance arrived. Someone had called the police and told them what was happening, and off Elizete and her little one went to the hospital. We kept Dejanira from going; she was in no condition to accompany her daughter. We asked Dona Rosa to go along.

I don't know the particulars of the rest of this story. Dona Rosa returned the next day without Elizete or the baby, and no one ever saw them again. Dona Rosa would tell nothing, and Dona Dejanira simply went on with her life. I'm sure she's dead by now.

****

I do though have a contrasting addendum to this story.

After we saw the ambulance off that day, I had to leave the favela to give an English lesson. For quite a few years, I'd been giving lessons to upper-class Brazilians, many of whom I'd known for years and had become quite close to; they'd made me feel a part of their families. Knowing that I needed the money from the lessons to continue my work in the favela, they were always generous and were great supporters.

But the contrast between their homes and those of the people with whom I lived and worked was so very great. This was Brazil: such an enormous divide between the haves and the have-nots.

And on no day was this contrast so clearly delineated as on this day. I left the scene I've described of Elizete giving birth to go to the home of a very well-to-do student who had just had her fifth child. I was welcomed by the maid and told that my student was upstairs in the nursery. I climbed the stairs of this beautiful home and was warmly greeted by my student. She was seated in an expensive rocker in a room decorated and equipped for her new son.

I sat down and congratulated her on her new baby, whom I had not yet seen. A nurse came in and asked if she was ready to nurse the baby and brought her a tray with a silver bowl and cloth to clean off her breasts and wash her hands. Then she brought the baby in and laid him on the mother's lap. The mother began to nurse.

I don't think she noticed, but my eyes welled with tears, my heart thumped and I was momentarily speechless. The contrast with the scene I had left was too much for me. The fate of this boy was sealed, a future of luxury, school, travel and whatever he might want, while the future of the girl I'd helped deliver would almost certainly be one of deprivation.

I told my student what was running through my head, and being the woman she was she understood.

I left her home that day, the condominium in which she lived, now ready to shed the tears I'd withheld. Where was the justice? Where was God? Why such fortune for one and such misfortune for another? Luck? Fate?

This well-to-do mother, my student, prayed; she was a good church-going woman, as we say. The other mother, an illiterate teenager, may have never entered a church in her life, and the only mother she knew was one whose life had been derailed early on by poverty and its consequences.

I asked myself, "Where is God in all this?" – that is, the God I'd been told of all my life. "Pray, and God will answer," I'd been told.

This pain, these questions, influenced me profoundly. This life here was challenging me. Everything I believed was in question.

My Caretaker

Dona Maria Gorda, a woman I shall never forget, was in her late sixties or early seventies when I met her. She was a plump ("gorda" means "fat," and is used in Portuguese affectionately), always-smiling black woman whose humble hut was across from the hut we used for our free pharmacy in Tavares Bastos. Her story is one of courage, fortitude and love, but I only know pieces of it – that is, what she told me in our many years of knowing each other.

She was born in the rural, impoverished state of Minas Gerais and came to Rio de Janeiro as a young woman, perhaps in her late teens, with her young daughter, who was paralyzed from polio before vaccines were available in Brazil. She had to find a job, but, being illiterate, domestic work was about all that was available to her.

Dona Maria Gorda had a way of speaking that is difficult to describe. Soft and friendly, it betrayed her naiveté. She had such a winning way about her, captivating and warm. She soon found a job available in a laundry – as a sacudideira, or someone who shakes out clothes to dry them – but in order to get the job she had to have documents. In Brazil at that time, this was often a problem. Mothers weren't allowed to register a birth, only the father could, and this was perhaps why Dona Maria Gorda didn't have a birth

Dona Maria Gorda

38

certificate: It's not unlikely that her father had disappeared, or perhaps she had never even known him.

Nonetheless, Dona Maria, with the help of others, succeeded in securing the proper documentation, and she rushed happily to her new employer.

It was a victory.

So now, each day, Dona Maria would carry her paralyzed daughter to work with her – not an easy task, for the favela was high on a hill overlooking the beaches of Rio. I can testify: It was quite a climb. Just imagine with a growing child on her back! She did this for many years.

All of this was before I came to the favela. By the time I arrived, her child had died, in her early teens, though Dona Maria was unclear why. She knew nothing of the names or causes of illnesses. Medicine for the poor was scarce, and often of not much good.

****

But now I want to tell you about the Dona Maria Gorda that I came to know and love. Soon after we met, she took on the role of my caretaker and Gus and I became hers until her death.

Dona Maria Gorda's very shambled hut consisted of one room that served as a living room and bedroom, a very rudimentary kitchen space and an open area for washing clothes. In this humble hut, she housed many a sick woman who, like her, had no family. She was always taking people in. If someone from a different area came into Rio de Janeiro and didn't have a place to stay, she would take them in. She would go to the open-air market and pick up scraps of vegetables that had fallen to the floor and bring them home for what she called her "medical soups" (though what we called them was "garbage soups.").

There was always a cup of coffee and a piece of bread for me when I arrived at our little clinic in the morning, courtesy of Dona Maria Gorda. The coffee was black and so strong you could barely drink it and the bread she made was tough and hard but made with such love that it couldn't be refused. She would always prepare something special for our birthdays. And though I often wondered how she could buy the ingredients to make it, she never spoke of it. It was her gift of love.

One day Dona Maria Gorda collapsed, and we rushed her to the public health center, where we were well known, as we were always taking folks there. It was quickly discovered that she'd had a stroke, was a diabetic and had high blood pressure. Having had no medical care up to this point in her life, she was completely unaware of these issues.

Gus and I took over. Dona Maria was very good about taking her meds, but getting her to stick to a proper diet was difficult. We watched her lovingly and she showed her love for us just by being there at the clinic each day with a little something to eat. Food was her way of showing her love and gratitude.

We then discovered that with a new government (this was not long after the military coup), there were new laws, and she was eligible for retirement – a monthly minimum salary of perhaps $150 to $200 U.S. – but it took a determined fight through the bureaucracy to secure it. We succeeded though, and now Dona Maria no longer needed to gather scraps for her soups.

****

In effort to further improve Dona Maria Gorda's health, we took her to a cardiologist, endocrinologist and neurologist. I'd like to tell a story about a visit to the neurologist, because it tells a lot about this remarkable woman.

Dona Maria was the kind of woman who talked to everyone, charming people with her sweetness and innocence. She would ask strangers questions like, "How much does your husband make?" and, "What size underwear does he wear?" When we would leave her for the long wait in a doctor's reception room, she would converse with all those around her, telling stories and asking personal questions. She'd get chummy with the doctors too. "How many children do you have, doctor?" "Where is your wife from?" Captivated by her way, they would always answer. One doctor even swapped recipes with her!

On this one particular visit to the neurologist, we dropped Dona Maria Gorda off and went on to do other things. When we came back, this is the story that was told to us by others in the waiting room.

It seems there was another young woman waiting for her name to be called who was nervous and kept pacing back and forth, mumbling. Dona Maria, in her special way, began to talk to her, saying something along the lines of, "Why are you so nervous, young lady? Be patient; sit down with us and relax."

"No," the woman said, "I have to get home."

"Why are you in such a hurry?" Dona Maria asked. "We have time."

"No; I don't have time," the woman replied. "I have to get home to nurse my son."

"Oh," Dona Maria said. "How sweet. And how old is your son?"

The woman smiled, charmed by the attention she was receiving, and now unwilling to continue with a made-up excuse. "Fifteen years old," she said.

Now all attention in the waiting room was on this woman. Dona Maria looked up at her and smilingly said, "Oh, my; how do you nurse him, sitting down or standing up?"

That is an example of our beloved Dona Maria Gorda.

****

There's one more story I'd like to tell of this extraordinary woman.

One morning when we arrived at the favela, Dona Maria was not there with my coffee and bread. Concerned, I crossed over to her home and found her on the floor in a diabetic coma.

In those days, ambulances would seldom come into favelas, especially one as difficult to reach as this one. So with the help of others, Gus and I got her to our car, and off we went to the closest hospital. But as we were trying to get her seen in the emergency room, we were reminded that documents were required proving that she existed and had worked at some time in her life. In the rush to get her to the

41

hospital, I had forgotten to bring her papers.

I lost it: I began to scream and shout all sorts of things, even threats. These were tenuous times in the country, politically speaking, and shy Gus had the wisdom to try to calm me down – but to no avail. The life of this woman I loved was at risk!

Well, I had an American accent, was middle-aged, my threats were making everyone uncomfortable, and the hospital staff determined that the best thing to do would be to take Dona Maria Gorda into the emergency room while sending us home for her documents. They told us to return the next day.

At six the next morning, we were back, documents in hand and anxious to find out how she was. We were now greeted with warmth and ushered to the infirmary. And there she was, our Dona Maria, holding court. She was sitting up in her bed, chatting away, in that special way of hers, with the other patients, telling yet another of her stories.

The head nurse took me aside and told me the director of the hospital had sat up with Dona Maria all through the night and wanted to see me. To make a long story short, he chided me for the way I acted upon bringing her in, saying that a woman of my age should know better, foreigner or otherwise.

I told him that if I *hadn't* acted that way, she would have died because she wouldn't have been admitted, and that would have been inexcusable. He said, "I can tell you're an American." I didn't ask what he meant by that, but we became friends.

I didn't need to ask him why he sat up all night with this patient. It didn't strike me as at all strange. She could have charmed him even in a diabetic coma. With our Dona Maria, nothing was impossible.

But she was not at all well, and she soon had a stroke. Dona Maria Gorda feared dying alone, and I wanted to bring her home with us, but she couldn't climb stairs. So, with much regret, we put her in a rest home for those with no money or family, but that didn't work out. We brought her home, and she had another stroke and went into another diabetic coma. She died in the hospital on the one day that there was no visitation. Given her fear of dying alone, I felt just devastated.

Dona Maria, if there is a heaven and I can get there, I'll explain why I wasn't there when you passed away.

I don't know that I could love anybody more than I loved her.

The Story of Dona Maria Emilia

Maria Emilia was born in the rural northeast of Brazil, in the state of Paraíba, an extremely impoverished area, in December 1925, to a family who survived raising cattle or doing very rudimentary farming on other people's land. In other words, they were dirt farmers.

It was a very difficult life. The family's house was made of wood strips filled in with mud and the cooking was done over a wood fire. All food came from their garden and the milk came from the one cow that was their own. The closest water was a well some miles away, and every other day or so the children would walk those miles, fill up homemade mud jars and carry them back on their heads. Woe be to the child who let the jar fall or otherwise spilled water.

Dona Maria Emilia

Entire lives were often lived in this region with no record of the individual's existence. There were priests who came yearly to perform baptisms and marriages, and they often promised to register births and deaths, and sometimes actually did – though not infrequently names were forgotten and new ones invented.

Social life was minimal: People would converse at the common well, and there would be the occasional wedding, birth or funeral, when all the farm families would walk or ride horses or homemade carts, often for a great many miles.

At these events, stories were told, often of accidents or deaths or of young girls given or sold to wealthy individuals

44

who came to this poor region looking for girls to work for them in the big cities, even as far away as Rio. These children would never see their families again, but were spared from starvation. Often, people talked the families into giving away or selling their daughters with the promise to send them to school – promises that more often than not went unfulfilled.

And it should be noted that the family member responsible for these dealings was always the father.

Maria Emilia was a pretty child, full of energy, daring, a tomboy who was to become quite a flirt as she entered her adolescent years. She attracted many young boys at the well or whenever farm families gathered. And among the young boys who were attracted to this pretty, vivacious girl was Antonio Jales. The two married while still teenagers and moved to the state of Ceará.

In 1944, Francisca, the first of Maria's ten children (not an unusual number for a poor northeastern rural family) was born. Then came William – and who could imagine that this infant from this very poor family would someday graduate from college and become an architect. But that's another story.

****

After the birth of Dona Maria Emilia's third child, Sonia, life grew more difficult for this young couple, leading to their separation. But then things got worse. After some months, her husband returned and took away the children, not for himself but to hurt Maria. He then placed the two youngest in a boarding school for the poor run by nuns. The oldest girl, Francisca, was placed in the home of one of his girlfriends, with instructions not to allow the girl to mix with other children.

But Maria Emilia, who never accepted "no" for an answer, fought back. Using all the cunning and artfulness she possessed, she began the hunt for her "treasure," as she put it – her greatest treasure, her children. She went from neighborhood to neighborhood asking questions of everyone, then followed up on every story she heard, every possible lead, and at last she found the boarding school where her husband had placed the younger children. She initially wasn't allowed to even see them, as she had no proof that she was their mother. But Dona Maria Emilia waited, patiently, sleeping outside the walls and watching closely, until she spotted them playing in the yard. Scaling the fence, she grabbed them and ran.

Maria Emilia took her children to the home of friends and set out to find her oldest, Francisca. After six months of relentless searching, she found the home of the girlfriend, and there – standing on her tippy toes washing dishes, dirty, with a charcoal-stained dress far too big for her – was her daughter.

Maria Emilia launched her rescue plan by making friends with the woman's neighbors. Again, she watched and waited – and when the moment was right, she swooped in, snatched up her daughter, and off they went.

Maria Emilia was now happy and once again complete; she had her children back – and for her this was paradise.

But reality soon set in. How was she to raise these children with no money, no job, an illiterate woman alone?

It was not easy, and the struggle is well remembered by these children. But Maria Emilia was an artistic and clever woman, and she began to crochet dishtowels, table clothes and the like. She did well, and earned enough to rent a one-room shack far from any member of her husband's family, once again making a home for her children.

She was a young woman, very pretty and full of life, and she soon again met a young man. His name was Luiz: young, handsome, a steady worker, and so enamored of Maria Emilia that he was willing to take on her children. Out of this union came six more children – Mario, Luiz, Itamar, Fatima, Selma and another who died in infancy – quite a lot of mouths to feed, but not unusual for the poor rural families of the northeast.

There is a common saying among the poor of Brazil, "What is good lasts only briefly," and once again ill fortune struck: Luiz died of a ruptured appendix, or so it was believed, as there were no doctors in the area to see him. Maria Emilia was alone again, this time with eight mouths to feed.

But again she stood strong, undaunted. Though ravaged by grief from her loss, she expanded on her artistic talents, learning bordering and sewing, and she found work as a maid, while also washing, ironing and delivering clothes to homes.

Within a few years, both her parents, to whom she'd often turned for help and guidance, passed away. Maria Emilia was now truly alone to raise her children. Many of her brothers and sisters had moved to Rio de Janeiro looking for better lives, to escape from the poverty of the northeast. She received letters from them in which life in Rio seemed like a paradise.

So she made the decision to join them.

****

Her children – who remember so fondly their mother's love – told me these stories. Even after so many years, their memories of those days remained vivid.

Having made the decision to move to Rio, Maria Emilia's task was to choose what to take and what to sell at any price, for the money she had would only pay for what was called a pau de arara ("parrot's perch"), a flatbed truck, standing room only, with wooden posts on the sides to cling to.

So with her brood – aged twelve years to eight months – she set out with but a few possessions on the twelve-day trek from Ceará to Rio de Janeiro. Her brothers were waiting upon their arrival, and off they went to live in the favela called Tavares Bastos, on a hillside overlooking Guanabara Bay – a picture-postcard view, a true socio-economic contrast.

Now how to feed eight hungry children? Maria needed to work, but how? Who would take care of so many children? It seemed there was only one solution: colegio interno, boarding school – a solution that broke her heart. But there seemed no other way until she was able to make a living for them.

She found a job as a maid, and the woman for whom she worked, admiring her determination, told her of an organization, Services of Assistance for Minors, that took in street children accused of misdemeanors. As Maria Emilia

47

puts it, "God was looking out for my children," and they were sent to public boarding schools, with promises that it would only be temporary. On her one day off a week, she would go, without fail, to visit each of her children, assuring them that they weren't abandoned.

But in order to bring them home, she needed to find a way to work at home, and one day she heard that the wife of the mayor of Rio de Janeiro would be giving a few sewing machines to needy families. Maria Emilia asked someone to help her write a letter to the woman explaining that she needed a machine so that she, a widow, could financially support her eight children.

Her neighbors laughed at her. "Imagine," they said, "that the mayor's wife will even read this letter." But Maria Emilia prayed and waited, and one afternoon a truck with the mayor's name on it climbed up the mountainside to the favela and asked where a Dona Maria Emilia lived. It was to deliver her sewing machine.

Wooden shutters and doors opened all along the path as her neighbors peered out at the men carrying this wonderful thing, and they cheered. With this sewing machine, Maria Emilia began to sew clothes, dish towels, sheets and more, and very soon acquired enough clientele to guarantee a steady income – enough to bring her children home. It was the victory of a courageous and determined woman.

****

Maria Emilia, a widow, thirty-three, attractive and full of life, was a good catch for any man. And she was ready. And sure enough, it happened. She met a widower, a man named Vicente from Minais Gerais who had two children and was willing to take on another family, Maria Emilia and her eight children, to become now a family of twelve in this favela hut. Vicente was unable to read and write but took on any work he could find.

Time passed and all was going well with the newlyweds, when, sure enough, they soon added a child to the family, Roberto. Maria Emilia and Vicente managed to feed and clothe this brood and the older children found after-school jobs, helping with the expenses and leaving no time to get into trouble, as so many slum kids did. Despite the hardships, these children were brought up quite well.

And in time, Maria Emilia gathered the fruits of her many years of sacrifice and struggle. One day, William, the oldest boy, came home and announced that he had purchased a house for the family. Of course, Maria Emilia at first thought it was a joke, until he showed her the key – the key to a house not in the favela but in the suburbs of Rio. The house had a yard and much more space for this large family. It was old, and not in good condition, but it was theirs. Maria Emilia felt fulfilled.

And there was more joy to come. The hardworking William, driving a taxi and attending college in his off hours, graduated with a degree in electronics and soon became a member of the prestigious Engineering Club of Rio de Janeiro. Three of Maria Emilia's sons were also able to work their way through college, receiving degrees in various fields.

What an example of the determination and dedication of a woman whose life had been one of sacrifice and difficulty. But it had all paid off. Maria Emilia's children are all well aware of their mother's value. She is a woman I feel privileged to have known. During this time, the family suffered a tragedy, the death of Maria Emilia's son Itamar, still in his twenties, of health problems that no doctor could treat. But her life was full; all of her children married and she was blessed with twenty-four grandchildren.

The girls – Francisca, Sonia, Fatima and Selma – were not even considered for higher education, nor did they want it. This was typical of women's status at that time in Brazil. The roll of a woman was to marry well and bring up her children. This they did, with their mother as an exemplary role model.

Mammy Yokum

How to describe Dona Cecilia? The closest I can come (for those of you old enough to remember) is L'il Abner's mother, Mammy Yokum. Dona Cecilia was a real life Mammy Yokum: measuring less than five feet and weighing maybe eighty-five pounds, kerchief on her head and a pipe in the corner of her mouth, puffing away and talking out the other side.

Dona Cecilia spoke the part as well, with her backwoods rhythms and colloquial slang. Her standard attire was a housedress, with large diaper-like pins on one side, either to hold the shabby dress together over her skinny body or to apply to one of her grandchildren's items of clothing.

I didn't know much of Dona Cecilia's life before we met, except that she came from an extremely rural area. She had three daughters, but may well have given birth to more, for infant mortality was high in remote areas in those years, as was maternal mortality, though no one then bothered with statistics.

I knew she was a widow, was illiterate, had never seen a doctor and was very backward in her thoughts and ways. Why and how she came to the favela, I don't recall her ever saying, nor did she ever mention her husband.

By the time I met her, her daughters – Geralda, Vilma and Maria – were grown and lived down the hill from the central part of the favela. Dona Cecilia raised chickens and sometimes pigs, and the animals ran freely about, both outside and inside the home. There was, for a time, an old, scrawny dog, and always there were cats.

I can see them all now on the long open porch in front of Dona Cecilia's shack, her daughters, now married with children of their own – including one, Vilma, who was our godchild – sitting beside her, one scattering feed to the chickens, the dog chasing the cat and barking at the squawking chickens – a scene truly right out of L'il Abner. Dona Cecilia sucks on her pipe as her oldest daughter tells her how to better care for herself, as she was prone to accidents. Some of the stories of those accidents were funny, though sad as well, due to her ignorance.

For example, there was the time she cut her hand on her rusty stove handle and came over to our little health care hut for assistance. I was sitting at the desk taking a blood pressure when her daughters brought her in with her whole arm bandaged. The wound was not too bad but the skin was broken, so I told them to take her to the public health center to get a tetanus shot, knowing she'd never had one in her life. She was probably in her late forties, early fifties, and I knew it would be a traumatic experience for her, but that it had to be done.

Dona Cecilia loudly protested, and when her daughter tried to pull her up she pushed her away and told her to mind her own business, that she'd had cuts before and there'd been no consequences. She knew how to care for herself, she said, and all she wanted from us was to treat the wound, as she had nothing in her hut to put on it. In the area she came from, there were all sorts of plants she would have used, but her daughters wouldn't let her use them in the city.

"Ya know," Dona Cecilia, said, "just because these girls have had some schooling, they think they know everything!" (The girls had only the equivalent of a grammar school education.)

But the daughters won this battle, and took her to the public health clinic to get a shot.

The next day though, Dona Cecilia was back at my desk with that same hand now badly burned, covered with water boils, and she was in a lot of pain.

"What on earth happened to your hand?" I asked.

Her daughter, Geralda, sighed. She had told her mother that heat would help cure her hand and relieve the pain, so Dona Cecilia had boiled water and dunked her hand in it.

There are other stories of Dona Cecilia to tell. She, like so many of the favela women, washed and ironed clothes for

51

the well-to-do families that lived down the hill. Dona Cecilia would climb up and down the hill, fetching dirty clothes and delivering clean ones, folded in newspaper or flour sacks and balanced atop her head. One of her daughters always accompanied her, usually Maria, the youngest, who was slightly developmentally challenged.

One day though, Dona Cecilia was delivering the clothes alone. When she reached the bottom of the hill and started down the well-known route to the apartment where her customer lived, she encountered something unexpected: There were yellow wooden barricades in her path, hindering the passage along her familiar route. A subway line was being constructed.

Dona Cecilia stopped, began to turn around, but was confused by the barricades and the many people who were turning onto other routes. She was lost, and she was dizzy. Gathering herself, she devised a solution: If she backed up the way she came, she would get back to a familiar place. And that's exactly what she did: The package of clothing atop her head, she backed up. This was Dona Cecilia.

This final story, however, is the one I think captures her best. Her daughters Vilma and Maria came to me one day to tell me they had noticed that their mother had an odd smell, and that they thought it was coming from the lower part of her body. There was no piped-in water, and bathing was done with buckets of water behind a sort of shed. They'd tried to catch her taking a bath to see if they could determine what might be wrong, but had been unsuccessful.

So one day, while Dona Cecilia was lying down, they sat on her, removed her skirt and underpants and saw that she had a discharge with a sour smell.

This they told me, and that they didn't know what to do. So I said I would make an appointment with a gynecologist I knew, a woman, which I thought would make the idea more palatable for Dona Cecilia, remembering that she had never before been examined by a doctor.

The day came and her daughters fooled her into coming, saying they were taking Maria to the doctor and that Dona Cecilia should come. We took them, and when it was our turn to enter the doctor's office I just pushed her in and closed the door behind her. She hesitated, but sat down, nervously clearing her throat. Dr. Paulinha, who saw all the women I brought to the clinic from the favela, quickly and accurately assessed the situation, and the extent of Dona Cecilia's discomfort with it all. Dona Cecilia was trembling; the throat clearing had become incessant.

"Well, Dona Cecilia, what brought you here today?" Dr. Paulinha asked. I patted her head and told her that since she was here anyway, she might as well tell the doctor if she had any problems.

"Oh," she said, "it's this hawking that I have; it keeps me awake."

Dr. Paulinha smiled and said, "Well, Dona Cecilia, step behind this curtain, take off your underwear and I'll examine you.

Now, you would think that anyone would wonder why if the doctor was going to check the throat she would ask you to take off your underwear. But Dona Cecilia, naive, nervous and frightened, did just as she was told. The curtain separating the examining table from the rest of the room was almost transparent and I could see Dona Cecilia being helped onto the table, her legs being placed in the stirrups. She had not let out a peep, and at that moment I was truly sorry we had tricked her.

Then I heard her groan. Not a word said, just groans, as the doctor began to place the cold metal of the instrument into the vaginal area. Then what happened, happened so fast that I can't describe it accurately. Dona Cecilia flew off that table and disappeared before our eyes – gone before we realized what was happening. Not bothering to collect her underwear, this tiny woman vanished as we stood there with our mouths agape.

She'd left her mark with her daughters though. On the way out the door, she had reached up and slapped them both, screaming indecipherable words of anger.

We searched for hours, but couldn't find her. She had no money, and we were twenty minutes by car, with a tunnel to go through, from the favela. Where could she go?

That evening, she was brought back to the door of the clinic by a woman who found her begging at a bus stop and suspected she didn't know how to get home.

Needless to say, I had to work hard to win Dona Cecilia's confidence again, and it was days before she spoke to her daughters. The end of the story came two years later, when her uterus collapsed and she ended up in the hospital for a hysterectomy.

The Story of Alice

Alice is a mixture of all the races that represent the beauty of the Brazilian people. She has both indigenous and black features, and surely her DNA would show some Caucasian as well. I don't know much of her early life; she spoke little of her parents. But I do know that as a very young girl, perhaps not even yet a teenager, she was working as a maid for a well-to-do family in the new capital of Brasília.

Brasília was the ambitious project of one of the more famous Brazilian presidents, Juscelino Kubitschek. Bahia was the country's first capital, then Rio, but the idea was to move the population from these coastal cities to the interior in order to advance the area's development. So while the capital was moved to the center of the country, for many years it had little employment to offer. Nonetheless, the city grew, and became a huge metropolis.

Though Alice worked as a servant, her employers allowed her to learn to read and write. As a teenager, she met a young man, Trajano, from the poverty-stricken northeast of Brazil, where the mixtures of races were similar to hers. People always joked that northeasterners had short necks because their parents would constantly pat their heads, saying, "Go, my child, to São Paulo," where good jobs were to be had.

Why this short-necked young man, Trajano, unskilled and illiterate, stopped in Brasília, I don't know, but it was here that he and Alice began their life together.

****

From Brasília they headed to Rio, perhaps hoping to move on to São Paulo. But that was as far as this very young couple, now with a young son, had the money to reach. Trajano was a typical northeastern man, very macho. Women were to have children, keep house, obey their husbands and

55

be totally modest in all ways. Such was Trajano, and Alice trailed behind him and accepted whatever he said.

Very soon after settling in their hut, Trajano and Alice came over to our pharmacy, having heard that we helped people arrange for doctors' appointments and would also assist with the paperwork necessary to receive public services. Their little boy, Jeronimo, who was more than a year old, had a twisted foot and was unable to stand. Trajano was getting only very low-paying jobs, and there was just barely enough money to buy food. They also had no documents; Jeronimo had no birth certificate. Without the paperwork, no hospital or doctor would treat him. So our first task was to secure the paperwork. This took months, while the boy's foot grew more deformed, but eventually we were successful.

By this time, Gus and I had been working in the favela for some time, had come to know numerous doctors and public health administrators, and knew where to go to get the proper referrals. The process, including surgery and physical therapy, took almost a year. But by the time Geronimo was two and a half, his foot was almost straightened out and he was well on his way to recovery. He did have a limp, and still needed therapy, which Alice helped him with in their tiny hut: Hour after hour, together they would exercise rigorously.

But Alice was not a happy woman. Trajano often beat her; his sexual appetite was too much for her, and she feared getting pregnant again and would sometimes refuse him, and he would beat her. There was no birth control available at the time. But even if there had been, Trajano would not have allowed it. Alice had one miscarriage and one stillborn baby. The family barely had enough to eat, and only with donations were they able to buy medicines and other necessities.

****

Then came a change in their lives – an unexpected and, or so Trajano thought, wonderful opportunity. The government wanted to build a road into the Amazon to help develop the northeast, and a great deal of labor was needed for what would be a risky adventure. So an offer was given to poor families to homestead along the highway they were to work on. A piece of land was promised as well as sustenance while they settled in.

Trajano, unable to find a job and unskilled, fit the bill, and jumped at the chance. Without consulting Alice, he signed up for this venture.

Alice was devastated and afraid, worried about, among other things, Jeronimo's healing foot. With little choice, she agreed to go, but only on the condition that Trajano would make their union legal. To be married – to have a name and an honorable reputation – was the dream of all poor women in those days, and was especially important to Alice, who had no other family around her.

This seemed simple enough for us to arrange; there would be the usual red tape, but we could handle that, as we had done it for so many others. But Trajano insisted on having his parents present. In fact, what he wanted was to help them leave their difficult, impoverished life in the northeast. He knew there were agencies that helped families be rejoined, but needed our help. He knew only how to write his name, and the paperwork was beyond Alice's skills as well.

So we agreed to help, and within a few months Trajano's father and mother had arrived. But Alice had just had a miscarriage after a beating by Trajano, and things were tense. We were then shocked to discover that the parents didn't approve of the marriage, and everything was at a standstill.

The time was coming to leave for the north, and decisions had to be made. Why did they not approve? Though Alice had indigenous features, her skin was dark, and they convinced Trajano he shouldn't marry her.

Alice, shocked, asked us to take her and Jeronimo in. She said she would work for us till she found a solution. We agreed, and she packed up and moved into our house. Trajano took his parents into their little hut, and for several months we didn't see him.

But he learned that the government wouldn't accept single men into its homesteading project; wives were required, presumably to keep the men contented in their remote surroundings. So Trajano turned over his and Alice's hut to his parents and married Alice without their blessing. They were now off. As Alice hugged me, she said she would return with a child for us to baptize.

****

What happened to this young couple next is unbelievable, and further evidence of women's strength in spite of extreme hardship. Yes, they were given a piece of land along the highway to be constructed and material to build a home – that is, a meager shelter from the wild terrain they were to live in. Trajano had to walk miles to haul back the supplies that weren't provided. Everything was purchased from the government, to whom everyone remained in perpetual debt.

There was no water, so a well had to be dug, and prayers were said that it wouldn't run dry. Rainwater was collected in whatever container could be found.

But Trajano was young and strong, and Alice worked at everything: hauling water, planting, making clothes out of flour sacks, fashioning screens to protect them from the mosquitoes and other bugs. She fought off invading animals when Trajano was away and continued with her son's physical therapy. Often she would have to carry him on their long walks to the well.

There was, of course, no electricity, so water had to be boiled over a wood fire, for which wood had to be found. As you can imagine, diarrhea and other illnesses were rampant; infant mortality was a part of life. When someone became very ill, a neighbor with a horse or one willing to walk the miles between the homes would spread the news, and women who were able went to help. Men often were called upon to make a stretcher to carry a very sick person to the nearest medical center, which was several days' travel away. With no means of communication, patients' fates were unknown until they returned home or died.

It was into this environment that Alice's second child was born. Upon learning she was pregnant, she prepared what would be needed and informed Trajano that he would have to stay near as the time approached. She saw no doctor. Her medications consisted of leaves, bark and other of nature's gifts.

The time came. Alice boiled water and sterilized a knife, prepared her bed and told Trajano to go fetch a neighbor. He hadn't gone far though when he heard Jeronimo screaming and saw him hobbling after him. There was no time for a neighbor. Instructed by Alice, Trajano delivered his second son.

****

In the next few months, there were several deaths among the homesteaders. Supplies weren't coming in as promised, and the exodus began. Trajano, Alice and their two sons returned to their hut in the favela.

Alice brought us the godchild she had promised, Ernani, but she was a different woman. She had matured far beyond her years, and we hoped that Trajano too had matured, for they would have to begin all over again, now with a larger family. They had suffered much together, and had been each other's only companion. Their relationship had changed.

But even with all this experience, Trajano was still an unskilled worker. His parents had taken over his hut, so he would have to rebuild; they would really begin all over again. He had no job to return to, just a little compensation from the government for his work with which to begin a new life.

In the following years, three more sons were born to the couple. They built a new hut, and Trajano, unable to keep a job, set up a tiny shop in the favela where he sold fresh vegetables and other such things that he purchased down the hill at the open markets, carried up the hill and sold at a higher price to the favela dwellers. This was a boon to the dwellers, in that it saved them the long trek down the hill and was so convenient.

It was a difficult job and the family was always struggling, but as time went on Trajano was able to improve the family's life. The little favela, high on the mountain looking over the beautiful bay of Guanabara, with the statue of Christ in view, was developing into a more self-sufficient community.

We voted in a board of directors. We had a president, and Gus and I were placed on the board. I was in charge of health and he was in charge of electricity, which was now available. Not everyone had it, but they would wire it from one house to another, and it was Gus's job to make sure the city got its money for that. The city also piped water into the homes. Things were changing.

****

All of Alice's boys developed allergies, which resulted in bronchial asthma. There were so many times when Alice rushed to the emergency room with one or more of the boys in crisis. At one of the hospitals we frequented, a nurse told us of a doctor in private practice who made vaccines for allergies. The nurse had become a friend of ours because of our many trips there with the boys and others, and offered to write a letter to this doctor, who was a friend of her cousin's.

So off we went to meet him. The doctor was excited about trying out his vaccines on the boys and agreed to do so without charge if Gus and I would take watch over the applications. I was frightened at this untested experiment, and knew this type of procedure would never be permitted in the U.S. But Alice begged me to agree, as it seemed their only hope.

So for the next six or so years, these four little boys came to our hut on a regular schedule for their vaccine injections. I shall never forget how they filed into the hut and sat down on the couch to wait their turns. And after each one had received his shot, he would say thank you, even as he was shedding a few tears. Jeronimo would then collect them, and they'd file out. As they grew older, they still always came together, the older ones often dragging the younger ones. Their mother had taught them exemplary manners; she didn't want them to be like their crude father. She had dreams for these boys.

****

But Alice certainly wasn't content. Trajano had returned to his old self, and beat her quite often, especially when she refused his untimely sexual advances. His appetite continued to be too much for her, and she couldn't risk another pregnancy. She came to me, and I taught her natural means of birth control, which worked well enough. But as she refused him more and more, Trajano found another woman. His little store had grown more lucrative, and he had money to spend on his desires, but would give no money to Alice.

Alice wanted money for books and school supplies for the children; she didn't want her sons to be illiterate like their father. So she took in sewing and clothing repairs, and with that money bought what she could for the boys.

In Brazil, children are required to wear school uniforms, but Trajano refused to give her the money, so she made them. Shoes, though, became a problem. She couldn't make them, and they were expensive, especially Jeronimo's special shoes. So she sent them off to school shoeless.

One day, one of the boys came home crying. The teacher had sent him from school, saying he couldn't come back without shoes. Alice was undaunted. The next day, she took the boy back to school and explained to the teacher that she simply didn't have the money to buy shoes for five boys. Alice was a charming, polite woman, the type who attracted people with her sincerity. The teacher offered to buy one of the pairs in return for sewing lessons. And so it went. With each of her son's teachers, Alice traded her skills for shoes for her boys.

Of course, Trajano knew nothing of this, and neither did we for a while; we only learned of it when Trajano decided he wanted Jeronimo to stop his schooling and help in the store. As the boy was not a good student and still had some physical difficulties because of his foot, he was delighted to stay home. But it wasn't okay with Alice. She came to us, begging us to intervene, telling us of all that she'd done to keep the boys in school.

We tried to talk to Trajano, but it was of no use. He was going to train his son to do something "useful," as he put it.

Our only recourse was to go to the school authorities. School was compulsory, but no one ever checked up on the favela children. A school officer went to speak to Trajano and, as he had no license to operate his food stand, he was pressured into allowing Jeronimo to return to school.

But Alice paid highly for this, with beatings and humiliations. She was able, though, to keep Jeronimo in school until he was almost twelve, when he began performing so poorly that he was called to repeat a grade. Trajano then removed him and put him to work in the store.

Alice abided by the decision, focusing her energy on keeping the others in school. She knew that without an education, they had little chance in life.

Jeronimo did, however, learn how to run the store – which left Trajano with more free time to spend away from it with other women. Ernani, our godson, finished high school with difficulty, but he was a talented soccer player. He played in the minor leagues, but wasn't good enough for the top levels. He entered a rebellious period, but with his mother's insistence went to a trade school and became a porteiro, a doorman. He married and had a son.

The other boys finished high school. Two learned a trade and one was a natural with figures and became an unofficial accountant, helping people in the favela and handling the financial end of his father's business. And the youngest was an artist, a natural talent. With help from numerous people along the way, he attended art school and later got a scholarship to study architecture.

The boys, even as men, cared for their mother, and she needed it. Though Trajano allowed her to remain in the big house he had built in the favela, he moved out and built a house for himself and his new woman next to his expanded store. He no longer gave Alice any money, and she counted on the boys to supplement her limited income. Jeronimo brought her food from the store, behind his father's back.

I haven't seen Alice in years, but know that she had a stroke, followed by signs of weakening cognitive abilities, or what we know as dementia. What a sad end for such a woman of strength and determination. I certainly shall never forget her. She never knew her value. Her sons knew though, and they stuck by her.

Did they ever tell her what a magnificent woman and mother she was? I don't know. I hope so.

An Abandoned Dog and Baby

"Look in the back seat," Gus said as I climbed into our car after giving an English lesson.

I turned my head, and there in the back seat was a box and in the box was a pup, just a mutt, but, like all pups, cute and just yearning to be loved. Gus knew how much I loved dogs. But he also knew that when he told me how he happened to acquire the pup, I would be even more moved to keep it.

As he was driving down the hill from the favela, he had heard a series of tiny squeaks. Curiosity got the best of him, and he stopped the car and walked a ways into the woods. There he found a sack, torn at the bottom, with four pups inside.

The two pups on the top had worked their way out, but the other two were dead. So being a dog lover himself, and knowing what my reaction would be, he put the two dogs in the car. But, he thought, bringing two dogs home might be too much, so he rode down the hill and stopped at a small apartment building and called to the porteiro, a man he knew.

"Hey, Jose, know someone who wants a pup? I heard you were looking for one for your son."

The man came over and looked. He smiled and said, "Not really; but let me see." He picked them up, and seeing that one was a female, the other a male, he said, "Okay, I'll take this one." And he walked away with the male.

So the little dog in the car looking up at me, begging for me to pick her up was now our pup. Her name to be was Zuzuki, named by my daughter Judy.

I tell you this so that you might understand what this next story would add to my thoughts and questionings about love and justice, about humanity, about creation.

One evening a couple of years later as I got into our car when Gus came to pick me up from the home of one of my English students, I heard a sound. Though I could hardly believe it, it was the cry of a baby!

Gus looked at me and pointed his thumb toward the back seat. There, rolled up in a worn blanket, was an infant. I got out of the car and into the back seat and picked the infant up. Its umbilical chord was still on; it was a newborn.

In astonishment, I cried out something to the effect of: "What the heck is this all about? Where did you find this baby? What's going on?"

This is what Gus told me:

As he was coming down the hill from the favela, he heard a loud voice, a woman's voice, calling for help. He got out of the car, listened to find where the noise was coming from and followed the sound into the woods.

There, under a tree, was a woman, wailing. She wore a torn dress and was filthy, her hair wild and unruly. When she saw Gus, she raised her hands and wailed even louder. When he approached her, she tried to get up but didn't have the strength.

"I went to her and she shoved this baby in my arms," Gus said, "and said, 'Please; take him. I have to get away or they'll catch me. Take him quickly; they're after me.'"

He tried to reason with her. But in a burst of energy, she sprang up and flew off into the woods. And there he was with this baby in his arms, crying, wrapped in bloody newspaper.

I wondered if the woman was perhaps an escapee from the nearby mental institution. The baby was now clean, wrapped in a blanket and sleeping. Gus had taken him to Dona Maria do Senhor Teto's hut in the woods, and she had tended to him and nursed him. She said that she would ask around to see if anyone knew the mother.

As we drove home with the infant cradled in my arms, I couldn't help but remember the abandoned puppy Gus had found in the same woods. A pup abandoned, and now a child. Another life thrown aside, another life that hadn't asked to be brought into this world, now rejected. A child and a dog, each saved only by chance.

****

It seems only fair to tell you the outcome of this story. Dona Maria do Senhor Teto kept the little one to save us from going back and forth for the nursing. We went to the mental facility and learned that women often escaped; some came back or were found, others disappeared forever.

Before the baby was yet a month old, Dona Maria had found a woman in the favela whose baby had died soon after birth, still had milk and took over nursing responsibilities. She was happy to take the infant to relieve Dona Maria.

The end of this story is perhaps obvious: The woman fell in love with the little boy she was giving life to with her milk, and took him as her own. This was all possible in Brazil at that time. A boy and a dog, both abandoned, had found homes, but most of all had found love.

And I pondered this. Was I really living all this? Never in my wildest imagination would I have thought I would live such experiences. And as I was experiencing them, I needed to find meaning in it all.

A Woman's Tragic Abortion

The story I'm going to tell you now affected my life very deeply, and certainly shaped my future work in Brazil.

I'd been working in the favela for some time and thought I knew everyone and their families. But one day, I was asked to come look in on a woman in a nearby hut. There a young woman whose face wasn't familiar to me was stretched out on a cot, blood all around her; her sheets, soaked. I rushed to her side. Her body was cold, her eyes closed, and she was moaning.

There was another woman in the tiny hut and three young children. The youngest one was crying; but the older two, perhaps three and five, were staring, eyes wide, but silent.

At first glance, I assumed the woman had given birth. But since I'd never seen this family before, I could only guess. I asked if she'd had a baby. There was silence. The woman on the bed opened her eyes and spoke an almost silent word. I bent down to hear her, but she said nothing more. I took her pulse, and it was dangerously low.

Concerned for the children, I asked someone to take them out and someone else to call the police or an ambulance as quickly as possible. I knew that because of where this hut was, no ambulance or police car could get to it, but a stretcher and doctors were needed.

An older woman, whom I knew, then entered.

"Dona Barbara, she used a coat hanger; she used that coat hanger," the woman said, pointing to what I had not noticed: a bloody coat hanger that had been twisted into a sort of rod that I was told she had inserted into her vagina to abort.

The older woman told me she had sent the children out, locked the door and done it. When the children tried to get in, the door wouldn't open, and she didn't answer them, even though the youngest was crying. The neighbors broke in and found her as I had. She had spoken though, telling the neighbor to look in the drawer of an old bureau where she would find the telephone number of her sister.

As we were talking, the woman struggled again to speak. I could barely hear her, and I knew she was in very bad shape – that if help didn't arrive soon she would bleed to death. I was doing what I could, but there wasn't a lot that could be done.

Another woman I knew came into the hut talking loudly: "She's crazy! Didn't want help! Wouldn't speak to anyone, kept to herself and, well, she is irresponsible, crazy. We could have told her what to do!"

She was prepared to continue on, but I stopped her, and sent her out the door. Not the time for judgment.

I was alone now with this woman. Her eyes opened, she looked at me, and she said: "I'm so sorry to cause all this trouble. I'll be fine; just let me rest. Please, where are the children? Please tell them I'm fine."

I held her hand, and my tears flowed. Did she know she had so endangered her life? Did she realize the seriousness of her condition? She was shaking with cold and I put a blanket on her and waited for help. I held her hand, and she asked me to say a prayer for her. I did.

Could she even hear me? I don't know. I heard people arriving, the door opened and in walked two men in white. One of them began examining the woman, then asked me what had happened. I told him what I knew. He asked me who I was and what the woman's name was. I answered that I didn't know, and called a neighbor.

While we were talking, the woman gave a sigh, sort of trembled, and the doctor quickly moved to her side. She had stopped breathing. He took her pulse and blood pressure, and said she had died. No effort was made to save her.

****

A victim of ignorance, of the times, of poor health care, of poverty – of a culture dominated by men and the haves.

She was a woman and a have-not. She had died because of her ignorance of how her body functioned, or of her rights as a woman, or of a lot of things I wouldn't know, because at that moment I knew nothing of her. I didn't know what had brought her to do this. But I could imagine, and I knew that in the days to come I would hear stories and condemnations.

But I couldn't condemn her; she was a victim. What had caused her to do this? How desperate she must have been. But I was sure she hadn't thought she would die. She had other children to live for.

I wept. I cried for all the women who had been denied their rights to know about their own bodies. And as time went on, that became my goal in life, the reason I created a training course for community health educators. I knew nothing of this woman, but she changed my life.

There's a Native-American saying: "Never judge a man without walking a mile in his moccasins."

My mantra became: "Never judge a woman without walking a mile in her shoes."

My Chicken Story

This story is about my trips to the interior of the state of Rio de Janeiro, about four hours drive from the city of Rio, where Gus's godparents, Senhor Pedro and Dona Adelaide, lived.

When we traveled to the interior in those days, the 1970s, it was like going back a full century. They were farmers, raising pigs and cows. The sale of the milk and meat provided a meager income, and Senhor Pedro and his brother, Senhor João, who had a similar farm nearby, grew all the food for their families' consumption.

They lived far from anyplace where anything could be purchased and the milk was hauled in oxen-pulled wagons. There was no electricity or running water, roads were of dirt and the only transportation was by horse, a wagon or ox over very tricky roads. The homes of both these families were made of stone and mud or mud and tree trunks. The roofs were of straw, and when you were trying to sleep you could hear all sorts of noises, which we were told were straw snakes, mice and who knows what.

The kitchen was where the family spent most of its time. It had a dirt floor and a rustic stone cooking area to one side. There was but one window, with poorly made wooden shutters, and in the middle of the floor was a sort of indentation, almost a hole, where the animals huddled to keep warm.

Now let me tell you about these animals that kept us company in the kitchen. You had chickens cackling, a little pig that stayed in the hole, a medium-sized dog, a few puppies, several cats and the cow at the window. There was no fighting, just a few squawks from the chickens, and no one paid any attention to that.

The animals came in and out of the open door, and every once in a while Dona Adelaide would become annoyed and shoo them all out with a broom. The excitement came when she would throw a few bones into the center of the floor. It was a scurry then, in which you lost track of which animal was which.

****

Sunday dinner was special in the home of Senhor Pedro and Dona Adelaide, and so it was served in the dining room, which had a crudely built wood floor. The food was placed in the center of a homemade table, grace was said and plates were passed. As food was eaten, the bones and other scraps were dropped on the floor, and the scrambling began. You had to protect your feet as the battle ensued. No one paid any notice.

Senhor Pedro had a cow that he had raised himself. Her name was Estrela, or star. She gave milk but was treated as a pet and never came into the kitchen only because she was too big to get in the door. But she would come around to the open window and stick her head in to join the crowd.

Estrela and I became quite friendly over the years, probably because Senhor Pedro let me give her sugar. She became so friendly with me that if she was out in the fields when I arrived, Senhor Pedro would call her name and she would come bounding in to see me and to receive her block of sugar.

And if we were sitting on the benches in the kitchen and she knew I was there, she would poke her head in the window to have me scratch her. What a wonderful image this brings to my memory.

****

Gus and I still grow emotional when we recall Senhor Pedro's untimely death. He always worked barefoot – this big, simple, sweet-talking rural man, who loved his animals as if they were the children he never had. He had no clothes other than what he worked in except for the suit he was

70

married in, which was then too small for him to be buried in.

While out milking his cows, one of them stepped on his foot, and the wound became infected. It got so bad that he could hardly walk. His wife, brother and others kept telling him to go into town and see a doctor, but as he had no clothes and would have to go by horse, and with a fever, it was too much for him, until he collapsed. His brother then hitched up the horse wagon and they carried him the hour-and-a-half ride to Tres Rio's hospital. There Senhor Pedro begged for a tetanus shot, but was told it was too late. Lockjaw had set in, and he died within forty-eight hours, still in his sixties. This was rural Brazil.

But there's more.

It was unusual that Senhor Pedro and Dona Adelaide had no children; most women had more than enough. For example, Senhor Pedro's brother's wife, Maria, had given birth to fifteen, as I recall, though only nine survived. And their children, living in huts on the land and sharing the farm with them, had, at that time, an average of seven each, I'd say.

It was because of this that Senhor João's wife asked me to speak to the women in her family about how to stop having so many children. She made this request very shyly, unable to look me in the eye.

And here was a challenge: How to explain a woman's reproductive organs to women who may have had, at most, a couple of years of schooling and whose lives were dominated by their husbands – women for whom this subject was never to be discussed.

It was only because Dona Maria had been told that I, being a foreigner, knew of such things that she had the courage to say: "Dona Barbara, I know you can help my daughters and sons-in-laws' wives not have so many children. They're so tired, with the farm work, the children, and, well, they've lost so many, it's just so hard on them."

Yes, I could imagine. In addition to all she'd described, there was the matter of taking the children who weren't needed to work the farm to school on horseback and picking them up. They were the miracle workers, these wives and mothers, as far as I was concerned, and if I could help, I would.

****

I need to describe the farm on which Senhor João and Dona Maria lived. It was arranged like Senhor Pedro and Dona Adelaide's farm, except that the cow stable was in the front. That meant that there were cow flies, and excrement, all over the place. The adult children's homes were a distance away, but they spent a large part of their time in Dona Maria's home – farmwomen working together to survive a harsh life.

Outside the kitchen was a running stream and some ways down was the outhouse over the stream. There was also a hog pen, and chickens, dogs and cats running all over the place. This house was quite a bit smaller than Senhor Pedro's, but was still the family's gathering place for Sunday dinner.

So it was decided that I should come for one of these Sunday dinners and give my talk. When the time came, the men would be sent to the barn.

But first came dinner. When the food was ready, the men were served first, then the children and the women last. This made it possible for these some twenty human beings to eat their Sunday meal – theoretically together, in this tiny hut.

After dinner, the dishes were thrown into a huge stream water-filled barrel to soak. The men retreated and I sat down with the women: Dona Maria's daughters and daughters-in-law. I could tell they had no idea what the topic of conversation was – but here goes, I thought.

Dona Maria explained to the women that I knew some things that would help them control their "birthing," as she put it. All faces were upon me. These women, I remembered, had had some schooling, and though it may have been but two or three years, they probably knew more than Dona Maria.

I laid the cardboard doll on the dirt floor, with all its genital parts, and began to explain. Some looked at me eagerly, interested and taking note; others never raised their eyes, for this was a taboo subject and one that embarrassed them. Some asked questions. And though there was little I could really teach them in this one short lesson, I could tell that just the idea that there were times when they were more likely to give birth than others opened possibilities, and that they knew they needed to know more.

After they all mounted their horses or buggies and drove off, I told Dona Maria that I would try to come again within the next few months, but that she needed to encourage them so they would feel freer to question.

As I was getting ready to leave, she turned to me and said she needed to ask me something, but didn't know how to do so. She dropped her eyes and said: "Do you think it's wrong to deny one's husband when he comes in from the barn and wants to take me to the bed? He hasn't bathed and, well, you know, he does smell bad."

I was truly tongue-tied.

Yes, I did go back and give these women several more talks. And though I knew their husbands ruled the home and expected women to have children – after all, to them that was their role in life – I do think it made a difference in the women's lives.

And my thoughts were once again turned to the fantastic roles lived out by these women: Birthing and raising the children were just a small part of their struggling existence. Yet it was this that gave them their value in the eyes of their husbands, while the survival techniques they acquired weren't recognized. Their lack of education was, yes, a detriment. But to compensate, they had the stamina that hardship brings.

****

I just have to add this one other experience I had with these women – a tale on myself.

On one of these trips to work with the women, one of them gave me a gift, a live chicken, which for them was a very valuable gift. But for me, who had become a city girl, it was not the ideal gift.

I said thank you, put the chicken in the back seat, and off we went. For four hours, I listened to this chicken squawking and thought, "Now what am I going to do with this bird?" These women killed the birds themselves, and how would I do that?

Dona Adelaide had told me to ring its neck and Dona Maria had added that I should give it cachaca, a homemade alcoholic beverage similar to moonshine in the States, and gave me some to take home. These were the only words of instruction I had received; for these woman, this was a common chore.

When I arrived home with my prize, I placed the chicken in the yard, gave it some corn feed, and there it was for days, until I could no longer stand the squawking and the filth it left. The day had come and I would have to do it.

I prepared for the neck wringing by giving it the cachaca as told. It would be numbed for the murder – or so I thought! For the better part of a day, I chased that chicken around the yard, pouring cachaca down its neck each time I could corner it. I did it over and again till the drink was all gone. Cachaca is pure alcohol, and that night I found the poor thing dead – dead of an overdose of cachaca! The job was done; no neck wringing was necessary. It had died drunk but in no pain, and I was freed from a horrible task.

The next day, I was informed that the cachaca wasn't meant to kill the chicken. It was meant as a tenderizer.

I didn't eat that chicken, but I was told it was tender but bitter – an excess of alcohol, I imagine.

A Mother's Strength

The story I'm going to tell you now began after we had been working in the favela for some time. As I've said, we had acquired our little hut, which we'd made into a free pharmacy where the doctors' samples, which were given to us, were stored. Gus and I were now well known at the large public health clinic, a great distance from the favela, where each day we took people to consult with the doctors or for exams. The doctors knew what we did and were happy to donate free samples given to them by the drug companies. At that time, the poor in Brazil knew little about preventing or curing illnesses. There were no vaccines except for smallpox. We had our hands full.

I remember that when the measles vaccine came to Brazil, we had to convince mothers that it was safe to vaccinate their children. The main illnesses were parasites, pneumonia, respiratory infections of all types and tuberculosis.

The absence of birth and marriage certificates or other necessary documents was a big issue, and we'd do what we could to help people get those documents, so vital to their lives. In those days, you couldn't even enter a hospital without proof of your existence: a birth or marriage certificate.

We were witnesses to so many marriages of couples who had come to the favela from other areas and started families but weren't legally married. It took a lot of paperwork to go through the legal channels, and so many of these people were illiterate or semi-literate. Life was much more complicated in Rio than their lives had been in the rural areas they'd come from.

Dona Zeza was a marvelous example of the strength of women as they struggled in poverty to raise their children. She had a son, Elias, who had a sever developmental disability, and she did everything for him. He had to be fed

75

and changed, and this loving, overworked woman did all these tasks.

There were so few places at that time that worked with children with developmental disabilities, but we found one where Elias could stay during the day and receive therapy and group work. Getting him there though was a task. The favela, Tavares Bastos, was high up on a hill overlooking the beaches of Copacabana – among the most famous beaches in the world. What a great distance the favela was though from those beaches, both literally and socially. It took twenty minutes to ascend from the bottom of the hill to Tavares Bastos, a slow, steady climb.

Dona Zeza had to carry Elias down that hill each day – and this was certainly not like carrying a healthy child: Elias was unable to hold his head up. Once at the bottom of the hill, they would board a bus for a forty-minute journey, then walk a couple of blocks to the school. They'd then repeat the routine in reverse every afternoon.

This was Dona Zeza's life, in addition, that is, to also raising a little girl. Because of this rugged schedule, we didn't see much of her. In time, Elias grew too large for Dona Zeza to carry him, so she had to give up taking him to the school. She then attended a class that taught her how to do much of the therapy herself. Such a magnificent mother!

****

One day, Dona Zeza came to our little hut and told us that her next-door neighbor had left in the early hours of the morning to accompany the man the woman lived with, Senhor João, who was a street vendor, and had left the man's four-year-old son, Joãozinho, alone all day in their home. The houses in favelas have shared walls, and all the sounds from one house can be heard in the next.

Dona Zeza and the other neighbors were furious. The little boy would cry and stick his hands out from under the door into the alley and beg for water or food, which the neighbors tried to squeeze through the door crack.

Very little was known of this couple; they were fairly new in the favela. Dona Zeza had heard that the woman,

Maria, was Senhor João's second woman, but that was all they knew.

Gus and I, with help from the angry neighbors, broke down the door of the hut and carried the starving, crying little boy out. We took him to the doctor, got him some medications and brought him home with us.

Senhor João was furious when he returned home and learned what had happened, and the neighbors told us he beat Maria and blamed her. Joãozinho was terrified and didn't want to return home. With the help of some lawyers who were students in my English classes, we were able to get a restraining order until the juvenile court appointed us as temporary guardians.

We put Joãozinho into a day-care program, and in time he became a happy, though still fearful, little boy. As he opened up, he told his teachers of horrible beatings and punishments. We also learned that he had a real mother whom his father had beaten and abandoned. We worried for the future of this innocent victim.

After some months, a solution materialized. It seemed that Joazinho's mother's sister had decided to come for the boy. This happened while I was in the States visiting family. We had left Joãozinho with Dona Lola, a neighbor of Senhor João's who had known the boy since the family had moved in. I was naive in thinking that Senhor João would do nothing to harm his little son, whose life was now so much better. Even though he would be much freer to live his life without this responsibility, he wanted to keep his son. To a man, a son is a son, and, despite the court's judgment, which he had witnessed, he wanted him under his control.

Senhor João haunted Dona Lola's house, waiting for the moment when he could grab the boy. Dona Lola's husband feared for her, and so he contacted Joãozinho's mother's sister. Joazinho's aunt arrived and took him away with her.

Joãozinho was placed by court order in his aunt's custody, and off they went to another state in Brazil. We never saw him again.

This little boy whose life we had shared for more than a year was gone, just like that. But I comforted myself knowing that his life was now better. Clearly, this woman truly wanted him; if not, she never would have come for him. She had no children of her own.

But there was another reason, which the woman revealed to me the last time I saw her. Joãozinho's birth mother had been very ill, but had given birth to a little girl, and died soon after. The man she had lived with had taken the little girl and disappeared. What a tragedy, I thought, but felt there was little I could do. What I didn't know at the time was that Senhor João knew of this little girl's birth and, for some strange reason, wanted her.

And so now he went after this child, named Monica, and brought her home for Maria, his woman, to care for – the same woman who had so neglected Joãozinho. I wondered if he was doing this to make his neighbors think he was not so bad a father.

****

For a few months, according to the neighbors, all seemed well. Senhor João went off to work and Maria stayed home with Monica, hung her clothes out on the public line, chatted with neighbors and carried Monica with her up and down the hill when she went to help Senhor João sell clothes on the streets of Rio.

But this seemingly good behavior lasted but a few months. Soon Maria started leaving Monica at home while accompanying Senhor João to the streets. She would come home at lunchtime and tend to the infant and then go back to the streets until sometimes as late as eight. This lasted a few weeks, and then Maria stopped coming home at lunch. So Monica, now about four months old, was left alone all day with only the bottle she was given early in the morning.

One day, Dona Zeza, accompanied by Dona Lola, came to tell me that for the past several days they had been hearing the infant cry at various times during the day, but on this day they had heard no sound at all and were worried. We went to the hut and broke in once again. What I saw will live in my memory for the rest of my life.

There, strapped to a chair with pieces of cloth, was an emaciated Monica, with sores on her body, some open and raw, covered with feces and urine. She wasn't crying; she was too weak.

While the women bathed and cleaned up the baby, Gus and I prepared to once more take a child from this house. We took her to a public hospital, where I spent the night with her while she received intravenous feeding and the doctors' care.

When the immediate danger had passed, I was questioned by the social worker at the hospital. Who was I? Where was the baby's birth certificate? What had happened to her?

I was told that I would have to go to the juvenile court before I could take Monica home and that the father would be called. How could I leave her at this moment when she was so weak and frightened?

I asked to call the priest so that my story of who I was could be verified. He came, and I was allowed to take Monica home with me. I was given a letter from the hospital to take to the juvenile court.

So there we were again in court with another child. Senhor João was called three times before he finally appeared. He denied everything we had told them. We were then called to court to face Senhor João.

I knew that my being an American wouldn't help in this situation; Senhor João was the father. But the day of the audience, he didn't appear. Two days later, social workers from the court arrived in the favela and we took them to Senhor João's house. He wasn't there, but Maria was, and under pressure she told her story.

Unfortunately, she later received a severe beating for helping to save Monica's life.

Monica's Story

So began our life with Monica. She was placed in our custody and was visited monthly by social workers. She was a sweet and loving baby. She and my youngest daughter, Judy, bonded right away. We took Monica with us wherever we went. We became parents of a small child again: walks in the park, games and so forth.

Our devotion to her though would be tested and tested again. Monica seemed so healthy, but when she was about eight months old I discovered what looked like a tumor, or cyst, a lump in her groin. It didn't seem to be painful, but it was alarming.

We took her to the doctor, who knew her whole story. She was put on antibiotics, but the doctor was unsure what was wrong. Then another lump appeared in her neck, which, like the first, didn't respond to antibiotics.

We went from doctor to doctor, but finally our friend, a pneumonologist, did a skin test for tuberculosis. Monica developed a huge sore, and we remembered then that it was tuberculosis that had killer her mother. Yes, the diagnosis was TB of the glands.

Monica was given a year of prophylactic treatment. Judy stayed with her most of the time and took care of her when she was not in school. Through it all, Monica was a happy child, and our bond continued to strengthen. But Judy was growing up and was not home as much, and our work in the favela and my night classes kept us from giving her the life she deserved. Plus, I knew that Gus and I might not spend the rest of our lives in Brazil. I was already in middle age. I needed to think of what was best for Monica.

****

One day as I sat watching Monica play on the playground, a woman sat down beside me and we began to chat. It was

80

obvious that Monica wasn't my blood child – she was mixed race – and the woman, whose name was Francisca, asked me whose child she was. Was she my maid's child? No, I said, and told her, briefly, Monica's story. She told me she had a daughter in her late teens who took lessons with a tutor nearby and that she always came to the park to wait for her.

She then said: "I would surely love to have another child. My husband travels all the time, my daughter's nearly grown, and it's lonely. I love children, you know. I wanted more, but I was unable."

Dona Francisca and I began to meet regularly in this park, sitting and chatting while Monica played. Monica took to her immediately because she had a great big pocketbook and always let her look in. Monica loved pocketbooks, so one day Dona Francisca brought a small one and gave it to her. She was thrilled, and carried it everywhere she went,

Monica

filling it with rocks, flowers or anything that would fit, and Dona Francisca would sometimes bring little gifts for her to put in it.

Monica began looking for Dona Francisca when we went to the park, and her face would light up when she saw her.

The writing's on the wall, isn't it? As I struggled with Monica's future – one that would allow her to remain in her country, safe and secure – I thought of Dona Francisca. By now, I knew quite a bit about her. She was a woman of means; her husband had a good and steady job, their daughter went to private schools. She and her husband were just a few years younger than Gus and I, but Dona Francisca didn't work and had a maid.

Gus and I talked about it and agreed that we should suggest this adoption, though convincing Judy wasn't easy

– and, in fact, the process proved harder on all of us than we could have known.

I wasn't prepared for the enthusiasm and joy Dona Francesca immediately showed when I suggested it to her. She paused and said a prayer of gratitude, then, with tears in her eyes, picked Monica up and hugged her. I told her I wanted to do this properly – that though we had custody of Monica, we hadn't adopted her. She agreed and said she would discuss it with her husband immediately.

The decision had been made, and, though I knew it was the right thing to do, my heart was heavy. Monica knew us as her family and was happy and developing well, but my future was uncertain. We loved her dearly, but it had to be done.

I told Dona Francesca that we should go to Romão Duarte, an orphanage run by nuns where children were often taken when their families hadn't the financial means to care for them. It was a well-known place. It had a door that moved in a circle: You put the baby in a cradle, closed the door and then cranked it to the other side so that the mother remained anonymous. She agreed, and I made an appointment.

****

The orphanage was a large building, very warm and welcoming. I told the nun Monica's story and what we felt had to be done for her and why. Many years have now gone by, so I don't remember exactly what she said or whether I felt she agreed with my decision to have Monica adopted. She wanted to meet Dona Francisca and her husband as well as Monica.

The next step was for Dona Francisca's husband, Senhor Jesus, and Monica to meet, and that went perfectly.

We met at the orphanage. When Monica and I arrived, she jumped from my arms and ran to Dona Francisca and opened her pocketbook. Senhor Jesus smiled and immediately bent down to talk with her. The nun was observing all this. She chatted with the couple, looked at their documents, asked questions about their private life and if they knew that

82

Monica had had tuberculosis and that little was known of her parentage. Yes, they were aware, they said.

We were asked to come back several times. On the final visit, Dona Francisco and Senhor Jesus brought their daughter, who immediately bonded with Monica. The nuns then called a lawyer, and the paperwork was done; Monica would be adopted. The reality sank in, my heart skipped a beat, and tears came.

Dona Francisca took me in her arms and said, "I can imagine how hard this is. You have given us the greatest gift, and we understand what this means to you. You don't have to let us take her now. Let's do it gradually."

"Oh, thank you," I said as I dried my eyes. "This is going to be so hard on my daughter too." The nuns agreed, thinking this would be better for Monica as well.

So we made a plan. Dona Francisca would come to our house once a week while I went to work in the favela and when I gave my English lessons. She'd have Monica to herself.

In time, she began coming twice a week. After about two months, we decided that Monica should spend a day at Dona Francisca's home. She then began to go there several days a week. The bond was becoming stronger between Monica and her new family, as we struggled to break our ties.

Then Dona Francisca asked if Monica could spend the weekend with them in the room they had decorated for her. Yes, we said, of course. She was returned to us on Monday, happy to see us, but watching as Dona Francisca left.

Monica began to spend more weekends in her new home, always returning happy. It was getting harder and harder.

Then one day, Dona Francisca called and said that this weekend they were going to take Monica to their summer home in Paquetá, a beautiful island off the coast of Rio. It would be a longer visit than usual. This is right, I told Judy; she needs to spend more time with them.

On Sunday, the day Monica was to return, there was a torrential rainstorm, so typical of Rio. As evening wore on, we began to worry. It just poured and poured. They would be returning by boat from the island, only to then have to

83

face the terrible traffic jams so common to Rio in the rainy season.

We were worrying about this when the phone rang. It was Dona Francisca. She told us that they couldn't make it back because of the weather and not to worry, everything was fine with Monica. I sighed and said what I knew was right.

"You don't need to bring her back, Francisca. You take her to your home, her home now. We'll send along all her things. The adjustment time is over for all of us."

I hung up, went to my room so that Judy wouldn't see me, and cried. It was the right thing to do. But, oh! How it hurt! Love sometimes hurts. Love can be painful. Love sometimes means sacrifice! I thought of all the other women I'd met who'd given up their children.

****

Months passed. I didn't call them; I couldn't. And I had asked Dona Francisca not to call me. The pain eased with time, for I knew Monica was happy and she would forget. We might not, but she would.

Then six months or so later, Dona Francisca called. At first, I was worried that something had gone wrong. But no, she wanted to ask Gus and me to be Monica's godparents – a big honor and responsibility in this country. I was surprised, but thrilled.

"We're thrilled and honored," I told her. But before I could say yes, I needed to make a very important request. We didn't want Monica to know of our roles in her life, how we found her and what we knew of her past. We wanted her to know us simply as her godparents, good friends of the family.

Dona Francesca agreed, and on the day of Monica's baptism I cried, not with sadness but with joy. It was right! Monica had a guardian angel with whom we were attuned. She would have the life she deserved, and if we were privileged to have a part in it, we would be grateful.

She's a grown woman now with a daughter of her own. She separated from her husband and went to the northeast, and I lost track of her. She went with another young man and her daughter stayed behind with Dona Francisca. It was not unusual that grandparents raised their grandchildren as their children sought a freer life.

Unanswered Questions

In 1980, two important events occurred on the same day that brought change to my life: My father died and my first grandchild was born. Was it now time to leave? I was torn.

But something else was happening to me. I was questioning everything I had ever believed in my life, about God, faith and religion; social and economic justice; and the U.S., my country.

Coming from a middle-class family, never having been without in my life, I was asking "why." People were starving in Brazil, Africa and elsewhere. There was corruption everywhere. Why these people, why not me? Was it an accident of birth? Why were women treated as inferior when, in fact, they were such heroines? Why didn't they rebel?

I knew that suffering people and abused women were praying, but nothing changed in their lives. I lived in the midst of injustice; I knew that these people prayed for life, for food, for medicine. But for most, these prayers weren't answered. Why?

I knew that nothing would change *unless* we humans brought about that change

I came from a family of girls. Both my mother and her mother were strong women, but they were nothing like these women I had come to know. They couldn't be compared because they had never known poverty, social injustice, helplessness in the face of political abandonment.

These magnificent women I had come to know in Brazil, with whom I cried and who I prayed for, had introduced me to women's roles so different than any I had known, to the roles women play in a third-world society. In spite of the odds against them, they survived, they laughed, they sang, they rejoiced – they were powerful. But they weren't aware of their own value, their own power.

In Brazil in 1967, I was told that women couldn't even register the birth of their own children; only the male could. This had been the case with my partner, Gus. His father disappeared when he was very young and Gus and his sister could have lived on with no documents to prove they existed, would never have been able to go to school. They would have been, in the view of the state, nonexistent.

But Gus's mother, Dona Maria, was well known in the little rural town of Minais Gerais, and it was also well known that her husband had abandoned the family. Dona Maria knew she had to have birth certificates for the children in order for them to go to school. She didn't want them to be illiterate, as she was. She was yet another exceptional woman I came to know. She went to the local officials, who, knowing her and her story, made an exception, allowing her to register her own children in her own name and without a father's name on the children's registry.

Each day, women went down the hill to do housework for wealthy families. These women were the backbone of our favela community, no matter what their age. They would go down that hill to work each day and come back up it each night. This was something I'd never experienced prior – this level of sacrifice and suffering – work without end, all for the sake of their children.

And yet they were second-class citizens. Though the well-to-do could get around a lot of this, poor women's rights were ignored. The saddest thing was that they didn't even realize it. These women, as I saw it, had developed a survival theology – a crutch theology – that offered rationale for the things that happened in their lives, good or bad: "Se Deus quiser." If God wishes.

A husband will survive a work accident or a gunshot wound if God wishes. A baby will be cured if God wishes. The surgery will be successful if God wishes. If these events didn't yield the hoped-for result, it was God's wish. They thought that if a baby died, it wasn't because there was insufficient health care or no affordable medicine, or because the patient was malnourished, or because there was no transportation to get to the hospital – it was because God wished it so. God decided everything. Social and economic injustice played no role.

I didn't believe it. But as with the woman whose longed-for baby had died, and who I was confronted with having to comfort, I knew of no way to offer that comfort except with that which I knew would provide it for her: the crutch theology; survival theology. It was God's wish. God knows best.

So had I been sleeping all my life? Was I awakening? And if I was, what did it mean? And what was I to do about it?

So I left it all behind, all the people I had grown to love, a life so meaningful though difficult. I had trained several women in things like taking blood pressures, and the president of the favela was very supportive. So I left it in her hands.

I wept for days, for it was a sad awakening, and I knew I was fleeing from the responsibility of this awakening. I was returning to my old life, to find answers, to escape the poverty and find new meaning, though at that moment I knew not how. I was recently divorced, and I wanted to marry Gus, which we couldn't do in Brazil, divorce being illegal. In the U.S., we could begin a new life.

My First Days in Wisconsin

I can hardly remember, it seems so long ago. I was such a different person then than I was in the fall of 1967 when I went to Brazil.

We had moved to River Falls, Wisconsin, and I was seeing my country through Gus's eyes. Everything was so new and, though it was my country, I had not been a part of the many changes that had occurred since 1967.

So much had happened to me, and thus I saw things so differently.

But I tried to look through the eyes of my fifty-year-old Brazilian husband-to-be who had dreamed of the USA since he was a child, reading books about the country and watching as many movies as he could find about it.

He commented immediately on how clean the streets were – no papers or garbage thrown around – and I had to agree, for one of the first things one notices when entering a favela in Brazil is the garbage and disorder on the streets. On the other hand, the streets were always full of people, a lively atmosphere no matter the hour or the temperature. He noted this difference too, and, yes, the streets were so quiet. Where were the people?

Now closer to my family, I dug in to make a life for us. Financially, all we had was what we had saved in Brazil from the sale of our home and possessions. Since Gus couldn't speak English, I would have to go to work. And what experience did I have? In my generation, working wives and mothers weren't that common. I had been a nursery school and first-grade teacher and junior high substitute. Beyond that, all I had to put on my resume were my nursing courses and experiences in Brazil.

With the help of family and friends, I went to work in the local hospital as a nurse's aide. But I was lost; it was all so different from the work I'd done in Brazil. There were wonderful people to help me, including my oldest daughter, Carol, but I cried often and continued to feel that I didn't belong. Something was missing.

****

We searched for a place to rent, and I remember a funny comment Gus made as he tried to grow accustomed to life in a new country. One day while I was looking through the newspaper at all the garage sales and commenting on them with Gus, he looked up at me and said, "Why are you looking for a garage to buy if we don't even have a house?"

The few things that we'd had sent from Brazil at last arrived. I remember sitting on the floor, and as I unpacked them the memories took over. Gus was at an English class, and I began to cry and couldn't stop.

Suddenly, the doorbell rang; I dried my eyes as best I could and opened the door. It was the pastor of the First Congregational Church, United Church of Christ – the church we had attended the previous Sunday – Rev. Dick Hoblin. How was I to know at that moment that I had met the person who would change the path of my life?

Being the super-sensitive man that he was, Rev. Dick immediately knew I had been crying, that I was unhappy and disoriented. He knew little about me, but he stepped in to help.

He introduced me to Mariann and Wayne Wolfe, who were very involved with Latin America, mainly Mexico, and they welcomed us with open arms. Meanwhile, Rev. Dick got to know more about my life. He saw me struggling with my work at the hospital and Gus's struggle to find work. He took Gus under his wing, and soon Gus became the janitor of the Congregational Church in River Falls (later the singing janitor!). Gus was loved and he loved. He took English lessons with other foreigners from a volunteer, Bobbie Kuhn, in this college town and got involved in the community.

Not so with me. I struggled in the hospital and wondered if I should go back to nursing school. But how? I had to work.

Once again, Rev. Dick stepped into my life to open a path – a path I'd never contemplated! He came to the house one day and told me that the University of Wisconsin-River Falls was looking for a campus ministry director.

"A who?" I asked. "I'm not a campus minister. I'm not clergy!"

He said, "It pays very little money, but I think with your experiences you'd be really good with these young people."

I was having trouble seeing it. Nevertheless, I allowed my name to be submitted.

I will never forget the evening of my interview. It was in the campus ministry house and the interviewer was Bill Romoser, a member of the Methodist Church and professor at the university. I didn't know him and so was a bit on edge. This whole idea seemed strange. Me working as a campus ministry director!

Bill then took me around the building, and as we walked into the kitchen I saw two young students with scarves on their heads washing dishes. They were Mark Christopher and Wade Brezina, whose lives would be entangled with mine. They took all the stress away, greeting me with such warmth and welcoming.

We chatted for a bit. Then Bill took me into the campus minister's office, and, truly, I don't remember much about what he told me or asked me, except for one question: "Where on a scale of one to ten would you say you stand theologically: one being very conservative and ten not at all conservative? Where would you place yourself?"

My answer came without hesitation: "I'd be right off the scale – ten, eleven, twelve ..."

He looked at me for a moment, and that was all.

I went home that evening and said to my mother, who was visiting us, "Well, I blew that one."

I explained why. In my mind, Bill Romoser, a longtime member of the Methodist church, a member of the campus ministry board of directors – and though pleasant and polite, a bit stern, it seemed to me – certainly must have thought that Dick Hoblin's suggestion of me for this job was very foolish. Or, as another member of the board later put it,

"Why hire a fifty-one-year-old Girl Scout leader as a campus ministry director?"

As I was talking with my mother, the phone rang. It was Bill Romoser, offering me the job! Unbelievable! Maybe there just weren't enough candidates, because I certainly didn't have the proper profile.

But the job was mine, as was a better salary than what I'd been making. Gus and I were relieved. And over the years, dear Bill Romoser became a warm friend and an avid supporter of my later work in Brazil. All these people entered into my life, helping lead me to what I now believe was its purpose.

But there was more to come. Once again, Rev. Dick Hoblin became an instrument for more change in my life, suggesting that I apply for entrance to the United Theological Seminary in Minneapolis.

Not possible, I thought. But he convinced me to at least give it a try.

So on a very snowy day, Gus and I set out for an interview at the seminary. Gus had no experience driving on the highway in the snow; visibility was poor, and we skidded and ended up in a ditch.

I began to cry. "Let's go home. This was never meant to be," I told Gus. I didn't want to go any farther.

But my husband was undaunted. "No, we're going, and you are going to have this interview," he said. And so on we went, a long and scary drive.

I had the interview. I was enchanted by all that I learned about the courses, the student body, and I was accepted, entering in the fall of 1982. I was able to keep my half-time job as campus ministry director. A scholarship allowed us to make ends meet.

Rich Experiences

Seminary was a rich experience and, though my theology has since changed, my studies included many things that remain with me.

But at one point, I almost gave up. It was my first semester and I was feeling so out of place. I was much older than the others, my life's experiences were so different, and I was having a hard time relating.

Telling my story was also so difficult. One day in a course called Theology of the Human, I broke down and left the room when the professor corrected me for something I said that he felt was out of place or irrelevant. What was I doing here anyway!

That afternoon, there was a note from the professor in my box asking me to come see him. To make a long story short, he told me he felt I wasn't seminary material, that perhaps I should think of some other career, etc.

I left his office sad and angry. "Yes, I guess he's right," I thought.

But as I further considered it, I thought of Rev. Dick. He had believed that this was what I should be doing. So I couldn't give up. And I didn't.

I remember at my graduation, the pastor who gave the sermon, the Rev. Reuben Sheares, an African-American, said something to this effect: "If you came to seminary to find the answers and you think you've found them, then you shouldn't be graduating today."

I felt then that I was in the right place. I should be graduating, for I had not found the answers – just one. And that was that I needed to return to Brazil to continue what I had been doing, now armed with more tools with which to work.

****

There were many seminary experiences that were important to me, but I guess the one that stands out is my summer internship as a pastor in a Native-American congregation in Black River Falls, a Congregational Church on a Winnebago reservation.

As a student who had lived in another culture and whose husband was a foreigner, and aware of what a rich resource the Native-American culture was in that area of Wisconsin and Minnesota, I was interested in knowing more when I met Rev. Mitchell Whiterabbit, a professor at seminary. I found his teachings of the Native-American culture so interesting.

Then an opportunity came when he told me of a mission UCC church on Winnebago land where I could do a summer internship.

My first impression of the church and the land was one of awe. What a beautiful place. There wasn't much time though to take in the scenery: Soon this little church was my charge alone. I had barely become used to the activities and the area when the pastor fell ill and left and I was asked to take over the congregation.

I had already learned that there were a lot of family conflicts in the congregation, and if it had not been for

Winnebago reservation, Black River Falls, Wisconsin

94

Rev. James Savides, the UCC's Northwest Association conference minister, and Rev. Whiterabbit's encouragement and support, my time there would not have been such a wonderful experience.

I learned so much about these wonderful Native-American people, but I remember the women most vividly. Officially, the men made the tribal decisions, but behind every decision was a woman's hand. They were staunch and dignified and I had an opportunity to know many of them and to witness their strength and their quiet power in their families and community.

As a pastor, I visited the sick and hospitalized members of the community, and one in particular gave me a chance to glimpse into their family life there. I called on Mrs. Deerfoot, who had broken her leg and was in the local hospital after surgery. I walked into the room and introduced myself to this woman who radiated dignity and control. She didn't respond to me or even look at me. I continued to talk, but there was no reciprocation, and so I bid her goodbye and left. I'd learned by then that the women of the Native-American community could seem rather aloof and that reaching them could be difficult, so I wasn't disturbed. This was their way, and, after all, I was a white woman with whom they had nothing in common.

However, because of where Mrs. Deerfoot lived and the poor accessibility of her home, she stayed in the hospital longer than normal, and I made it a point to visit her at least twice a week. We established a friendship, and the key to unlocking it was that I had lived in another culture and she was interested in knowing about it. We talked a lot, and as time went on she could look me in the eyes – two women, of different cultures, looking across the chasm, building a bridge of friendship.

Then one day she told me she could walk on her own again and was leaving the hospital. I told her I would miss her. And she responded in her slow, quiet, dignified way that she would send me a message as to when I could visit her.

****

And sure enough, within about ten days a message was sent to my office to come see her, with directions, as she lived a good distance from the church and parsonage.

I entered a different world, rather primitive to me. Mrs. Deerfoot lived deep in the woods, far from any other living quarters, and the only road there was a deeply rutted dirt road. Fortunately, it was winter; had it been summer, the house would have been totally hidden by foliage.

It was certainly a different kind of dwelling from those around the church. On one side of the land was a rounded dwelling with a straw roof with branches on it; the bottom half was made of stone. The sides of this house were open to light. To the left was a covering, a low hut of stone where hot stones were kept. It was the sweat lodge where their religious sessions were held. Behind this was a wooden structure similar to the ones closer to the church. This house, I later learned, was the house where the women stayed during their menstrual periods. Another world!

I found my way to the entrance to the house, where Mrs. Deerfoot – in her so very regal, dignified way – invited me in. In the middle of the room was a homemade wood-cooking stove that also served as a fireplace for heating. All the pots and pans and utensils were hanging on or piled upon a flat surface used to prepare meals. There were built-in benches along the walls. So much light poured in from the rustic-type windows all around the house that it was almost like being outside. Mrs. Deerfoot told me to sit down and served me some type of tea.

One of her married daughters was there helping out, and while she acknowledged my presence, only her mother spoke. And though, because of the center stove and a wide pipe that provided ventilation for the stove, I didn't see him at first, there was a man sitting on the other side of the room. He wore a heavy blanket on his shoulders and a fur hat.

Assuming it was Mrs. Deerfoot's husband, I greeted him. He didn't raise his head or acknowledge my greeting. The daughter looked over at me and nodded as if to say, "Don't bother with him, that's just his way."

I later learned that he hadn't wanted me to come. They didn't frequent the church, and he felt my visit was an invasion. He didn't speak to me the whole time I was there. I said goodbye to him when I left, but he didn't raise his head. Neither his wife nor daughter explained his attitude, but I understood.

I told Mrs. Deerfoot that I hoped to see her again, and she said that would only be at the powwow, which would be in a few months. She didn't leave her home except for such occasions, her daughter explained.

****

And I did see her at the powwow, where Gus and I were welcomed as honorary members of the tribe. She only nodded to me though, with no indication that we had been good friends. I danced in the circle with them, and she nodded each time we passed.

Gus, who has Brazilian indigenous blood in his ancestry, was given a special commendation and made a member of the tribe by the chief. And once again, as I danced in the circle with all the women, I was reminded of how regal they were, the dignity and power of these women, who, in their own way, within their culture, were the backbone of the tribe.

The oldest woman of the tribe was Grandmother Lydia. She didn't speak English, so I had to ask her son to translate as I chatted with her. She told me stories of her people of the Winnebago tribe, so many of whom were her relatives and who she regarded with great respect. She told me of her people's respect for nature and the spirits within all living things.

"We do not cut down trees unnecessarily," Grandmother Lydia told me. "But if we have to, we ask pardon of the tree's spirit, as we do when we have to kill a deer for food." She told me of how when one of her people died, they would be buried with moccasins and food for the journey.

She told me how the white man's money changed her people and caused a rivalry in the church community, which I had noticed. This magnificent woman told me of her life, and truly she was an example of her people, of whom she was so proud, while acknowledging some of the problems that arose in dealing with the white people's way.

****

One day, I received a call from the sheriff's office. One of the members of our congregation was in jail, having gotten involved in a barroom brawl. I recognized his family name but did not know him. He was sixteen and in trouble for being drunk and breaking some things in a bar.

So off I went to talk with him. A deputy led me into a small room and then went to get the young man. The door opened and in walked a huge boy; he looked like a giant. This handsome boy was at least six feet tall and weighed two hundred pounds or more. All I could think as he walked in was, "If this boy got violent with me, he could whip me down in a second with one swing of an arm!" I felt uneasy.

He sat down, his head lowered, never looking me in the eye, and told me what had happened.

He was walking to the bus stop to go home and some boys called him into the bar. For the most part, this young boy, being a Native American, was isolated in school, had no friends in his class and suffered what we today call bullying. So he was happy to be invited to join the group.

But these young boys didn't have such good intentions. They got him drunk and then began insulting him and his people. With the alcohol in his body, he became angry and hit a man who was taunting him. Others joined in, and soon it was a brawl. The police were called and the boy was taken away.

As he finished his story, giant tears began to fall down his handsome face.

What could I do for him, I asked myself. He looked at me and asked me to explain to his mother what had happened. He did not want to disgrace her. He wasn't a drinker, he said. He wanted me to apologize to the bar owner to save face for his family.

Then he said there was one more thing he wanted, and that was to see his mother on Sunday, which was Mother's

98

Day. He didn't want her to see him in jail though; that would hurt her too much. "We are a proud people," he said, "and I do not want to humiliate or shame her."

So I asked the sheriff if he would allow the boy to sit in front of the police station with his mother on Mother's Day. I saw him hesitate, and I told him I would take responsibility, that the boy wouldn't do anything foolish that would disgrace his mother.

And so on Mother's Day, after church, I took his mother and two of his siblings to the police station and we sat out in the yard and talked. My experience with the Winnebago people I knew was that they didn't show emotion, but that it was there. I saw the respect and concern this boy had for his mother, who, in her dignified way, listened to his story of what had happened, nodded her head and said something to him in their language. And I felt the boy's relief that all would be forgiven and that his story was believed. His family had not lost their honor.

The judge who heard the young man's case also believed his story, and his sentence was community service.

Once again, I was reminded of the strength and power that women have as mothers and wives as they cope with their roles in family, in community, in life.

Planning My Return

My job as campus minister also proved to be rich in experiences. There were quite a few foreign students at the university, and we held international dinners and other gatherings in which the students shared their different cultures.

I noticed right away the differences between the status of the women students from other countries and marveled at the courage of the Asian and African women and their determination to defy their status by coming to the U.S. to study.

Of course, to be able to come to the States and study they had to come from wealthy homes. The most oppressed I observed were the women from Iran, who came not to study but to accompany their husbands who were students. Some of them were not permitted to leave their homes unless accompanied and the dress code for women in Iran had to be maintained.

I wondered though how, upon returning to their native lands, they would be changed by having lived in the U.S. and made friends with American women.

I thought of the women I had worked with in Brazil. Being all from poor families, they couldn't be compared to these women who, though of lower status in their countries than men, had the distinction of being from well-to-do families, with all the advantages this allowed them.

But while I was in the U.S., things were beginning to change in Brazil. In spite of now being well adapted to our new life in the States, my longing to return to Brazil was returning.

But how? The United Church of Christ had no specific work there. And after my experiences in the Native-American mission church and with others, I felt that my calling was not as the pastor of a church but to continue what I had been doing in Brazil, though now with new tools and training. I wanted to help educate women: to help them raise their self-esteem so that they would be active participants in their own life stories. My education was changing me in so many ways. But it seemed impossible to find a way through the church to do the work I felt called to do.

****

I participated in the annual River Falls March of Dimes ten-mile walk and my partner was Jo Wilson, the Christian education director at the River Falls Methodist Church.

It was a gorgeous day and we were walking through beautiful farm country, but Jo began to feel ill and could go no farther. We stopped at a farmhouse and she called her husband to come pick her up.

So I continued the some six miles remaining alone through the beautiful farmland, so typical of the area. I remember so well that as I came to a crossroad at the end of a pasture, I looked across the road and on the right side was a wooded area from which was coming the sound of birds singing. Their songs were so loud, echoing in my ears, and I had to stop. I was filled with a feeling of such calmness, of peace, overcome with the beauty all around me.

And suddenly I knew that my instinct to return to Brazil was right and felt certain that I would get there. It was such a powerful feeling that I began to cry. And I bent down on the dirt road to give a prayer of gratitude for this experience and insight.

That same year, Dom Hélder Câmara, the Catholic archbishop of Recife, in the north of Brazil, who had been nominated for the Nobel Peace Prize, was invited by the Catholic Archdiocese of Milwaukee to speak.

Rev. Dick Hoblin once again stepped into my life. The organizers of the program were looking for someone who could speak Portuguese to help with the translations. He offered my name. So there I was, before one of the most important Brazilian men of the times, Hélder Câmara, who

101

knew the pain of poverty and injustice in his own country, as he came from one of the poorest areas of Brazil, the northeast.

He repeated to the audience in Milwaukee what he had said when he made his speech upon being nominated for the Nobel, "As long as one child in the world goes to sleep hungry, there will be no peace in the world."

He also said, "When I give food to the poor, they call me a saint. When I ask why they are poor, they call me a communist."

And now here was this man, tiny in size but a giant in stature, before me. He looked at my nametag, saw my Brazilian name, and took my hand. I told him who I was and we chatted. I had just been told though that he did speak English and wouldn't need an interpreter. I was preparing to leave the room when he took me by the hand and led me to a seat right in front of where he was to speak.

I don't remember all he said to the ecumenical audience there. But I do remember that when he finished and asked if there were any questions, a woman pastor stood up and reminded him that the Catholic Church did not ordain women, and that as he could see, there were many women pastors there. What did he think of this?

I'll never forget his answer: "My grandmother used to tell me that, yes, men are the head of the family, but," placing his hands around his neck, "women are the neck!"

After the program, I went down to the lobby of the church. Dom Hélder had been led away and I hadn't been able to say goodbye. I saw a crowd of people around him, but he was so small, I couldn't see him. I made my way in the direction of the crowd, doubting that I would get to him.

But somehow he saw me and called to me. I went to him and he took my hand. I had told him earlier that after ordination I wanted to return to Brazil. I repeated that desire. He patted my hand and said, "Yes, my dear, you will get back to Brazil. And when you do, you must promise to come and see me."

This tiny man, my height, looked into my eyes and smiled. I felt a strong urge to kiss his robe as I had seen so many Catholics do in Brazil. As I started to bend, he stopped me and gave me his blessing.

Yes, I now believed I would return. I just needed to finish seminary and a way would be found.

****

My last year of seminary was a busy one – writing papers, writing my ordination thesis and looking into all the possible ways to return to Brazil. That spring, the University of Wisconsin-River Falls had a program on Central American issues, and representatives of the American Friends Service Committee were there as sponsors and speakers. One of them was staying in the home of a church member who had a copy of my ordination paper, and read it.

In the UCC ordination process, a candidate's ordination paper is circulated throughout the churches with which the sponsoring church is associated – in my case, the Northwest Wisconsin Association. This is in preparation for its presentation to the Ecclesiastical Council in one of these churches. Mine was scheduled to be presented on April 30, 1985 at the First Congregational Church in Eau Claire, Wisconsin.

My ordination thesis was my faith journey in religious terms, and mine was quite different than the other candidates' in that it was primarily about my experiences in Brazil.

After the pastor introduced me with a quick summary of my experiences and readiness for ministry, he called for questions, as was the custom, so that I might defend my thesis. There was silence; no questions were asked. I panicked.

Then a gentleman rose and asked me a few questions about my work in Brazil. When I finished answering, others asked similar questions. I had passed; I would be ordained.

But the surprise came a few weeks later, when the American Friends representative who had read my paper called me and asked if I would consider going to Brazil with AFSC to work with women!

I had received my "call"!

****

As I've said, I'd already come to realize that my calling was not as the pastor of a church but to continue what I had been doing in Brazil. In my ordination paper, I wrote about an experience I'd had with a woman named Umbelina. It was in this dying woman's face that I saw how a health worker could be the hand of God, the presence of Christ. And these thoughts never left me as I struggled through seminary:

One day, a nun came to see us in the little hut that served as our clinic in the Tavares Bastos favela and asked me, as a health worker, to come visit a home that had been converted into one-room apartments, with one bathroom per floor. The halls were common property and no one was responsible for cleaning them. It was a horrible place to live.

The nun told me that there was an old woman who was very ill and asked if I would look in on her, that she had not been seen by any of the other tenants for several days and no one answered when neighbors knocked.

So I went, and I knocked and knocked, but no one answered. With the authority I had from the nun, I demanded the key from the landlord. Upon opening the door, the stench of sickness and filth overwhelmed me. I gagged! The room was dark, and it took me a few minutes to recover from my feelings of nausea and find the bed. What I saw, I will never forget.

I saw eyes – huge, suffering eyes in a face so thin that one could see only eyes. I thought she was dead.

"Dona Umbelina," I called several times. There was no response. I was filled with an agony, and I sat down beside her and held her hands that were only bones. My tears began to fall and I cried out loud, "Oh, God, where are you?"

"Help me, Dona," I heard a voice say, a voice almost too weak to be heard. "Can you give me a glass of water?"

I was startled. "Dona Umbelina. It's Dona Barbara. Are you all right?" I asked stupidly.

"Can you give me a glass of water?" she repeated, and suddenly faded out again.

I shouted her name and felt for her pulse. Water, that's what she wanted. There was no water in her room, no refrigerator or faucet. I rushed out calling at the top of my voice, "*Water, water!*"

There was no sound. Desperately, I screamed out. A door opened a crack and someone handed me a cup of water and I ran to her bedside. I lifted the bones that were all that was left of Dona Umbelina. Her huge eyes opened for a minute and she swallowed, but most of the water ran down her chin. She choked, and I became frightened.

"Are you all right?" I cried. She looked up at me and her huge eyes glazed, and she smiled. Yes, she smiled, and said, "Bless you, senhora. It was God who sent you. Thank you, God."

She looked into my face, and with the tenderest expression I had ever seen, she died!

"Oh, my God", I cried out. I shook her, at first gently, then a bit more roughly, then felt for her pulse. I began to cry. I knelt on the floor beside the bed and called out to what seemed like an absent God.

Life in São Paulo - 1985-93

In early December 1985, Gus and I – having married in River Falls in 1981 – set out together for our new mission assignment for the American Friends Service Committee. We would first visit the northeast of Brazil. We would travel to Recife, the capital of Pernambuco; João Pessoa, the capital of Paraíba; and Salvador, the capital of Bahia – each with different cultures and stories to tell; each place leaving its mark on me and helping shape my plans to work with women in a country in which at that time they had no voice or power over their lives, with so many living simply to survive.

The bus ride to the northeast of Brazil was like traveling back in time. As we drove farther north, I saw sights along the roadside that made me feel as if I were going back a hundred years. I had lived and worked in a city favela and seen poverty, but what I saw along the road was unimaginable to me: huts made of mud and wooden slats, roofs of plastic or straw, no windows, just a door for ventilation. There were also tent-like homes made of plastic.

These primitive scenes were right along the highway we traveled. Alongside the road were crude stands with women and children selling bananas or other fruits that grew in their yards. The children worked alongside their mothers and were often the ones shouting to advertise their wares.

The yards around the houses were just dirt, and in some you'd see chickens running about or a pig or two, with maybe a couple of vegetables planted. There were children, often many, in all sorts of attire, but mostly shorts and seldom shoes. It was obvious there was no electricity or running water. Water came from shared wells or from pails that collected rainwater.

The women wore long skirts, heads covered with rags, and as we rode along I saw the many tasks they had to carry out: taking care of the children; tending to the chickens and the garden; cooking, mostly on wood fires and in makeshift outdoor kitchens; scrubbing clothes in basins or barrels. They were everywhere, and took no heed of the passing cars and buses. "Where are the men?" I wondered.

As we got closer to a city, the dwellings improved a bit, but it was only when we got very close that there was electricity. The roads were now busy with cars, buses, horses and buggies. I felt like I was reentering civilization, though still nothing like the U.S.

Dom Helder Camera had told me to visit him when I arrived in Brazil; he had been certain that I would find a way to return. And here I was now in Recife, eager to see him. I called and spoke with him briefly. I was afraid he wouldn't remember me, but he did, and we made an appointment to have breakfast. Unfortunately, that never happened. His secretary called to tell me that he was ill, and I was bitterly disappointed until I received a note from him wishing me luck in our work among the poor of Brazil.

"Never give up your struggle for justice," were his last words to me.

****

Our visit to João Pessoa was unforgettable. We stayed with a woman named Magdelene who was active in her church's ministry work among the poor. Her home was an extremely humble one, but there was electricity and running water.

But we saw neither of those when Magdelene took us to the area in which she worked. There was one place in particular I'll never forget: the city garbage dump, surrounded by the poorest ramshackled huts I had ever seen. The huts were made of all the cast-off scraps of other homes, with absolutely no comfort or much protection from wind or heavy rains. The families who lived in these homes lived off the city's garbage.

We entered a shack, and the woman, though at first uncomfortable talking to us, finally did so, offering a glimpse of her life. She had five children, but never in our

107

conversation was any reference made to a husband or father. Her shack was cluttered with all sorts of junk. There was a dirt floor and a large basin for washing piled with aluminum dishes and broken utensils waiting for the woman to fetch water from one of the drains nearby.

She would wake early, go into the dump and find something there to feed the children or to a nearby bakery to beg for a few leftover scraps. After breakfast, they all set out across the road and into the dump to pick up things they could use or that they could sell or trade to earn enough for more food.

Magdelene led us into the dump, which was full of families with sacks collecting what they could. There were children as young as three or four collecting garbage. When something really good was found, a shout of joy could be heard, which brought others running to see the prize, with fights often breaking out as people scrambled to share in the loot.

We saw a child pick up what looked like a leg or an arm, then throw it aside. We were told that the local hospital emptied its garbage there too. Shocked, I had to stop to catch my breath, wondering how this could be. Was I really seeing this?

Magdelene then led us away, and I asked her about schools. Shouldn't these children be in school? Yes, they should, but their help was necessary to the family's survival. Beyond that, there was no money for school uniforms or shoes and many of them didn't have a birth certificate.

As we were leaving, I glanced into a shack and saw a table with a black tablecloth on it. I asked Magdelene if someone had died and the family was waiting for a priest to come and pray over the body before burial. Before she could answer, the "tablecloth" arose and flew into the air. It was no tablecloth, but flies, so many that they covered the table! Garbage attracts flies, disease and premature death. I turned away with a gasp.

Such poverty, such injustice, and where was God in all this?

****

I asked the same question of the archbishop of João Pessoa, Dom Jose Maria, the only black archbishop in Brazil, when I had the privilege of visiting with him. He acknowledged the poverty and the tragedy of families forced to live on garbage. He said he was fighting for the city to prohibit the hospital from throwing its garbage in the dump. He showed in his face the pain he felt over the situation. And I thought, then why does it go on, and remembered another experience we'd had with our friend Magdelene.

There was to be a women's gathering in one of the poorer sections of town near the garbage dump, and our friend would lead prayer and discussion. We had arrived early, and decided to take a walk around the neighborhood. We came to a mud hut, and our friend said she wanted to invite the woman to the meeting.

When we entered, we saw a girl of about five or six changing the ragged cloth that served as a diaper for an infant just a few weeks old. My friend asked for the mother and the child told us, over the wails of the hungry baby, that her mother was at the garbage dump. Never had I seen such poverty, and I thought, "How can this situation be tolerated by those in power in this city – a five-year-old caring for an infant in the most unsanitary conditions possible?"

We then went to the hut where the meeting was to be held and as I was introduced to the women and heard their stories; the absence of a permanent male figure for so many was apparent. They discussed their problems, the problems of extreme poverty, and were promised help, even food baskets at the church. Prayers were said, and I could hardly keep from crying. Ah, that prayers could solve such misery.

Once again, the strength of women came to mind: their resilience, their faithfulness to their children and their daily struggle to keep them alive; the pain they suffered as the little ones died of hunger, dehydration and disease – and their lack of knowledge of how their bodies functioned, how to prevent pregnancy, how to care for their children, simple preventative measures that could save lives.

The objectives of my mission were beginning to take shape. I was to work with women; that was my assignment. I now knew I would teach them about their bodies and those of their children, about disease prevention and birth control, and I was reminded of the woman who died of a botched abortion. Wouldn't that be the best way to help? Little did I know how right I was.

****

I remembered all this as I talked with Bishop Jose Maria and he told me of all the work the church was doing. But there were so many obstacles: a lack of schooling, the time spent in the daily struggles for survival, the exploitation of the poor by the wealthy.

Things had once been better in this city, I was told. Some years before, the city government had invited large companies, some of them multinationals, to establish themselves in the city free of taxes for five years in order to create jobs and improve the life of the inhabitants, as there was no lucrative work to be had in João Pessoa. Families who wanted a better life had for many years migrated to the big cities like Rio de Janeiro or São Paulo where these unskilled workers hoped to find a better life, but ended up in the cities' favelas.

So for five years, relatively well-paying jobs were available. Tourism grew in João Pessoa, which is on the water and has beautiful beaches. The city changed, buildings went up and life improved; fewer families had to leave in search of a better life.

But when that five-year grace period expired, the incentive to stay was gone, and one by one the companies left. When we arrived there in the early months of 1986, the city had returned to its former plight – with no jobs to keep the young from fleeing and with the infrastructure beginning to crumble.

Dom Jose Maria told us this story and of the church's struggle to do what it could. He then took us to visit a nun who was working with women who had turned to prostitution in order to feed and clothe their families. The sister offered the women spiritual guidance as well as classes in parenting and in skills in other trades. They lived in a very poor area, isolated from the city, on the waterfront. They all lived together in rooms connected to one another and had a central room for meetings and socializing. This was my first experience with women who earned their living trading their bodies for money – or in some cases, food, when that was all the man had to pay with.

I saw no condemnation in the sister's eyes, only concern, patience and love. She asked them to tell me their stories, how they were surviving and raising their children. They talked about sharing the care of each other's children when they had clients, of discipline, diets and natural healing techniques when the children were sick. They also talked of their hope that someday they could send their children to school.

I just listened. This was a first experience, but there was absolutely no condemnation in my heart, just sadness at their lot. They looked just like any other woman struggling to raise a family. I could only admire them for their positive attitudes, their survival techniques.

Does that sound strange? I felt at moments such a love for these young women whose lots in life were so difficult, and I didn't even think to ask how they happened to become prostitutes. They were just women to me, mothers living in poverty.

Each experience I was having only confirmed my belief that women had much more power than they realized and much more resilience than they would acknowledge. All they needed was to know this, know their own value, be empowered. Little did I know that some years later I would work among women of the sex trade, as they were called, to prevent the new menace in their lives: AIDS.

And so I left João Pessoa with all sorts of ideas as to how I could work toward women's empowerment. And our next city gave me more to think about: Salvador, Bahia, and the black culture.

Salvador, Bahia

When the first slaves were brought to the Americas from Guinea in Africa in 1538, the largest percentage were taken to Brazil's northeast region. Given their large numbers, they were able to maintain much of their African culture. Their own religious practices were prohibited, but the slaves syncretized their gods with the Catholic saints. This deeply influenced the development of Brazilian culture. Each of the Catholic saints has an African name that is accepted by Catholics. God was called Oxala; Jesus, Zanbe.

Salvador, where we visited in 1986, was the capital of Brazil from 1549 until 1763 and is known as the African soul of Brazil, the darkest city in terms of skin color. The symbols of Candomble, this mixed religion, are seen everywhere.

The colored beads around the necks of the followers represent their deities. The place where they carry out the rituals of Candomble is called the terreiro and is led by a Mae de Santo or Pai de Santo: mother or father of the saint. There's singing – which sometimes seems like a chant – and dancing, done in a circle, with everyone dressed in white.

The Mae or Pai de Santo smokes cigars and the smoke symbolizes the purifying of the terreiro and the participants by taking the evil away. There are many other parts to this service that are purely African, and they're carried down through the generations.

Gus and I had the privilege of visiting a Mae de Santo in her home. One of the nuns where we were staying gave us her name, and off we went. She welcomed us, even though she had no idea who we were or why we had come. She was an impressive woman, very dark skinned, tall and large, wearing clothes appropriate for a leader of the religion: a long white dress with a large blouse over it and all sorts of beads around her neck and arms. As we walked into her house, there was a huge statue representing the devil: Black and dressed in red, carrying a arrow, he's called Exu, and represents the evil that one can do to another. She, as a Mae de Santo, was called upon to control him.

When we entered her home, the woman waved her hand above us, a sign of purification, and welcomed us very warmly. We spent several hours listening as she told us the meanings of the symbols, and she invited us to the ritual. I asked her about her involvement with Catholicism, since she was known by nuns and priests in the area. She told us that one of her sons was a Pai de Santo but that her daughter was married to a Protestant pastor and was involved in the church. Another son was involved in politics in Salvador and another was a priest. This was true syncretism, as is common throughout Salvador.

The city is divided into two parts, Cidade Alta and Cidade Baixa. There are large, magnificent Catholic churches everywhere. In the higher-elevated part of the city, Cidade Alta, we entered into several of the churches, which are decorated in gold: Everything from the altars to the magnificent ceilings are designed in gold, while outside, beggars were everywhere. The contrasts throughout Cidade Alta were shocking: streets paved in stone, full of potholes, prostitution and neighborhoods of degradation; we had been warned to look out for pickpockets.

But there were also singers and musicians in the streets, children running around. Food and other wares were sold everywhere, the vendors singing out the advantages of their particular items. It was truly a colorful scene, though poor and unkempt, with the hint of violence.

We were told of the Slave Museum in Cidade Alta, and so we made our way there. Our guide was a young black woman, well dressed and very knowledgeable. We were spellbound with the stories she told us as we followed her around. There were statues of slaves in chains, paintings of the terrible suffering they experienced in the crowded boats, shackled to blocks of wood with iron chains, a marketplace where they were being sold, some with iron neckholds.

We talked with our guide about the differences between slavery in the U.S. and in Brazil. One thing was clear before she even spoke of it: Miscegenation was practiced from the very beginning, thus the makeup of the Brazilian population today, the large majority of mixed race. She told us a folklore story I have never forgotten:

João, among the first settlers, left his wife and children in Portugal to find the riches of Brazil. He had heard gold and precious stones were to be had, and so he set out to find them and to build a life there for his family, who he would send for later. But upon arriving, he found he couldn't do this alone, so he took himself a companion, an African woman, with whom he had several children.

Meanwhile, as the years went on, his wife, Maria, in Portugal, was growing impatient. She was having a difficult time raising their children alone. She was tired of being put off by João's excuses. So she wrote him, warning him she was coming to Brazil and to be prepared. And so she did, with all the children. João met her and brought her home, where she was surprised to meet his companion – and even more so, their several children.

But life was difficult for the settlers; extra hands were always welcome. Thus Maria, her children and João's "wife" all lived happily together, helping create the makeup of the Brazilian people.

⁓

Irma Dulce: A Saint?

Besides the Mae de Santo, there was another whose life and dedication I will never forget.

Irma (meaning "sister') Dulce was a Franciscan nun who died a few years after I had the privilege of meeting her – this holy woman; that is how I felt about her – a tiny person, who I'm sure didn't weigh a hundred pounds, but whose eyes and enthusiasm made her face glow.

Irma Dulce spoke quietly, and her voice radiated love. She dressed in her order's black habit (though the day we visited the patients in her hospital, she wore a white habit), but what stuck out was the huge hat that was part of it. It was pointed on both sides, and those points stuck out such that you could only see her face if you looked straight in from the front.

Irma Dulce was born in 1914 to an upper-class family. At thirteen, her aunt took her to a very poor section of a city in the state of Sergipe. She was so impressed by the misery that poverty causes that her life was changed and her future set. Out of this experience, she began to care for the homeless and beggars in the neighborhood into which she moved, finding food and shelter for them, even bathing them and cutting their hair.

Despite her father's objections, at eighteen she joined the Missionary Sisters of the Immaculate Conception of the Mother of God, in Our Lady of the Carmel Convent, and set about finding shelter for the sick and homeless.

Then in 1939, in Salvador, Bahia, after being evicted from her home, she went to the mother superior of her convent and asked to use the convent's chicken yard to house her patients. The mother superior consented, with the understanding that Irma Dulce would also care for the chickens. This simple structure later became the Hospital Santo Antonio, a large medical and educational facility that continues to serve the poor.

In 1959, the Charitable Works Foundation of Irma Dulce was launched.

There are several moments that stand out in my mind from the time I spent with Irma Dulce. One is of her sitting on a board to talk to us, a board, it turned out, upon which she slept. I was startled, and had to ask her why this bed. She said she had been sleeping this way for some time due to her bad back. But I learned later from one of her assistants that it was more about being in solidarity with the homeless. And, I was told, she slept little, roaming her hospital even in the wee hours, checking in on her patients, especially the newly arrived or those who were very ill.

She worried constantly about the children in her care. She took us to the children's infirmary, where she spoke to each child by name. Her habit, with that conspicuous hat, never daunted the children; her show of love for them had a soothing effect. She kept the children there longer than they needed to stay, as many had no place to go, or such poverty to return to that she couldn't bear to let them go. As we passed by the beds, she told each child's story, and we felt her pain and love.

She told us to return early the next morning to visit the outpatient clinic. We arrived at seven, and were spellbound. A line of people stretched around the block and beyond – people in homemade stretchers; children on the backs of their parents or with crude crutches, some crying out, begging for help. I looked at this line and thought to myself, "No matter how many doctors can fit into this clinic, there is no way they can all be seen today."

I said this to Irma Dulce. Her face immediately showed pain and anguish. She clutched the cross she wore and said she prayed each day that all would be seen by a doctor or other health professional. And we learned that, miraculously, the majority were. Those who were more seriously ill were admitted as inpatients, even when there were no beds. How and where, we never learned. We only know that no one left that day without treatment or a promise of help. This was confirmed by her staff, many of whom were concerned for her health and stamina, but knew that nothing would take her from her calling.

We left this tiny, giant woman in whose face I saw sainthood.

I shall never forget that when she said goodbye, she asked us to pray for all these people who came to her for help.

Simple Favela Life

With all these experiences behind us, Gus and I returned to the city of São Paulo to begin the work that the American Friends Service Committee had sent us to do.

Our friend Padre Alamiro took us to an area far from the center of the city of São Paulo, where we were living, to a very poor area full of small favelas and little infrastructure. We knew we wanted to live in a favela, and we found a hut close to a small church – a base Christian community, as it was called.

Gus and I had lived in a favela hut in Rio, but only for about six months. In São Paulo, we lived in one for four years. It consisted of a small room that we called a living room, then a passage space to the tiny kitchen – so tiny, in fact, that it was smaller than our guest bathroom in Rio. In

Our favela hut

the passage space was our bed and a portable closet in which to keep our clothes. The kitchen had only a small sink, a stove and a table. At the end of the kitchen were a shower and our refrigerator, in which I kept our money in a plastic container. We'd go to the bank in the city, bring cash home and place it in the refrigerator – which proved to be a smart thing, as I'll soon explain.

There was an air space between the top of the rough-faced building blocks and the tin roof, and in the winter we could see our breath. We'd go to bed early through those winters, retiring to the little hallway that served as our bedroom.

My children worried about the cold and gave us an electric blanket. So here we were in a tiny, poorly built alley hut, with an electric blanket!

Yes, we did have electricity, but only if it didn't rain. And when it did, the patter against our tin roof was so loud that it made conversation impossible.

Life was so simple, but full, and that's what made it so wonderful. Our hut was at the bottom of the favela, off to the side of the main entrance, and to get to the upper area everyone had to pass in front of our hut. Thus we'd get news of what was going on, who was sick, etc. People would stop to visit.

Our neighbors were our friends. We hung our clothes out on the line together and watched their children if they had to leave for a bit. We were godparents of a few of those kids. We shared meals, as well as domestic and neighborhood arguments – one of which I broke up with the sweep of a broom. I never thought of myself as living a sacrificed life.

We were respected. It was known we were church people; in fact, I was thought to be a married nun! It was assumed that was the reason I lived among the poor, and the rumor spread – a married nun. My nun friends and the priests who worked with us went along with it.

****

We soon added a free pharmacy, stocked with donated medications, in the yard of the church. It was frequented by people from all over the area and became quite well known. We also kept a few medications in our hut for me to use for first aid, wound care and so forth. As I said, the news spread, and with it the idea that maybe we had narcotics too.

One day, Gus had gone to the airport to pick up an American friend who had come to visit us, and I remembered I had to go to the public health center for a meeting. With no car, I went to the little church office to ask one of the priests if I could borrow his, and off I went. When I returned, there was a big hullabaloo going on. The alley in front of our hut was full of our neighbors. Something had happened.

Apparently, a member of one of the local gangs had notified a gang member of a nearby favela that the "nun" had left her hut and that she kept drugs there. So a few members of this gang entered the alley, shooed everyone away with guns and threats and broke in. There were no drugs, but there was a TV, a camera and a few other items of some value, including our gas tank for the stove, which they took. Of course, they never thought to look in the refrigerator, where we kept our money – cold cash!

This was the talk of the community for some time.

Then one day as I entered the alley to our home, the gang leader – or at least the guy we knew had control of the illegal activities in the favela – approached me. He asked me if I was missing some things – that is, had our hut been broken into.

I said yes, knowing, of course, that he already knew. He gave a signal, and out of a bend in the alley appeared four young men. "These are them," he said. He then turned to them and told them to return what they had taken. They did, looking rather humbled, I thought. The only thing they didn't return was the TV, which they had sold immediately.

I looked at these young men and proceeded to give them a small lecture, telling them what I thought would happen to their lives, knowing, though, they were already hooked and could never get out alive.

Within the next five months, they were all dead, victims of fights between gangs or over drugs. The head of their gang was shot in front of our hut sometime later.

****

Which leads into another story.

This gang leader was in his late twenties or early thirties, and was one of the first AIDS patients we knew and tried to help. His wife, or female companion, also had AIDS, but she was getting help at some of the new public centers treating AIDS patients. She was in bad shape, she told me the many times I visited her hut, which was just down the alley from ours.

Her primary concern was for her son, a fourteen-year-old whom I knew well, as he was a severe asthmatic and very slow. He didn't attend school, spending his days, between asthma attacks, flying his kite. I had gone to his hut so many times when he was having an attack, trying to help. I wanted to take him to a doctor, but he had no birth certificate, a nonexistent child!

One day he was flying his kite in front of our alley, where there was a bakery (there's one on every street corner in Brazil – the poor at least eat bread), when a car drove up and two armed men jumped out, entered the store and robbed it. The owner called the police and in minutes the cop cars arrived. Out jumped the men, with guns in hand, while all during this drama our young boy continued flying his kite. Suddenly, a cop ran up to him, yelling, knocked him to the ground, and they took him away.

Three days later, his mom came to get me; the boy was having a severe asthmatic attack. She told me that at the station, the police had beaten him, thrown him on the ground in a pool of water and stomped on him. There was a bruise mark on his back where he had been kicked. Of course, this brought on a severe asthmatic attack, so bad that the police brought him home, and there he lay before me, sobbing, but angry – a potentially violent, nonexistent teenager.

So his mother, ill as she was, took him away to one of the poorest areas of Brazil, in the northeast, from where she had come, knowing that his life was in danger if they stayed.

I never heard what became of them. But surely the boy's mother died soon: In the rural north, she would have found no health care, nor, at that time, would anyone there have known what AIDS was, if she even told them.

Another woman showing the strength and sacrifice that millions and millions have shown.

Creation of the Health Course

I had observed first-hand in my days working and living in the favela in Rio that women knew nothing about their bodies. What brought my attention to this fact were the many preventable diseases that were so prevalent. And the fact that there were so many large families indicated that women knew nothing about contraception.

I would talk with the women in our little makeshift hut where I kept the sample medicines that doctors donated to me. I would explain to them why the doctor had prescribed the medicine, information about the illness for which they were being treated and how it could have been prevented. From 1967 until 1981, working out of that little hut, I taught the simplest things about health and nutrition.

So when I returned to Brazil as a volunteer for the American Friends Service, I knew that I would use this

Training community health educators

health knowledge to educate women and thereby empower them, as I had done before.

I began with small groups, the first one meeting in the AFSC's Office of Peace and Justice. The women I was teaching had little education, some barely knowing how to read and write. Thus the challenge of how to teach such things as what a virus or bacteria is and the importance of knowing the difference.

In the initial groups, I used poster-making and all sorts of games, like guessing games with puzzles the women made. We would act out sicknesses, creating our own dramas, which the women loved. Each new group came up with different ideas, and so my skills in teaching improved with each.

As time went on, I felt the need to organize all that we were learning. We would start with what causes diseases and then go through the systems of the body: respiratory, circulatory, urinary, glandular and so on – and, most important, the sexual organs, male and female, followed by contraception. We'd then learn about children's diseases.

A methodology was developing. First the system, its different components, how each functioned, then the diseases that affected it, ways to prevent these diseases

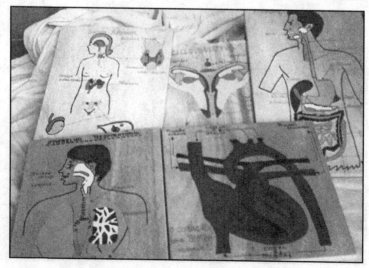

Body-part puzzles used as teaching tools

124

and treatments that doctors might prescribe and how these functioned.

And I began to see the changes that would come over these women. When we discussed the nose and throat, I had them look into each other's throats and then go home and examine the throats, eyes, ears and so on of their family members and neighbors. We gave them a little flashlight and a thermometer, and they were beginning to build their own health educator kits. They made little bags to carry them in and drew pictures to explain the procedures they would perform.

It astounded me to see the effect this had on the women as they went about examining their neighbors and recording what they learned.

But the most apparent change came when we began to study the circulatory system and I was able to get donations to buy each woman a blood pressure kit and taught them how to use them. Once I knew they were all proficient in the procedure, they were sent out with their bags to read the blood pressures of their families and neighbors.

For women whose value was simply to care for their humble homes, take care of the children, who had little or no education, this was an exciting and empowering experience. As one woman put it, it made them feel important! If someone's blood pressure was too high, they would urge the person to see a doctor; they were improving the general health of their communities. With these changes came the desire to learn more and more, and, over the years, many women went back to school – some even finished primary school and a few went on to further education.

****

What happens is that women begin to learn the wonder and beauty of the sexual organs, how well they are intertwined, the beauty of menstruation, why it occurs and what causes it, the magnificence of the act of fecundation, and they see the sperm entering the egg at just the right time for fecundation. It's all so beautifully designed, and their admiration grows for a part of their body that many of them felt ashamed of, or just never dared to talk about. I would then ask them to go home and look at their vaginas. When I would first suggest this, as we began to study sexuality, I would hear, "Ugh!" "Awful." "Oh, I don›t want to see that; it's so ugly!"

Then a change comes; though, in reality, some come along slower than others. But they begin to appreciate that it is, in fact, beautiful, and it occurs to them that there must be a designer behind all this with a purpose in mind. And this for them is God. Beauty, design, purpose = God.

Next step: If this designer, God, created this, for what purpose? First comes the thought, "To have children, to be mothers!" They see the beauty of birth, the miracle of another life coming from their bodies, as part of the design, the reason for all this, the purpose. And, of course, contraception comes in here, as they come to understand the fecundation process.

Next step: If this is my body, if this belongs to me and there is pleasure included in this design for the woman – the clitoris – then that part of the purpose is for women to have pleasure as well, not just men. And this pleasure can be just mine, or it can be shared with someone I love.

These steps take time – longer for some women than others – but it is the acceptance that the God they believe in, the creator, made this magnificent body for them to enjoy, appreciate and find pleasure in, and to be able to choose when and where and how they might have this pleasure. That means being the subjects of their own pleasure, not the objects of another's pleasure.

And this also includes their ability to control the number of children they want, because now that they're more knowledgeable about how it all functions and realize that they can control it, the empowerment process is growing.

Beauty, miracle, purpose, creation, ownership – all part of a plan in which they are the subjects.

****

After eight years developing this course in many groups in various poor areas of São Paulo, I began to focus on what had been one of the original primary objectives of the course:

126

for the women I'd taught to become multipliers – to teach others what they had learned, empowering others. Some of the women suggested that in order to accomplish this, we should put all the things they had learned into a teaching manual.

A good idea, I agreed. But if they were the ones who would be using this manual, it needed to be in the form they felt would be most useful. So I invited women from the many groups I had taught to meet with me and help design this manual.

And thus the Community Health Educators Training Course was born. We spent many months meeting and putting the manual together. They wanted to stick to the order in which I had taught them. They wanted to use the pictures they had chosen that I had xeroxed for them or those they had drawn. Thus we started with a picture of the body system, pictures of the components of the system, illnesses that affected the system, symptoms, preventions and some of the treatments the doctors might recommend. When the ideas were put together, I was pleased, but began to wonder how I would ever get it published. The women had made paper copies, but more would be needed in the future.

It took a year, but the manual did get published. By this time, I had moved back to Rio de Janeiro, where I was blessed to meet a well-to-do retiree named Mark Boyd, who had learned of my work through Rev. David Vargas – who was in charge of the Latin American division of the Disciples of Christ – and was excited about the course.

One day as were returning from visiting a group, he turned to me and said, "What would you need to publish the manual?" I gave him an estimate, what I thought was probably a high-end one. He pulled out his checkbook and wrote me a check for that very amount.

The manual was published in Rio de Janeiro, where I returned in 1993 when I became a missionary of the Global Ministries and was called to the Institute of Religious Studies to work on a project called Women, Theology and Citizenship.

But that's getting ahead of myself.

Health Education: A Way to Empowerment

I never imagined that this simple health course would have the impact it did – the hundreds of women whose lives have been changed by it, who see themselves now in a different light, as transformers of their own lives, as subjects of their own lives, now able to participate in their communities, in society, as well as being better mothers.

Thinking back now, it's hard to describe what I was seeing in these women. The course would begin and ninety percent of them knew nothing about health, disease prevention or causes, nor did they have any confidence they could ever learn. Some were so shy that I could hardly get a word out of them.

Of course, as time went on, and TV became more accessible to the poor, the world was opened up and women saw more. But still, their hands were often tied, and only in church-sponsored programs did they have the freedom to discuss issues and learn. That's why most of the courses were done within churches, as church activities were permitted by the men in their lives.

As the course progressed, it was amazing to me to see the creativeness the women used in displaying what they were learning, their self-esteem growing to the point that a shy woman could get up and show a poster she'd made or act out a scene about a health issue (play-acting was a very successful methodology). I watched as the women came to know one another better, working on group assignments and sharing their lives, comparing and comforting.

I remember in one group, four of the women became widows during the almost two-year course, and one by one they appeared in class with short haircuts. Men wouldn't allow their women to have short hair, and when I asked them what was going on, they all said, "We're now free to do as we want!"

As I said, many of these women went back to school, and some took specialized courses to become, for example, nursing assistants. Some went on to college with financial assistance from churches in the U.S.

Making dolls for sex education in the Community
Health Educators Training Course

****

There are two particular points in the health course that have the most impact on the women. The first I've already mentioned: when they receive their blood pressure kits, learn how to use them and then take them out into the community. For so many women who'd never felt important, this was the number-one life-changing moment.

At about the same time, they learn to take temperatures; examine the throat, nose and neck; and listen to the lungs.

I remember one woman telling me of being home fixing dinner, her husband watching TV, when a neighbor came in with her little girl to have the woman take her temperature and look at her throat. The woman told her neighbor that

129

the child's tonsils were very red and enlarged and that she had a fever. She suggested that the mother take her to the public health center.

When the woman left, our student's husband looked at her as if he thought she was crazy. "Do you really know what you're doing, lady?" he asked.

In the weeks to come, as more and more women came to his door to ask for his wife's help, he began to change his attitude. Then one day he came home from work with a sore throat, and, lo and behold, who did he ask to look him over? Victory! At least the start of one.

The next big apparent change in these women is when we get to the sexuality part of the course, which is about halfway through it. By then, they've built up self-esteem, are comfortable with the other women and are ready to get into this long-forbidden subject about a part of the body most of them knew little about, even their own.

I believe that what they learn is almost theological. They realize that sexuality is about them, and that they too, like men, are allowed to experience pleasure. The words "masturbation" and "homosexuality" are discussed – shyly

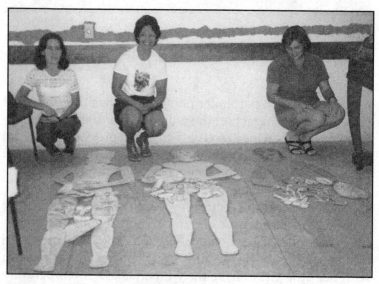

The finished dolls

at first, and then in the spirit of discovery. When AIDS began to be discussed in Brazil, these women were prepared to discuss it.

Their homework was to then go back to their communities and give talks about what they had learned, using dolls with sexual organs to demonstrate.

Naturally, all this affected their marriages – some for the better.

   ℴℽℾℽℴ

Testimonials of Students of the Health Education Course

The areas on the periphery of São Paulo where the women with whom I worked lived had little or no infrastructure. In most areas, sewage ran out in open valleys and garbage was thrown into the streets or onto vacant land. Public health clinics were few and far between, often with but one doctor and nurse on duty and an insufficient supply of medicines and supplies, while what was available was generally in very poor condition.

Measles, mumps, chickenpox, whooping cough, tetanus, diphtheria, meningitis and even polio were still prevalent in the years I was in São Paulo, between 1985 and 1993.

The average salary for a favela dweller was the equivalent of about a hundred to a hundred and fifty dollars a month. Nutrition was poor, homes were poorly built and schools were poorly equipped. In short, it was very difficult to live a dignified life.

And so this was a primary objective of the health educator course – to help build self-esteem, to help empower these women to take ownership of their lives. At the end of the course, almost all of the women agreed that they were not the same person as when they'd begun.

****

Up until just a few years ago, going to college was out of the question for a poor child, or even a lower-middle-class one. The public schools were so bad that the graduates couldn't compete on the entrance exams. In the early 2000s, the Catholic Church started a night-study program to prepare poor kids to take these exams, also providing tuition discounts, but most had to turn down these offers because they had to work to help support their families.

I tell this by way of context for Cida's story, which I believe is a remarkable one:

I came from a poor but proud family of six: my mother, father and three siblings. I was the oldest of three girls. Ten families shared a common space, called a cortico.

My father did everything he could to ensure that our family had as much privacy as possible. On a piece of land in the back of our living quarters he built an outhouse and a place where clothes could be washed, all from wood left over after construction jobs. Around this space, he and my mother had a small vegetable garden and a chicken coup, so we had fresh eggs every day.

Cida

Up until I was ten or eleven, I lived this way, and did not feel badly about being poor – to the contrary, I had a happy childhood. There were many children to play with, and we played all the usual girls' games, though I preferred the boys' games, like flying kites, playing marbles with small rocks, riding carts.

As I grew older and met new people, I began to feel embarrassed that I lived in a tenement slum. I was ashamed to bring my friends to my house. I never invited anyone over and gave excuses for why I couldn't host study groups.

At age fourteen, I had my first boyfriend, a neighbor, who until this time I hadn't even noticed. We met at a community dance; he took me home and I experienced my first kiss. Our romance began, but not at my insistence. I dreamed of studying more, getting a better job and gaining my independence, which would give me the ability to have a different and better life than my parents.

My parents had worked very hard to give a better life to their children. My mother worked as a maid and at home washing, by hand, and ironing clothes for her clients. My father worked in a factory, putting in extra hours and doing repair work at home. During his compulsory vacation from the factory, he loaded the four of us and a bicycle onto the train and took us to our grandparents' home in Santos.

My mother never went; she had to work, and she didn't get along with my father's family anyway.

My parents were not really happy together. I could see their unhappiness and dissatisfaction with their marriage, and I wanted to live differently. I wanted to find happiness.

But, unfortunately, I didn't have the courage or maturity to pursue my dreams, and I gave in to the desires of my mother and my boyfriend: I got engaged at seventeen and married at eighteen. I had my first child, Priscilla, at nineteen and my second, Clayton, at twenty-three.

My husband was a very kind and simple man and was satisfied with our life as it was, a very traditional life, with a wife who stayed at home and cared for the family. I was so disappointed, still believing in the fantasy of an enchanted prince – which my husband was not.

During my children's first years, my dreams were put aside and my time was filled with caring for them, which made me happy and fulfilled. But as they grew older and became more independent, my desire to do something different with my life returned. I became involved with the activities of a group called the Society of Friends of the Bairro. The children and I participated in ballet classes, gymnastics and other activities.

Around this same time, I was invited to take a training course for community health educators, the ultimate objective of which was to take the skills learned in the course and become multipliers, to teach others, forming groups in our communities. I didn't get any encouragement from my husband; but I believed it was a chance for me to feel important, to prove to myself that I was capable of taking on a challenge.

I began the course and met Barbara de Souza, and we clicked right away. She was strong, intelligent, determined and a defender of women's rights. I began to pass on to my community what I was learning. I read blood pressures and gave talks to women about disease prevention and how their bodies functioned. I was feeling very good about myself. I was beginning a new phase in my life and seeing different possibilities.

Barbara's receptiveness allowed me to feel free to open up to her, to reveal my true feelings, dissatisfactions and dreams for my life. I told her my whole story and of the changes in the path my life was taking. I always felt a great deal of support from her, and in the most difficult hours I could count on her affection and attention.

134

Participating in this course made it possible for me to think in a new way about sexuality and sexual rights, to overcome my fears and insecurities, making me a more courageous person, woman, wife, mother and professional, because I was looking at it all with new eyes, those of a woman with the capacity to learn, to teach others, to create and re-create, to escape from a limited world, transforming it into a world where women could be the subjects of their own life stories.

My marriage was now in crisis, because as I grew and changed, feeling better about myself and more important, my husband felt less important and would not accept this new me.

At the same time, Barbara asked me to begin teaching health educators courses. I saw in this invitation a recognition of my dedication and capabilities. It was an opportunity to develop myself professionally, contributing to the awakening of other women so that they might write their own stories, in which they would be the subjects, and possibly become financially independent. With such a big change in my life, it wasn't possible for my marriage to continue, and so we separated.

With my two children, I went to live with my parents. It was very difficult. My children suffered from the separation from their father, and returning to live with my parents after thirteen years was not a good situation. Though they were my parents, our lives were now very different. After six months, I rented a tiny house and went to live there with my children. I now felt that I could finally live out my dreams.

After some time, I met someone to whom I was attracted, and we began a life together. We had much in common. We enjoyed each other and our life together, and I was now experiencing the pleasure of loving someone. He liked my work and contributed a lot to it, but I still felt that I needed to do it all alone. I wanted to conquer my own space; I wanted to become a professional respected for my own accomplishments. In spite of having much in common, we had our own ways of seeing life, of living a married life, of dreaming.

So after ten years of living together, we decided to separate for a while; we didn't want to separate, yet we couldn't live together either, as our differences were getting in the way of our lives' paths. We moved into separate houses, but remained in constant contact. This was our way of reconstructing our lives, our dreams, and of meeting our own needs – of building a life for two that was pleasurable for both. Ten years have passed; we are still together, more mature, even better friends, but in separate houses.

During these ten years, I've grown a lot. I was able to buy my own apartment and a car. I went to college and earned a nursing degree, and I feel accomplished professionally. I know that I can contribute. I've worked in a home for street dwellers, worked in a program in the public schools on sexuality and knowledge of one's own body and am now part of a foundation called the Social Education Support Center for Adolescents.

But I also try to be a multiplier of all that I learned in the health educators course, which made me able to make my dreams a reality. My daughter completed her college degree in psychology and my son is in physical education. My daughter married, and I now have a grandson. I feel victorious, in that I was able to consolidate the various roles women play – that is, be a wife, a mother, a professional, a friend and, most importantly, a modern woman true to myself.

****

"Don't talk like that! You have to be a fighter. You can't just sit back and give up – you're such a fighter. How can you give up so easily?

"He was a no-good in life and now even worse in death. How could he do this to the children? Never mind me, but they are his children, just as much as the child of that other woman!"

She was crying now, but differently. She got up and walked out of the room. Then she came back again. She came back because the one thing she had been able to do since her husband's death was become a student in my community health educators course.

Genilda's case was a familiar one for Brazilian women: the injustice of the legal system at that time as it related to respect for women's rights, and the injustice of the economic system, which suggested that money could buy anything.

Genilda was born to a large rural family and married when still in her teens. Marriage was an escape from the endless tasks that define the lives of rural women. Like so many of them, she believed that marriage would offer relief. The man she married had a high school education and would take her to the big city of São Paulo, where life would be better and there would be more employment opportunities.

This is what people always said about that big city.

So Genilda went to São Paulo with dreams of improving her life. For a while, things seemed good; her husband was earning decent money, they bought a piece of property out along the periphery of São Paulo, where land was relatively cheap, confident that in time they could move closer to the city and its conveniences.

They struggled to build their house. There was no piped-in water, no sewers or paved streets. And, worst of all, no public transportation, which meant that Genilda's husband would leave for work on Monday and not return until Friday.

When she became pregnant with their second child, Genilda's husband was angry. At this rate, he said, they'd never improve their lives. There were no medical facilities nearby, and so Genilda had no prenatal care and no access to information about birth control.

Though the area did eventually get public transportation, her husband was now returning home only once or twice a month. Other improvements came: running water, an asphalt road within a half-mile of Genilda's home, an elementary school and talk of a public health facility.

With the help of neighbors and her husband when he was home, Genilda made a few improvements to the house. She had to beg money from him for these improvements and the children's necessities. And even though he claimed he was doing well in his job and rising in the firm, there was consistently less and less money for the family.

When her husband was home, they argued and argued. He wanted no more children. And though Genilda agreed, she still wanted affection, but got none. She then had to agree with her neighbors – that her husband must have another woman.

Genilda knew that she had to get on with her life, and, after months of contemplation, decided to take a part-time job as a cleaning woman. She took her younger child with her to work each day, while a neighbor cared for the other. Things got better; she felt more independent and bought new clothes for herself and the children.

Her husband, on one of his few visits home, noticed the differences and discovered that she was working. He was angry, and left the family permanently. Genilda was reconciled to the fact that she was now alone. He had left her, but she had a house and the children would soon be in school, at which point she could get herself a full-time job in the city. Though it would mean that she would be away from her home all day, the children would be fine; the neighbors would watch them till she arrived home.

****

It was at this time that I met Genilda. She became a student in our course when the company she worked for offered it to members of their staff as part of a program for creating health care alternatives for the rising city population, which had little or no health assistance. Genilda asked to take it, believing it would be useful, given the health conditions in the area in which she lived.

Right from the start of the course, Genilda was engaged; she loved what she was learning. She caught on right away, and as the months went on and her health knowledge improved, so did her poise and self-esteem. She freely shared her experiences with the other women as they learned how their bodies functioned and how they could better care for themselves and others. She was excited about the preventative measures that could be taken and was eager to share them with her neighbors.

And that's exactly what she did: She went back to her neighborhood and began to practice and teach what she had learned. She got involved in a government program that distributed free milk tickets for families in need.

But Genilda was changing, and though she knew that the milk tickets were meeting needs, she saw it as a paternalistic means of keeping people quiet and more dependent on the government. As she organized her own groups to teach preventative methods for controlling illnesses, she began addressing other issues, such as low salaries, especially for women. She discussed sexuality and birth control with women. Whatever she learned in my classes, she now passed along, and loved doing so.

She felt important and empowered with the health knowledge she was gaining. She and those she had helped organize began to fight for sewers in the area, where parasites and diarrhea left undernourished children with little strength to survive. She talked with the women about the importance of fighting for more equitable salaries. A leader was born. "When sleeping women awake, mountains will move."

****

Then, suddenly, Genilda's husband died of a stroke, and she learned that he had forged her name to divorce papers, remarried and had a child. He had been financially successful, but in his will he left all of his assets to his new wife, even the house in which Genilda and her children lived. There was nothing left. Genilda now sat before the women in our group and cried.

But this was a new and empowered Genilda, who would fight now for her rights, who would not give up. She was no longer immobilized by anger or frustration – and she had all of us in this group rooting for her. The group had been together for more than a year now, and we were ready to help Genilda evaluate her options, as well as herself.

Her courage built up, she went to her dead husband's other wife to make a case for keeping her home. She found a frightened and confused woman. She told this woman that though her marriage was illegal, she would not try to press charges. All she wanted was for her home to be put in her name; his illegitimate wife and child could have the rest. The now-empowered Genilda was able to see this woman and understand her.

The story has an interesting ending. Genilda saw immediately that this woman was much like the Genilda of the past. They became friends and the woman later became a student in my course. Surely, this woman owes her empowerment to Genilda.

This community health course proved that empowerment could be attained through education – even a simple course about the systems of the body and how they function. It challenged these students to go forth as multipliers of the course, thus empowering others. It proved to be not just a course in health education but one in which women were given the freedom to share their lives and encourage each other to work together for a more just society in which all have a right to the basics of life, including human dignity.

****

Dona Julieta was one of the students of my first health education course in rural São Paulo.

Her mother died giving birth to her and she was passed along from one member of this poor rural family to another. She was an awkward child, plump and, in her rural one-room schoolhouse, often the brunt of jokes. She was called fat, ugly and dumb by the members of her own family.

Julieta

When she became a teenager, she was no longer able to go to school, needed at home to take care of the younger ones and do the chores, difficult ones. There was no running water. Life was very hard, and she was an unhappy girl.

Then came a day that Julieta thought might bring relief, a new life. The aunt with whom she had lived the past two years gave her to a salesman who was passing through their rural town selling his wares. She doesn't know how the transaction occurred, only that the priest came and performed a marriage and she was told to pack her clothes and accompany this stranger.

So off she went, about sixteen years old, with this man who was now her husband, to São Paulo. The man worked at home as a carpenter and controlled his wife's every move.

140

He had been told that she was stupid, unable to learn, and so he gave her no money except the coins she needed to buy food. When I met Julieta, even the priest suspected that she was in an abusive marriage.

I was invited to give my health education training course in this priest's community. It was announced during mass that the course would be offered and that it would be a real benefit to this poor community, given that public health services weren't readily available in the area.

Julieta had to have her husband's permission to leave the house, and she knew he would not allow her to attend the classes. By this time, she had two young daughters. To take this course would have been an escape for her. She told the priest how much she wanted to get out of the house occasionally, so he said he would speak to her husband. He went to their home and the men talked, but the priest could see that it was of no use.

So Julieta spoke up, something she would not have been allowed to do if it had not been for the priest's presence.

"But there's prayer group on Wednesday, isn't there, Padre?" she said. Wednesday was the day of the classes

The priest went along and persuaded Julieta's husband to let her come to church for "prayer group" each Wednesday afternoon, with the stipulation that she would bring their seven-year-old daughter with her.

On the first day of classes, I asked each of the women why she wanted to take the course. A number of different answers were given, but when it came Julieta's turn she said she didn't know why, as she didn't read or write very well and found it hard to learn new things. She had been brainwashed from childhood, and my heart broke to hear her speak.

This would be a challenge for me. As I've said, a primary objective of the course – and at the core of my work for the American Friends Service Committee – was to empower women, to help them build up their self-esteem. I had chosen health as a way to achieve this. And here was a perfect example of a woman who needed to love herself, to learn her value. Her self-esteem was so low; there was much to do.

****

As the weeks went on, it became evident that Dona Julieta *could* learn; she was not dumb nor lacking in talent. One talent – unrecognized up to this point, even by herself – was drawing. She was a natural artist. Though she could barely read, she was good at the organization and drawing of posters. These women I taught had little formal education – some only two or three years – and so we would incorporate posters, dramatizations and other creative teaching methods.

Julieta's talent made her immediately popular and in demand. All the women wanted her to be in their work group, and she would go from one to the next, adding her touch or offering ideas. Now much surer of herself, she was beginning to build relationships.

As her popularity grew, Julieta came out of her shell. Before my eyes, a new woman was being born. In the first weeks, she barely spoke in class. Now she asked questions – and yet another talent emerged: She was also a born dramatist. When we did our role-playing and dramatizations about health issues, she shone. She could dramatize anything, and within her groups she was the leader. When we had quizzes, she was among the first to pop up with an answer, often doing so dramatically.

With this new sense of confidence, Julieta began to change her appearance. At the outset of the course, she would show up in wrinkled clothes, her hair uncombed, really a very dumpy appearance. Now she arrived in well-ironed clothes, her hair styled, and, in her simple way, she was becoming quite pretty. But what I think made her most attractive was her smile, and her newly acquired happy nature. She had become a lively member of the group, even encouraging others. In the eight or nine months the course had been going on, she had bloomed. A new woman was being born!

****

Then one Wednesday, Julieta didn't show up. She was ordinarily one of the first to arrive, and her absence was well noted. The next Wednesday, still no Julieta. Now we all were worried. One of her neighbors who was also taking the course said she had not even seen her in the yard. We suggested that she check on her, but she said Julieta's husband didn't allow her to have visitors, that he was a very rude and often violent man. No one wanted to check on her. She was missed.

By the next Wednesday, we were extremely worried and were discussing asking the priest to go to Julieta's home, when the door opened and in she came. Her blouse was torn and her hair was disheveled. She had a skinned knee, several bruises, and her daughter wasn't with her. The women rushed to Julieta, hugging her and asking what had happened. This is the story she told:

At lunch that first missed Wednesday, Julieta's husband told her he was tired of her going to prayer group, that she belonged at home. When she pleaded, he became shocked at her audacity to question him, struck her several times, pushed her into her room and locked the door.

The next Wednesday, as she prepared to leave, he asked her where she thought she was going. When she said the prayer group, he shouted at her and once again dragged her to her room and locked the door.

At lunch the following Wednesday, Julieta again asked her husband if she could go, reminding him that she had missed two weeks and needed to be present. He laughed cynically and asked his daughter what they did at this prayer group that made it so important.

The daughter, innocently, said, "Oh, Papa, they don't always pray. They make naked dolls and put all the body parts on them, and Mother is so good at that."

Furious, he rose up, and this time really laid into Julieta, to the point that her daughter cried out. He dragged Julieta to her room by the hair and locked her in.

But this was not the same Julieta of months ago. She now had friends and had acquired enough self-esteem to help her understand that she had rights, that she was not a prisoner. She recognized her importance to the group. She had gotten a taste of being loved and feeling important, and so she climbed out her bedroom window, dropped hard to the ground and ran to the church.

It was then that she told us her story, of being an orphan, passed around from one house to another, and that no one in her family had loved her, convincing her that she was ugly and stupid and should be ashamed of herself. But now she could look in a mirror and see someone she loved.

The women stood up and encircled her. It was a beautiful scene as they hugged her and formed a prayer circle; there were tears in all our eyes. Other women related their stories, of years of feeling inferior, of not feeling loved, and some of abuse. They too acknowledged that in learning to love one other, in working together in this course, they were also learning to love themselves.

The priest visited that afternoon and the women told him of Julieta's plight. They asked for his help. We don't know what he said to her husband, but though things didn't change at home – the abuse, both verbal and physical, continued – Julieta did not miss another class.

This was one of my first groups and I was still developing the program methodology, but in Julieta my objectives were being realized. Education empowers; even a simple health-education course, teaching how the body functions, could empower. And then lives like Julieta's are transformed. She became my encouragement. I dedicated myself to continue teaching and perfecting this course.

****

But that's not the end of this story. As the close of the course neared, we began planning a graduation ceremony. This was important; no one in this group had ever received a diploma. The priest and I wrote them, rolled them up and tied them with ribbons. They would be given out in a special church service.

But there was more to do. The women had learned in the course about how all the parts of the body function, the diseases that can affect these parts and how to prevent those diseases. They had been given assignments – talking to neighborhood groups about certain ailments, performing dramatizations, presenting posters – and they had learned to take blood pressures and explain, with illustrations, how to control blood pressure, diet and exercise and monitor cholesterol.

And so they decided to demonstrate to the congregation what they had learned, and it was determined that Julieta should introduce the program, show the posters and do most of the talking. She told me she was scared, but would do it. She wished her husband would come, but she knew he wouldn't and had to be satisfied that her daughters would be there.

The day arrived, and though it was apparent that Julieta was nervous, she did a wonderful job, as did all the women, and fifty or so people stayed to get their blood pressure taken. This made Julieta late returning home, and her husband came looking for her.

As he was approaching the church, he spoke to one of the women, asking what was taking his wife so long. The woman told him what a wonderful talk Julieta had given and that she was now reading blood pressures. Visibly angry, he turned back toward home.

The woman ran to tell Julieta what had happened. We could see a flicker of fear in her eyes, and one of the women suggested they all accompany her home. Julieta paused, and then smiled. "No," she said, "I must face this myself now." We were seeing a new Julieta.

When sleeping women awake, mountains will move.

As Julieta approached her house, she steadied herself for the beating that would come. She opened the door, and there he was. "Listen, dummy," he said, "if I'd known you could read blood pressures, I'd have had you read mine and my mother's."

Does this sound like a victory? Well, it was. I can't say that her marriage changed; it did not. But Julieta had. She became a teacher of the course in her neighborhood, and I heard some years later that she had left her husband and taken her younger daughter with her to the city to work in a church, to teach others what she had learned.

Prostitution: A Way to Survive

To work effectively with women who make their livings as prostitutes, I learned, you must remove all previous notions about prostitution and, as a feminist, try to walk a mile in their shoes, to see them as women who struggle to survive, to raise their children and to hold onto some sense of self-esteem.

You must acknowledge that for most of them, this is the only life they have ever known, that they live within a reality that is much different than ours, but that it is theirs and should be respected.

And even more important, and absolutely essential, you must erase from your mind, and vocabulary, the notion of sin, and sit at the table – a round one, preferably, where all are equal – and share.

This was my experience, and some of these women became close friends who changed my way of thinking and helped make clear the true meaning of love.

****

One such woman is named Fatima – at least that's the name I'll give her as I tell her story. She was in her late twenties and had given birth to three children, though the first one died soon after birth. She'd delivered the baby alone in a bathroom of the house in which she worked as a maid. Like so many other young women, poverty had led her mother to give her away – to send her off to a family to work as a maid in return for room and board. Fatima was only ten when she went off to the city to live with this family. The woman who took her in became her patroa, and she a child servant.

The family had promised Fatima's mother that she would go to school, but she never did. She was up at the crack of dawn to make coffee and get the children of the family fed and ready for school, then spent the day at all sorts of chores – and so went the day till night, when, with the children tucked in, she could fall onto the sack that was her bed.

Such was her life until the age of fifteen, which is when it took a turn for the worse. An eighteen-year-old nephew of her patroa came to stay while taking a course in the city, and from the moment he saw Fatima he had but one thought: to take her for himself.

And so he did. In the wee hours of the morning, he would sneak into the tiny cubicle where she slept and talk to her of other places, other lives and things she never dreamed of. He bought her sweets, the ones she was never offered in this house. She was mesmerized by his stories and the promises he made to her of a future together: As soon as he finished his course, he would return to his home and take her with him.

And so she fell into his arms and dreamed with him of a bright future. But within two months of his arrival, Fatima knew something was wrong. Her body was not acting as it should. She hadn't shed her blood that month, and she waited. With no health education, no knowledge of anything about a woman's body, she couldn't guess. She had no real friends with whom she could talk, and never could she speak of such a thing to her patroa.

Another month went by, and still no bleeding. Her small breasts hurt and she was often so nauseated in the mornings she could hardly make breakfast for the children. She was growing frightened and needed help.

One day when she was sent to the market to buy fruit, she saw an older girl who was in a similar living situation and with whom she often compared lives. When Fatima asked her what might be wrong, the girl covered her mouth with her hand and said, "Girl, you are pregnant." Fatima, in her ignorance, just stared at her. What did she mean?

"Have you ever been with a man?" the girl asked. And when Fatima continued to give her that blank stare, her friend explained. Choking back sobs, Fatima ran home – that is, the only home she'd had for some years now. Her

147

only thought was to tell the young man who up till then had been her friend. He loved her, she was sure, and he would take care of her.

That night, he came, as usual, and she told him what she had learned. At first, he just laughed it off. What did she know of such things? He soothed her, telling her it was nothing to be concerned about.

But as the days wore on, he could see the changes in her body and knew he would have to take action. Not action on her behalf, as she thought, but action to save himself. He simply told his aunt he'd been called home, and left.

****

At first, Fatima was sure he would return, that he was just making arrangements. She listened attentively to all the family conversations.

Nothing; nothing. The months flew by, and it was becoming harder and harder to hide her pregnancy. She didn't know what to do. Terrified, she decided to beg help from the young woman who had explained to her that she was pregnant. The woman knew of others who had been in the same situation and had gone to an old woman outside the city who could "fix her up."

When Fatima learned what this meant, she was even more frightened. So she put off making the decision and continued to hide her condition. The fact that she was able to do this speaks of how little she was acknowledged in the household. The children were too young to know what was going on, though often, to her terror, they laughed and said she was getting a fat tummy.

One afternoon when Fatima was in the park with the children, she felt a pain in her back. Later, as she worked in the kitchen, it grew worse, coming in spurts. She barely made it through the evening, crawled to her cubicle, and her labor began.

In the early-morning hours, she lay in her small bathroom, struggling, at sixteen, to give birth. She passed out as the child was born. When she came to, she was on top of this tiny premature infant girl, now dead.

Fatima couldn't cry; she was unable to feel anything except weakness and fear. She got up, cleaned herself, and was ready just in time to get breakfast for the children. Since no one ever entered her cubicle or bathroom, she could wait till dark to clean everything up and make it shine again.

But what to do with the dead infant? She did the only thing she could think to do: She wrapped her up and carried her to where the garbage was collected. Then, finally, she wept.

That night, she put what few possessions she had and left her patroa's house to find the home of the young man she thought loved her. She wandered the streets for days, hungry and frightened; she often begged. She met a woman who had taken to prostitution to survive, and the woman took her in. She gave Fatima a room that she could decorate and call home. But in return, Fatima became something she had never known existed. She was offering up her body for survival.

****

Over the next few years, Fatima met several men whom she loved, for whom, for a time, she was theirs alone and who treated her well for a while. One of these men went off to São Paulo to earn a better living but left her some money and a promise to send for her when he found a job. She'd given birth to a son by then, and after a year or so the man sent more money and she and her baby went to live with him in a favela hut. Life was terrible. He couldn't find a good job, got involved with drugs. When she became pregnant again, he beat her and left.

Fatima was now alone with two children; she was illiterate and had no skills. So she turned back to the only profession she knew would provide enough money to care for her children. And it did; it enabled her to attend school at night and finish grammar school. When I met her, she was finishing high school, but still a prostitute. We met her through an organization that was doing work with these women known as Mulheres Marginalizadas, marginalized women.

149

When Gus and I had first arrived in São Paulo to work with the American Friends Service Committee, we stayed in the AFSC's Office of Peace and Justice. There we met dedicated priests, nuns and lay people working to make changes in the city after the fall of the military dictatorship. The office was in a very seedy part of the city. We slept on the floor of one of the vacant rooms, and from the window we could watch the nightlife. We witnessed assaults and observed the open market for prostitutes of both sexes. We didn't dare go out at night. In the daytime, we wandered about getting acquainted with the city and planning the work we would do.

These priests and nuns served as our guides, and I was taken to a large hotel where women were, literally, prisoners, owned by men who lived off their earnings. A city existed inside this building! There were stores of all types, hairdressers and so on. There was no need to leave, and, in fact, they couldn't, because the gate was barred. Guards let the customers in and out. Why I was allowed in, I'm unsure.

I visited these women's rooms. They were fixed as nicely as possible, each woman making as much of a home of it as she could. I say "women," but most of the ones we visited were still in their teens. There were many stories of how they got to this place, most of them so tragic: girls sold to pay off debts or whose mothers were unable to care for them.

Most of them came from the northeast of Brazil, where many of them had spent their first years hungry, begging for food or forced already into prostitution to feed themselves and to help their mothers. Some came willingly, but others were dragged there, frightened, knowing nothing of what lay ahead.

We could see that they were bonded, arranging themselves into little groups and living as families. Some talked of trying to find a way to escape; others were content, for as far as they could see, no other life was possible.

****

And then there was Anna. I was told her story in one of our Ministry for Marginalized Women meetings. Anna came from the northeast region. In her middle teens, she

150

was forced into an arranged marriage with a man she barely knew and soon learned that marriage was not a good thing. She was a victim of the machismo that was so much a part of the culture of the northeast. She was her husband's property and he was free to beat her whenever he pleased. Which he did, and often. He gave her no money except when he sent her shopping. She had to account for every centavo and if he thought the accounting was wrong, he beat her; or if he thought she had spent too much, a beating would come.

After their first baby was born, Anna thought her husband would treat her better; he had been kinder during her pregnancy. But as soon as their little girl was born (he had wanted a boy), the beatings returned.

Anna was miserable and began hiding a few of the coins left over from her shopping, enduring even more beatings for not returning as much money as her husband expected. Finally, when the baby was a little over a year old, she could stand it no longer.

One day, after her husband had gone to work, she gathered up her child and the little money she had hidden and went to the bus station. She gave the money to the attendant and asked how far she could get with it. He asked her where she wanted to go. She said São Paulo – the only city she knew for certain the name of – and was told she had just enough to get there. She had heard a new life could be found in São Paulo, a city with streets paved of gold.

****

It was a long trip, about four days and nights, and when they finally arrived at the São Paulo bus station – a large station, full of activity, people everywhere, restaurants, stores and beggars – she was hungry and lost. People ran about, bumping into one another, dragging their heavy bags. It was chaotic. Anna had never been in such a place. She had no idea where she was or where to go – a rural, illiterate country girl with no money and an infant to care for. She truly was lost and alone.

She wrapped the baby in a blanket and curled up in a corner and waited – for what, she didn't know.

For two nights and three days, she lived this way. The vendors noticed her and the baby, and the fact that they had no food, and they offered her what they could. They asked where she came from, where she was going and if she needed help finding her family. It was a common situation, the exodus from the northeast to São Paulo – people hopeful for a better life arriving daily.

By the third day, Anna was growing desperate. She had ventured out to the street, but it was too busy for her, cars and people everywhere, and she'd rushed back to her little spot.

She had no idea what to do next – perhaps she would beg – when she was approached by a woman who asked if she could help. Anna sobbed out her story. The woman said that she had arrived in the city a few years prior under similar circumstances and that she could offer a solution.

And thus Anna's life as a prostitute began, having accepted the offer of a way out of her predicament from the only person who had offered one – a woman who had herself turned to prostitution to survive. The woman opened her tiny room to Anna and her daughter.

****

It was stories like Anna's that prompted me to become involved with the Ministry for Marginalized Women. Most of the women who worked there were nuns (though they never wore habits). There were two or three women pastors who joined us and also some priests. It was a wonderful group of dedicated people to work with. The prostitutes who heard of our support group must have liked our ideas, because they invited others, and our weekly group meetings were wonderful.

As the women became more comfortable with us and with one another, they opened up, talking about their lives, their hardships, their children. They offered help to one another, especially to the younger ones. We had prayer sessions and some Bible study. They were so often moved by Jesus's words and the stories from the New Testament about women. Jesus's love for these women comforted them.

On other days, we held bazaars in which they brought in old clothes and traded them or sold kitchen items or books. We had potlucks, where those who could brought in lunch dishes or recipes. Later, we acquired sewing machines, and those who knew how to sew taught others and some made clothes for themselves and their children. We had parties and played games.

There were heavier days, when one of the women would come in with a story of abuse or neglect, and advice and comfort would be offered. There were so many stories, and we women could relate. We all became friends; relationships were built. Some of their issues were very different from mine, of course, but there was a solidarity and affection that I will always remember.

****

I remember one older woman, probably in her sixties, who had been a prostitute since a teenager, with whom I became friends. She was the leader in a group within the marginalized women's project that met with some nuns and pastors to talk over individual problems and learn household skills – sewing, for example – as well as about health, their bodies and how they functioned, which was my task as a health educator. They shared clothes, shed tears together, shared their everyday lives – all the things that women share when they get together. They talked of their worries, their losses and their victories.

One of these victories was the story of a special friend, who, with money earned in this profession, had sent two sons through college, one becoming a doctor or a lawyer, I don't recall which. However, her sons were unaware of her profession, and she didn't want them to ever find out. I asked her why. Was it because she was ashamed of how she made her living? No, she said. But she didn't believe her sons would understand.

I considered this: This woman whose children had received a higher education with the money she'd made as a prostitute, or a woman of "ill repute," was to me a mother trying to give to her children what she'd never had. Doesn't that sound like other mothers?

What I had discovered was that there were no women of "ill repute" in the way I had always been taught; rather, they were women who used the only thing that was theirs to sell; they used their bodies to earn a living for themselves and their children. Often they'd had no choice; they were children of prostitutes or had been sold as sex slaves and knew of no other way of life. And they had been awakened with the hopes of better lives for their children. They were mothers; they had the same worries and concerns for their children that most mothers of the world have. They, like other mothers, aspired for the very best for their offspring. In all but their profession, they were, in my eyes, like any other mother. I heard their stories, I watched them protect one other, and when new women entered the group, especially if they were very young, they were taken in with love and concern. They looked out for one other.

When we would hold Bible studies, I was profoundly touched by the healing effect the stories we read would have on these women. God loved them, and they must love themselves.

I knew that the world of prostitution was one of many ugly aspects – politics, drugs, cruelty. I may have been naive, as I was not only in a different world but a country that was very much male controlled, in which women were still second-class citizens. I only know that I understood and truly cared for the women I met. I saw them as women struggling in the world into which they had been thrown, striving to make it one in which they could survive.

****

The AIDS epidemic came upon us, as to the rest of the world, as a shock, and the world was unprepared for its consequences. And, of course, for prostitutes it proved to be devastating.

In the beginning, so little was known of the disease's contagion. There were rumors of contamination on

154

silverware, glasses, etc. There was panic everywhere. But as can be imagined, the spread of the disease hit prostitutes and drug users the fastest. And our roles as health educators became vital as we tried to stop the spread among these woman. The health ministry gave out condoms on the streets. I can remember going with others of the ministry to the streets where the prostitutes waited for customers to give them boxes of condoms and try to persuade them to insist that their customers use them.

Nevertheless, they became ill. Some lingered; some went faster. A home for those with AIDS was opened and supported by the churches. There they went until they died. There were volunteer doctors and nurses and women like us in the Ministry for Marginalized Women. Nuns opened small homes for women with AIDS, and for children born with AIDS, many of them orphans. It was a sad time.

I remember visiting a woman who had been in our group, a friend. She was so thin that it was hard to hide the shock on my face at seeing her. She knew she would not last long; her concern was for her children, who were with her mother.

Was there regret for the lives they had lived? I don't know. None of the ones I spoke to expressed it, though some talked of God's forgiveness and asked for prayer, not necessarily for themselves but for their friends and loved ones. I witnessed some of the most beautiful scenes of love and support as these women cared for one other in their last days. No condemning, just love and concern.

How can one not be changed after witnessing all this love, and all the tears and pain? And how can one condemn these women as living a life of sin, when for most this life that was leading to their death was one of survival?

The ones I knew well were my friends, group members whose lives I shared for a short time. Who was I to condemn? I repeat that Native-American saying, "Never judge a man or woman until you've walked a mile in their moccasins." Like me, they wanted to love and be loved.

They were sleeping women, but were awakened by this tragedy to the power of love and healing, of connection. They

155

moved mountains as they learned how to heal one another and how to love in spite of the greed and victimization they had been exposed to. I personally never heard one of them blaming or condemning others – men, mothers, no one. The eyes of near death were loving.

****

Because of this tragic situation and my increasing involvement with the world of prostitution, I had to develop my health course in the context of AIDS prevention. I had been exposed to an underworld, one of exploitation, drugs, injustice, violence and illness – and death. But also of love and solidarity.

The following story captures this world. It was told to me by a seventeen-year-old street girl, a prostitute.

My father sold me when I was twelve. Yes, that's what I said, sold me, for that is how I feel. He received a sum of money and I became a slave of a household: domestic servants, they call us.

One of the members of this family, a boy of sixteen, the oldest son, began to abuse me soon after I was hired and continued to do so. Serving him thus became one of my "household" duties, until I became pregnant. As soon as this was noticeable, I was thrown out of the house. Of course, I was a disgrace to my parents, and my father would not take me back. At thirteen, I went to the streets. There I was taken in by the "gang."

My baby was born on the streets and died on the streets.

I found after a few years of begging and stealing that to be safer and earn more money it would be better to become a prostitute. The only thing I could sell was my body. As time went on, I had two more children, also born on the streets, but I gave them away, and it's a good thing I did, because now I have AIDS. What would I have been able to do for them? And I don't even know how long I will live. But at least I know my children are safe, and I didn't sell them like my father did me! I gave them to good people, so I don't have that sin to pay for.

I was reminded of Jesus's words, "Let he (she) who is without sin, cast the first stone." This girl, like so many, was a victim of a corrupt society, of poverty and machismo, but she was my friend now. I wept for her wasted life because her days were numbered, though she had not really yet lived. She was blameless; to my mind, society was to blame. My task then was to help her live for the time she had left, in dignity, knowing that she was loved.

****

As I said, we would sometimes go to the streets to hand out condoms. We had learned that the use of condoms was not an accepted practice among the prostitutes' clients. So the women were initially adamant in their refusal to demand their use, saying they would lose their clients. But as time went on and the victims of the HIV virus grew, we felt we must take action, and decided to go to the streets.

Armed with packages of condoms, we went to the areas of the city where the prostitutes waited for their clients. We gathered groups around us and talked with them, telling them about the contagion and the precautions necessary to avoid being contaminated. Some of the prostitutes resented our talking to them, and, in fact, our mere presence was probably hurting their business.

On one of these occasions, a nun and I were standing in front of one of the walk-up rooms where the women worked. A group of perhaps seven or eight prostitutes was listening to us talk as we handed out the condoms. We had our backs to the noisy street as we talked, and thus didn't hear the noise of an approaching police car, nor did we see it when it stopped behind us. But the prostitutes did. Suddenly, before our unbelieving eyes, the women scattered, mostly running up the steps to the rooms in which they worked. Surprised and a bit startled, we turned around to find ourselves face to face with two policemen.

"Okay, ladies," they said, with what I might call sinister faces. (I should add here that the nun wasn't wearing a habit.) "You know this is against the law, soliciting your wares. You can just come along with us."

My nun friend was much younger than I and seemed quite tongue-tied, so I spoke up, explaining we were educators working on AIDS prevention. As I spoke, I saw the men's expressions change. One looked at the other in surprise, as if to say, "What do we do now? This middle-aged woman's accent tells us she's not a Brazilian. She must be telling the truth!"

They smiled sheepishly and went on their way. We sighed with relief and climbed the stairs to find the women, who told us what would have happened if they had been taken to the police station. They would have had to clean the bathrooms and other areas and then practice their profession before being released. A night lost, one of them said, plus the humiliation.

It grieved me to think of these women's dignity being incrementally destroyed. Most certainly, they had dignity. Over my years of working with them, and weeping with them, as more and more became victims of the AIDS crisis, many leaving orphaned and sick children behind, I came to see them as women struggling for survival in the only way they'd found possible. And I loved them!

Understanding Rural São Paulo

As I mentioned, most of those who left the rural northeast of Brazil in hopes of finding better lives for their families and themselves went to São Paulo, because that was where most of the industrial development was going on. There were jobs, but there was always a lot of competition for them.

Still, it was worth risking the unknown, because life was so difficult in the northeast. There was no infrastructure at all. Families often had to walk miles, maybe two to four hours, to get water. Toilets were often mere holes in the ground, covered up when full. Garbage was thrown into pits, then burned.

Once every two years or so, a priest would travel to the remote areas to marry any couples who were living together – group weddings – and also to perform baptisms.

Rural São Paulo

The priest would then take the register of these marriages and baptisms to the nearest city to put in the public record. That is, sometimes this would happen and sometimes not. Or sometimes names would be recorded incorrectly, and it would be very difficult, if not impossible, to retrieve the documents when they were needed. And if you had no birth certificate, you couldn't go to a hospital, let alone work.

In these remote areas, it was taken for granted that a woman's function in life was to bear children, and her value was judged by how well she carried out this task. A husband could return a barren woman to her family – a disgrace to all. And if a family had a daughter who was still unwed at twenty, they would fear that she would never marry, an old maid, which was equally a disgrace and a financial burden. Unions tended to come early, with girls as young as fourteen or fifteen often married off to men much older.

I was told the story of the owner of a small store in a remote town who had a daughter – let's call her Maria das Dores – who was well past her twentieth birthday. She had twice been engaged: one fiancé died, the other got another woman pregnant.

Rural São Paulo

160

So here was her father, anxious, nervous and wondering what people in the town were thinking of his spinster daughter. All sorts of comments were made, many of them right to his face. He was desperate.

Then the mayor's wife died in childbirth and the man needed someone to care for the infant and his three other children. Maria das Dores's father went to the mayor and offered his daughter in marriage. Even though the mayor was some twenty years older than his daughter, the father knew this would be a good marriage for the family. Not only was he the mayor, he had land, which made him rich in everyone's eyes: a man of means. This union would not only free the father of the shame, and expense, of a spinster daughter, but there was financial gain to be had.

The wedding was a big affair for this small village. It took days to prepare for and lasted an entire day. When it was over, our young bride went off with her groom to her new home. This is how she related what happened next:

We came home and the children greeted us. I fed the baby, put the children to bed and then, looking at my husband, I waited for the next step. He took my hand and led me to our room. He sat me down on the bed and began to touch me in a way that was so different. I felt uncomfortable, so I pulled away.

He told me to get ready for bed, which I understood was to put on the new nightdress my mother had had the local seamstress make for me. I went into the bathroom – which was one of the few in the city that was inside the house – and changed. When I hesitantly opened the bathroom door, there he was, totally naked!

Terrified, I slammed the bathroom door and climbed out the window and ran the several blocks back to my family's home!

That was the end of that marriage, and when I met her at a seminar ten years later she was still the spinster of the family, but earned money taking care of the mayor's children.

****

One of the reasons birth control was not something poor women wanted when it first became available was because the more children you had, the more widely the burden of caring for the parents when they were old or sick could be divided. It was, and still is, thought that it's the duty of the children to care for their parents until death. Putting a parent in a home for the aged is considered neglect. Thus, multigenerational homes are common; old folks homes are nonexistent in rural areas.

There were two widely held, and contradictory, views of Brazilian women. One was that their value was in being able to "produce" – to bear fruit, so to speak. The other was that the woman was the core of the family; she was idolized as the most important person, the one who held the home and family life together. A male's sexual freedom was an accepted reality. The mother figure is venerated.

I remember a woman in one of the favelas in Rio in which I worked some years later who was a maid in a well-to-do family's home. She was from the northeast, and had no family in Rio. She allowed the son of the woman who was her employer to sleep with her so that she could become pregnant, even though she knew she would lose her job. But she would be gaining something more – status as a mother, something very valuable – and also the comfort of knowing she would have someone to care for her in her old age.

And I remember in the late 1980s talking with a group of women who had fled the poverty of the northeast, among the many thousands who arrived in São Paulo, causing the favelas to swell as they built their huts anywhere they could find a spot.

I began the conversation by asking each of them to say what state she came from and how many children she had. Almost all of these women had many children – ten, fourteen, one with seventeen – and then, from back in a corner, a woman answered, "Twenty-three!"

She was black, and unlike the lighter-skinned women who looked ten to twelve years older than they were, her skin was smooth. It was impossible to guess her age – but twenty-three children! And who knows how many she had lost. I figured she must have begun in her early teens and had one a year or maybe sets of twins.

162

I asked her how old her youngest was, and she answered, "Five." She then smiled and said, "My husband died." That had ultimately been her method of birth control!

****

Misinformation about pregnancy and childbirth was so very common in rural areas. If someone went to visit a new mother and was of the age that she might be menstruating, it was believed that if she sat on the new mother's bed the mother's milk would dry up. When a woman was menstruating, she couldn't cut her hair and often was forbidden from traveling far from home.

Once at a seminar, someone told me about a young woman whose mother had a baby about every two years, and each time she would go into labor her father or older brother would go off to get the midwife. The midwife would arrive carrying a big sack with everything she needed for the delivery. She'd close a curtain around the bed and then, after a while, would come out with the little one.

For years, this young woman thought the midwife brought the baby with her in her sack.

Another story I heard was about a young woman who was given away in marriage and moved to the city. When she went into labor at sixteen, she didn't know where the baby was going to come out. She thought, perhaps, it might come out of the belly button.

Teresinha's Story

It was into this environment that Teresinha was born, in 1944, in Jacobina, Bahia. Her father, Antonio, was a sort of traveling salesman type and was absent from the home months at a time. In spite of this, he fathered eleven children and ruled them with an iron hand. Dona Alexandre obeyed to the letter her husband's orders when he left the home for his travels.

Teresinha

Their home was made of wood and some homemade bricks; there was no electricity or running water. Garbage was buried in a large hole. The girls' clothes, made by Dona Alexandre and the girls themselves, had long sleeves and quite long skirts. One of the girls once cut off the sleeves of her dress to go to church. When her father saw it, he tore it to pieces and beat her.

Yes, there were many beatings. Teresinha said her mother cringed at her daughters' pain, but could do nothing. Their father didn't believe that girls should learn to read and write. "Never will a daughter of mine go to school," this illiterate man swore. "For what reason? To learn to read and write letters to boyfriends? There are enough domestic duties for girls to learn if they are going to be good and obedient wives."

Girls didn't need to be literate; their task in life was to raise children and care for the family, and he and his five sons kept close watch over the six girls.

There were no social activities except church. Each Sunday, the girls would march in line behind their father and brothers the three miles to mass. Every once in a while, there would be a church party encouraged by the priest to get these rural, isolated families together. Antonio allowed his children to go, but only if he was on hand to monitor their behavior. The girls weren't allowed to dance, only to enjoy the food and chat on the sidelines, watched closely by their father and brothers.

Once, at one of these events, Teresinha stopped to talk to a boy. When her father saw this, he yanked her away by the hair, pulled all the children out, and off they went home, where a good lashing was in order.

One of Teresinha's sisters once curled her hair with pieces of cloth and went to bed. When their father came home, he stepped into the room – all the girls slept in the same room – and when he saw the white strings in his daughter's hair, he screamed, "What is this?"

All of the girls awoke, but could say nothing. He called for scissors. He cut off, along with the hair, the strings of cloth that he couldn't pull out, as the crying and screaming of all of the girls filled the house.

With this kind of a life, there was but one escape for a girl: to be a nun, which meant to go off to a convent for preparation, which meant, of course, learning to read and write. This was the path Teresinha chose to gain her freedom. She wanted to learn to read and write. If she had to be a nun to gain this privilege, that's what she'd do – and, of course, to a father of many girls, this was a relief. Girls were a burden, and to have a nun in the family was an honor for the parents.

****

So off Teresinha went. She spent two and a half years in the convent, leaving at seventeen when she realized she didn't really want to be a nun. She couldn't go home to her father. He believed that she had been expelled from the convent because she'd had an affair and would therefore never find a man willing to marry her.

165

Teresinha went to live with an older, married sister who lived in the city. She continued her schooling and graduated from elementary school. She was invited to teach in the public schools, which she did for the next four years. She had been brought up by a religious mother, and even her father, cruel as he was, was a believer, so she also hosted prayer groups.

After four years of teaching, she met her husband, Darci, and set out with him for São Paulo, the city of jobs, to begin their family.

They had a son and a daughter, and when I met her Teresinha was an active member of a small church in a very poor area of the suburbs of São Paulo. She was already visiting people who were ill and was a perfect candidate for the health educators training course. She became my assistant and later a teacher herself.

Story of Yolanda

Yolanda died of complications of the HIV virus sometime around 1991. I'll never forget this woman who not only changed her own life but influenced the lives of so many, including me.

Yolanda was a young woman with three children when I met her; she was a volunteer in the Catholic Church's health ministry for undernourished children where I was giving classes. Her youngest was about two at the time and was undernourished and had asthma. She was a single mother who'd had an extremely difficult life. Her mother died giving birth to her, and her father, unable to care for an infant and six other children, took her to a school run by nuns in an interior rural city and left her there.

Yolanda was always sick, constantly anemic. At that time in Brazil, no one had heard of sickle cell anemia, and she was frequently sent to doctors for blood transfusions.

She was a quiet child and remembered the nuns as kind but offering little motherly affection. She was always interested in health and curing people, so when at the age of seventeen she was told of a sickly old woman who lived alone, she asked the nuns to be sent there to care for her. The nuns knew of Yolanda's wish to someday be a nurse and since they couldn't give her the education she longed for, they agreed that she could go and live with this woman, but was told that once out into the "world" she couldn't return to their school.

Yolanda left, and it proved to be the right move. The old woman gave her the motherly love she had so longed for and her life was enriched in this home, though it was a poor one. Yolanda took a part-time job in a shoe factory nearby to support them and proved to be an excellent worker and an eager student of shoemaking, which would later prove to be of great advantage.

But her happiness lasted only about eighteen months, when the woman died. Frightened at the prospect of being alone, she agreed to live with a young man who worked in the factory and had been wooing her for some time. She soon became pregnant and after the birth of her son, hard times set in and the young man left her. Yolanda became very ill, her anemia worsened, and once again she submitted to transfusions, the only treatment at the time for severe anemia.

Eventually, she was able to return to work in the shoe factory, but the factory then went bankrupt, and Yolanda, like so many others, set out for São Paulo. Unlike most though, she did have a skill, and soon found a job in a shoe factory. But though she worked long hours, she didn't make enough money to cover her expenses and, most probably out of financial necessity, moved in with a much older man and became pregnant again. Soon after her second son was born, the father died of a stroke, leaving her a bit of money. Yolanda decided to use this money to buy her own shoemaking equipment and began working from her home.

But it was a struggle, and under the strain Yolanda again became sick. In addition to anemia, she was suffering from the toxic fumes of the glue she used in her work. Once again, she found a male companion, and they joined forces in the home shoemaking business – she making the shoes, he selling them on the streets of São Paulo.

Yolanda became pregnant again, a little girl was born, and things were going well. Her partner was a good father to her boys and worked hard to make the business successful. But Yolanda was constantly sick, coughing a lot and feeling weak, and so she and her partner switched roles in the business.

****

It was then that Yolanda, sick and weak, came to the church where I was conducting a health course. Having always wanted to be a health worker – and with her little daughter undernourished – she began working in the children's health ministry, part of a program run by the Catholic Church with support from UNICEF. We would go into the favelas to weigh children and teach nutrition. Yolanda was a faithful worker, loving and caring, and she related well with the mothers of undernourished children.

Yolanda's health continued to worsen. It was at about this time that AIDS came to the attention of Brazilian health officials, but there were no tests available for the poor. And then yet another tragedy occurred in her life. Her partner was killed in an automobile accident, and Yolanda – sick, and now with three children to support – once again was alone.

But this remarkable woman, cursed with tragedy, remained undaunted. She continued working, making shoes, teaching the trade to her boys and, when she could, working in the children's health ministry.

This time though she had a lot of people concerned for her and her boys, who went off to school tired and smelling of glue. One day, while doing her volunteer work, she collapsed and was hospitalized. It was then that it was discovered that she had AIDS, not tuberculosis as we all had believed. It was this deadly disease for which there was no cure. Had she contracted the virus from one of her partners or was it the many blood transfusions she'd received?

I still remember the day she came to my home, weeping. "God is punishing me for my promiscuity," she cried, having been taught that it was a sin for a Catholic girl to live with a man outside marriage.

"I am being punished for being a bad mother," she sobbed. "I will go to hell, won't I?"

I had heard this before, and I cried too, for this beautiful woman, and told her, as I held her in my arms, that God was not punishing her, that God loved her and knew what a good person she was. I told her she may have gotten the disease from her transfusions, that God understood why she had lived the life she had, that God loved her the way she was. I told her what I wanted her to believe. For me, this woman's life was one of sacrifice, the sacrifice of love. And she was to further prove this before she succumbed to the disease.

****

Yolanda died about five years later. But what an example of love and inspiration she was to those of us who came to know her. At a time when anyone with AIDS was treated like a leper, afraid to even be suspected of having the disease, Yolanda spent the rest of her life as a health educator; unafraid to use herself as an example; giving talks in churches, schools and small community groups about AIDS. She became an AIDS-education teacher. She talked with groups of AIDS patients, encouraging them, even making shoes for them. She founded a shoe factory staffed entirely by AIDS patients. She helped them manage it and sell their shoes and divided the earnings with them.

She spent her last years visiting AIDS patients in hospitals, encouraging them and sharing her story, donating shoes made in her factory, visiting the homes of those who were dying, praying with them, holding their hands and giving them comfort, even as she, herself, was getting weaker.

She worried about what would happen to her children after she died. She had taken a leadership role in an initiative to find land where AIDS patients could build homes, as they were unwelcome in most places. A spot was found and very humble, makeshift homes were built.

A very different kind of community was born, one in which solidarity was the norm, and Yolanda was its leader. She moved her factory there, with her now-teenaged boys taking increasing responsibility as their mother grew more gravely ill. With help from the Catholic Church and her health ministry colleagues, she was able to put away money for her sons to support their sister, telling them that she was entrusting them with her care. So many of her admirers assured her that they too would look after the little girl. Though young, her sons were already responsible adults. Their mother had been their example.

****

I remember one Yolanda story in particular. A nun called and asked me to visit a woman in a nearby favela.

170

The woman had AIDS and a brain tumor, but there were no beds available for her in the local hospital. The nun said the woman was desperate, depressed and in pain. She was talking of suicide. Her infant child had been put in a home for the children of AIDS patients who no longer could care for them or those whose parents had died. This young woman was heartbroken and wanted to see her child and hold her once more.

I told Yolanda I was going to visit this woman, and she said she wanted to go with me. We went, and as I watched her with this woman, one dying woman comforting another, I felt love so strongly, God's presence. They were spiritual partners. They saw and felt God. Both dying.

Yolanda brought joy and hope to this woman and in turn to herself. She took the woman to have one last visit with her child, one more chance to hold her baby. I wept with them both.

The woman died a week after seeing her child, as Yolanda held her. I was not there, but I know she died in peace because Jesus was with her in the form of this magnificent woman named Yolanda, whom I was privileged to call friend.

Yolanda died about a year after this. More than a hundred people attended her funeral service, the majority with AIDS or HIV-positive and their families with whom she had visited and encouraged in one way or another.

My life was gifted by knowing this woman, and I would never be the same. I had seen Jesus at work, an awakened woman who moved mountains.

My Experience with the Landless People

A movement started in Brazil in the 1980s of those who were called the Sem Terra, the landless. They were families who lived on the estates of wealthy landowners and were held in virtual slavery. They had to produce for the landowner and could keep just enough to prevent them from starving. Whatever food they needed that they didn't grow themselves had to be purchased from the landowner's store, and since the families had no money the purchases were charged to accounts. The families were always in debt and thus tied to a piece of land that wasn't theirs. Those who fled formed groups called the Sem Terra.

Many of these families moved closer to the large cities, occupying open land, building their own favelas. Others chose unoccupied land close to where they had left and fought for their rights to keep it. While the wealthy owned hundreds of acres, these families wanted only a small piece on which to plant.

In many cases, the land had no registered owner and the families would attempt to claim it as their own. But since most were unable to read and write, they were largely unsuccessful.

The wealthy families would often enlist the local police or hired men to drive these people off the land. Their huts, mostly built of plastic or sheets, were destroyed, as were their crops.

But the Sem Terra formed a national organization, and in time became a political force.

****

Alzira was a wiry middle-aged woman, with a voice that made her seem larger than she was, who was active in the Sem Terra movement.

"They have no right to take our land away from us, destroy our homes with tractors, homes built with our sweat, blood and tears," Alzira said one day, speaking at a Sem Terra rally. "They have no right to come in, drag us from our homes and then destroy the few things we have. They have no right!"

The crowd around her was getting louder; banners were waving.

"This land is ours," she continued. "We don't want it for free; we want to pay for it. We want the rights to it! This land is for all our people, not just the rich and powerful. Give us the right to pay for it, the jobs and the salary to be able to afford it, and we'll show you."

On and on she went, citing more and more instances of injustice – the lack of sewers, water, electricity, schools and health and retirement benefits – from her own experience. She spoke with the passion of a woman fighting for the only home she knew, and with nowhere else to go. Her words echoed the experiences of all who shared her pain.

I had met Alzira when she became my student in the health educators course. She had little formal education, but a wisdom developed through years of struggle. She clearly understood the underlying causes of poverty, her own poverty. She was demanding work and a living wage, a right to live in dignity on her own land.

She knew that her children were malnourished because there was so little to feed them, so little choice, because their salaries were inadequate to provide even enough bread, the staple of their diets.

So as Alzira and her companions learned more about how their bodies functioned, they realized that they needed to organize and demand the changes necessary to make their lives safer and offer a better future for their children. As she learned the rehydration therapy taught in the course, designed to eliminate diarrhea and dehydration among the children, the major cause of infant mortality, she knew they needed sewers and potable water. She knew that her children needed a chance to go to school so they would not be semi-illiterate, as she was. She knew these were their rights.

"Listen, you folks; we have a right to sewers, adequate transportation, health clinics and, most of all, a decent place to live," she said that day. "The majority of us do not have enough of the basics. You know, they say that God created the land for all people, but that's not the way it turned out, is it? A few have a lot and a lot have almost nothing. Right, folks?"

There was a cheer from this crowd of some five hundred people. Alzira went on. She raised her arms above her head and shouted, "They're trying to buy our votes by promising us things. Well, we don't believe them and we won't until they fulfill their promises, will we?"

****

I have one very powerful memory of the Sem Terra. It was in São Paulo, along the side of a country road, where we came upon a group of families in their plastic-covered shelters beside a large field. The owner of this field had sent his men to circle the tents, and they were now firing their rifles in the air, demanding that the families leave at once.

That's the scene we came upon, a couple of my health workers, Gus and myself. I was called to a tent where a

The Sem Terra: "The Landless"

174

The Sem Terra

woman was in labor. The heat was unbearable. There was a makeshift table, blankets on the dirt floor, water bottles and clothes scattered everywhere.

The woman was lying on a bedroll beside the low table. Children were all about, and the two women attending to the woman in labor were trying to shoo them away. The men were standing outside the opening of the tent, attempting to get a fire going – and throughout it all, the landowner's hired gunmen were circling, sporadically firing their guns.

One of the children, an infant, began to cry, crawling toward the woman in labor. The child was dirty, wearing a soiled diaper, and one of the women carried her outside to bathe her in a water barrel beside the tent.

It was a sight to behold. I remember thinking, "Am I really seeing this? Am I really here?"

The women needed help. They knew nothing of doctors or medicine that wasn't homemade. But I was to learn that they knew a lot! One of the women looked up at me and asked if I was there because I was a midwife. She said the midwife who'd come with their group was ill and that she and some men had left on foot to find a doctor or a hospital, but none of them had yet returned. I was aghast at this scene, and at the thought of the others traveling the road beneath this unyielding sun, in search of help.

"No," I said, "but I do know enough to help."

We then began. One of the women went outside to where the men were heating water. She put some rags into the boiling water while the other woman and I got the mother as comfortable as possible and placed the cleanest pieces of material we could find beneath her. She was biting her lips, and as the pains came she cried out a bit.

I learned that this was her fifth child, but that two of them had died. Between pains, she told me a little about her life, the hardships the family had experienced, and that her children had died of diarrhea and dehydration, the most common causes of infant mortality in the rural areas.

As the pains increased, the infant, her youngest, came crawling to her, crying and hugging her mother. We tried to distract her, but the mother took her in her arms and laid her on her chest. "Just leave her," she said. "She's been so frightened since we left home."

Amazing, this scene, and what was to follow. Biting her lips and holding onto one of the women's hands, she gave birth to another girl. I did all that I had been trained to do – though it was these women who instructed me on what to use to cut and tie the chord: a kitchen knife and yarn.

They then took the newborn, washed her in water that was far from clean and wrapped her in a diaper that had been washed in the boiling kettle. Meanwhile, the mother was nursing her other child.

One of the women brought a glass with a green leaf in it, which I was told would keep her from hemorrhaging. Another of the women took a piece of bread with sugar on it and gave it to the baby as they took her off her mother's chest to place the newborn there.

A woman wrapped the placenta in ragged cloth and complained that she had no idea where she could bury it, as was customary among rural folk.

I let my tears flow. The miracle that birth is, the beauty of a new life, even in these conditions. I cried for these magnificent women who carried out the duties that women have been performing for centuries, brave women who didn't see themselves as special or brave. This was life, their lives, and whether this little baby would survive infancy would be a matter of luck – we all knew forces that were beyond these simple women's control would determine it. They would accept it as they accepted all the other hardships.

I became aware again of the guns circling us. The others didn't seem to notice, as they went about cleaning up after the birth and preparing a bit of food for them all to eat and some healing tea for the new mother.

These were not sleeping women; they had been awakened by the hardships of life. Would they move mountains? Perhaps, as they struggled to fight for the right to survive in an unjust societal situation. Magnificent women!

A Christmas Story

The hut in front of ours was larger than ours but strange inside, in that it was built around a curve in the road. In the first four years we lived there, two different families owned it. Then a woman named Cleide with four children bought it. She had no partner, and once she got to know me she told me that each child had a different father. We gave things to the children and I often wondered how she made a living for her family. Men would visit, and she became pregnant.

Cleide said nothing at first, but when it became obvious she said that the father had disappeared (like so many others) and that she had no money to buy medicines or even food. The church nearby had a food pantry and we took her there. The health educators visited her and determined that the children had what they needed. Her hut was spotless. And though the children didn't attend school, the older ones could read and, the woman said, she taught them what they needed to learn.

Cleide came to my hut often for medications that the doctor at the public clinic prescribed. She was friendly but discreet, though she did talk a lot against men. She made all her children's clothes out of scraps and we often saw her picking through garbage piles.

On Christmas Eve, just as we were leaving for the eleven p.m. church service, her son came to tell us that his mother was not feeling well. Knowing that her time to give birth was approaching, I went over to her hut. Cleide was lying on the blankets that served as a bed for the five of them and said that her pains were starting but that she knew it was too soon. I waited with her, trying to talk her into letting Gus take her to a hospital. But she refused, saying that three of her children had been born at home and that was what she wanted.

The pains grew worse, and I got a bit nervous. Time went on, and I could see she was having problems and was finally able to talk her into letting Gus take her to the hospital while I stayed with the children.

But no hospital would take her. At the nearest one, they were told there were no available beds; the maternity ward was full. At the second, no one even paid them attention: They were having their Christmas party. Then at the third, there was only one doctor on duty and he couldn't handle another patient.

It was Christmas Eve, and there was no room at the inn.

By then, Gus was running out of gas and there were no stations open. So they returned home. As we frantically discussed what to do next, another neighbor went to the street and found a police car, and the policemen set out with Cleide to find a hospital that would take her.

I kept reminding myself that this was Christmas Eve. I watched the children lying on the one family bed of blankets and thought of my own children's Christmas Eves, not at all like this. "Why?" I wondered. "Why are things this way?"

The next morning, just before noon, two police cars arrived, one with Cleide and her newborn, the other full of gifts for the children and bags of food.

We all celebrated Christmas together, the two policemen, this family and Gus and I. It was one of the most meaningful of my life. The story of another brave woman!

The Cat Secret

One night after bedtime, I heard a scratching sound on the kitchen window. I opened it, and in popped a tricolored cat. We were used to cats; there were so many of them roaming the streets of the favela. Kittens were often found dead in alleys or street garbage. Sometimes a whole litter was put in a sack and thrown in the muddy canal.

I'm an animal lover, and this was just unbearable to me. I did what I could and had rescued many. We'd leave food scraps each day for five or six cats that would visit our tiny open laundry area. They knew the hour to come and waited patiently for their meals. None of them had ever jumped into the hut. I knew them all by color and we had even given them names.

But this cat I had never seen before. She was striking because of her coloring: black, brown and white, all well designed. In spite of being dirty, her beauty was apparent. She looked up at me with her yellow eyes and won me over.

We named her Lady because she always acted like one. She would have nothing to do with those other cats. When they were around, she simply disappeared to the front of the hut. When they weren't, she would squeeze through the bars in the window and came and went as she pleased, but was almost always home at night to sleep at the foot of the bed.

Lady hadn't been with us long before I was sure she was pregnant. One day, she didn't want to go out as she normally did. She would usually leave when I did, jump on the roof and sit watching the alley till we came home for lunch. But now she stayed on my bed, so I suspected she was getting ready to give birth.

I put towels down in a box under a small wooden bench we used for a table. She wouldn't eat, so I was worried as we went off to work. When I came home for lunch, she was still there in the box, but restless, getting up and down and walking back and forth.

Then suddenly, with a sort of wail, a sac began to appear, and once again the miracle of birth struck me. As I watched her over the next few hours, I shed tears at the beauty of the act of nature I was watching.

With each kitten, she reached down and licked the sac, forcing the newborn to breathe, with the force of her tongue removing the sac. When each one was cleaned off, she took it in her mouth and placed it to nurse. She'd probably had other litters, but how could I be sure? I only know she did beautifully. Over the next few hours, four were born. The last one wouldn't come to life no matter what she did, and she abandoned it to tend to the others. It was remarkable to see.

At first, she hardly ever left the box. As her babies grew, she left more and more, but not for long. Then one day, I watched another act of nature. For some reason, the smallest kitten died. When Lady came in the house, I saw her nudge it, but it didn't react. I reached down and, yes, it was dead. After licking it for a while and nudging it around, Lady simply picked it up in her mouth, took it out of the box and dropped it on the floor. I could hardly believe her reaction.

The other two kittens developed normally, jumping on everything, knocking over all our dishes and so forth. Lady began to stay away longer and longer and the little ones soon learned how to jump in and out of the barred windows, just like their mom.

I didn't want to separate them and few people in the favela could afford to take on two cats, so it took a long time to find them a home. But one of the nuns knew a farmer and his wife and took them to their farm.

I cried as they left. Lady wasn't home and I worried how she would take this loss. At last, she came home and jumped into her now empty box. She smelled around, ran around the hut, and then out the window she went. She didn't come back for two days, and I shed many a tear waiting. Then there she was again as if nothing had happened, and life returned to as it was before.

181

****

I knew little about the sexual life of cats; I'd always had dogs. Lady soon began acting strange, meowing, like crying, and then I got the news. Cats go into heat soon after they stop nursing and stay in heat till they're mated. Lady was in heat.

Now what to do? We didn't want more kittens. So we closed the window, made a litter box and hoped she wasn't already pregnant. But she was, and the story was repeated, more kittens.

Soon after, I returned to the States to visit family, while Gus stayed to take care of Lady and to protect our hut. If you leave a favela hut vacant, another family will move in.

While in Wisconsin, I decided to get some expert advice and went to see the vet we had used when we lived there. She gave me the secret, which I am going to share with you now. She said that she used this method with cats that went into heat while boarded in her office.

Since a cat in heat remains in heat until she's mated, the vet said, we must mate Lady artificially – that is, make her think she's being mated.

"What?" I asked incredulously.

She explained the method. We must use a Q-tip to stimulate the mating act. She'll wail, as female cats do when they're being mated. But soon she'll stop, thinking she's been mated. This may take several tries over a few days, the vet said, but finally she'll settle down and wait for kittens that will never arrive.

There you have it: the cat secret!

****

So I returned to work in Brazil, armed with my new knowledge. Gus laughed and laughed. He said, "Well, this falls right into your line of work with women. Aren't you teaching them about sexuality and birth control?" I smiled, not dreaming the chore this would become.

Soon enough, Lady went into heat again. Now it was time for the test.

But Lady wasn't very cooperative. She wouldn't even let me touch her. It took days of listening to her meowing and desperately trying to find a way to do as I'd been instructed. I was beginning to think it was all a joke the vet had practiced on me.

Finally, after five days or so, Lady let me do it. It took multiple insertions and several days, but finally it was done and, lo and behold, Lady returned to normal. Now we would just have to sit it out till she went into heat again, which would probably be soon, as there would be no kittens to nurse.

So this procedure became a part of my life, with Gus grinning as he watched the procedure, often taunting me for my lack of technique. Lady was now a house cat; we couldn't let her out because we never knew when she would go into heat.

All our neighbors knew of the stunt and often joked about it when they heard her wailing. But the biggest joke was yet to come. I was called to a seminar in São Paulo and would be gone for almost a week. On about the third day, Gus phoned me, his voice in a panic.

"Barb," he said, "Lady is in heat." Sure enough, I could hear that familiar wail. "What am I gonna do?"

I smiled. "You're on," I said. "You have to do it this time!"

"No!" he said. "I don't know how."

"You've seen me do it enough," I replied. "Well, just do it the same way … and good luck."

To make a long story short, he did it, and so well that from that time on Lady preferred him. When it came time to do it, she would avoid me and back up against him for her treatment.

Everyone in the neighborhood – now familiar with what that wailing meant – would smile and call out to Gus, "You're on friend! She wants you! You're the lucky one!" It became the joke of the neighborhood.

The Eco 92 World Summit

What a privilege it was to be a part of the 1992 United Nations Conference on Environment and Development – also called the Earth Summit, or ECO 92 – in Rio de Janeiro. The group I was involved with that worked with prostitutes wanted to send representatives there, so I and one of the nuns registered to attend.

I said that I would find us a place to stay, and what better place than in my former favela hut overlooking the city of Rio. (Yes, it was truly a spectacular view from my old favela home.) I got in contact with my friends there and we set it up. I had to prepare the sister, assuring her that though it was a long climb to the top, it was worth it. I also had to convince her that it was not dangerous, that I knew everyone there.

People came from all over the world to the conference, and it was exciting to witness all the interaction. But the most memorable event was being a participant in the Women's

Earth Summit, 1992, Rio de Janeiro

Tent. I will never forget the many booths with women's wares and the many languages we heard. My strongest memory is of the African women in their colorful clothes, which made their faces shine with beauty. Once again, I was reminded of the creativity of women the world over, of their tenacity and courage in spite of the status in which they were held in so many countries.

There were two particularly outstanding experiences. One was a panel discussion of women from various countries describing their victories in the name of women's rights.

The woman who really stood out for me was a Buddhist from India who radiated peace and tranquility as she spoke – in sharp contrast to the fanfare of an American actress who came in after the discussion had begun, in a special car in which she stood and waved to the crowd, before climbing atop the panel table. She caused quite a stir, but since she was a well-known actress and author she could get away with it. To me, as an American, it was embarrassing.

After things calmed down, the woman from India, so beautifully clad in her native dress, took her turn to speak. The moment she began, a calmness came over the crowd; her voice was soft and melodious. I don't even remember what she said, just the sensation her voice gave me.

There was such a hush as she spoke. When she finished, she invited us all to take a candle, go outside the tent and form a peace circle. It was very emotional; women of so many countries, races, religions and cultures, united in one objective: peace for themselves and their children.

Each woman took a candle and lit it, and in total silence we walked, making an enormous circle that curled into itself, forming more circles, one inside the other. The only sounds that could be heard were the wind and the shuffling of feet. As the inner circles were formed, we passed women from all over the world, and we nodded or smiled, acknowledging one other. People stopped to watch, some joining in, even some men.

I don't know how long this lasted, but once again I felt a unity with all the women of the world. We all have one thing in common: We carry within us that miracle of life;

we can give birth. Though we American women have some problems with inequality, it can't be compared to those of women of the third world. Yet at this moment, we were all one, women of the world united by a Buddhist woman of peace.

Most of the plans made at this summit weren't carried out. However, as the years have gone on and I have talked with other women who were present, all agreed that this moment captured the power of women and their desire to create a world in which they could bring up their children in the peace and tranquility this woman from India embodied.

It was at the World Summit that I was approached by a Methodist minister, Pastor Rosangela de Oliveira of ISER – the Institute for Religious Studies – and a member of the group Women, Theology and Citizenship, who, having heard about my health educators training courses, invited me to come to Rio to work with her group to bring the course to the suburbs of Rio.

Returning to Rio

Arriving in Rio was exciting, for this was where it had all begun for me, the seeds of my awakening. But I was not the same woman who had left Rio in 1981, and Rio was not the same. Brazil had been changing even as I was in São Paulo.

There had been changes in women's roles. More and more women were working out of the home, though primarily in low-paying jobs. Favelas still existed, the same ones I had left in 1981, but many of them had improved; homes were better structured and better equipped.

There were supermarkets and shopping centers, and goods could be purchased on credit or layaway, making a lot of things more attainable, though more expensive, for the poor. Television was one of the most frequently purchased items; many of our favela friends had TVs, and soap operas, or telenovelas, were the topic of exchange among women. The world outside of the home was revealed, and things that never before seemed possible now did.

This was the Rio I came back to in 1993. Gus and I searched for a place to live but very soon returned to live near my dearest friend, Lea, whose hut we had purchased for our clinic years ago, when she, bettering her life, had moved to Jacarepagua. We found a home in the lower-middle-class community where she now lived and I began my work with the women's team at ISER, while Gus began his research of the area near our home, where there were a number of favelas.

With the help of the women of the Women, Theology and Citizenship team, I was able to identify the communities where I felt my Community Health Educators Training Course could have a real effect. The classes were all to be given in church communities, Catholic and Methodist, mostly in rural areas some distance from where we lived.

But one community I settled on was within walking distance of our home, a favela called Canal do Anil. This community would be our primary focus, and it was here that we were to one day open our free health clinic.

Leaving São Paulo after eight years was difficult, but I left behind women whose lives had changed and who were now moving forward to change the lives of others. So many of these women had been responsible for changes in my life too, my thinking, my awakening. I had witnessed so much transformation in these women and it never ceased to amaze me how a simple course in health and sexuality could alter the way women thought about themselves, how it could elevate their self- esteem. So many of these women who had hardly ever left their homes were suddenly active in their communities, taking blood pressures, visiting the sick, becoming involved in initiatives to improve the health systems in their communities and becoming aware of the need to speak out for women's rights.

In São Paulo, my students had asked me to write down the course curricula so that they could be multipliers of the course and form their own groups. So representatives of the various groups got together and we wrote the manual. I now needed to find a way to get it published for use. I felt it was time to move on, and Global Ministries, the United Church of Christ and the First Christian Church, Disciples of Christ approved my "call" to ISER in Rio.

****

In 1993, I began teaching the Community Health Educators Training Course in the local Methodist Church in the remote city of Itaguaí.

Itaguaí is about forty miles from Rio de Janeiro and was then very calm and underdeveloped, though it no longer is today. The main street had a few family-owned businesses and stores, but once you left it you knew you were far from Rio: Few residential roads were asphalted; sewers were scarce, and water often ran down the streets. There were few cars, and the ones you saw were old and not in good condition. Fruits and vegetables and other wares were sold on the streets.

The mayor was one of the people, in that he was of humble background and perhaps did not read and write beyond grammar school level. Corruption was part of the culture, and in rural areas such as Itaguaí at that time the mayor decided who would be punished for crimes – minor as well as major, including murder – as he wished, depending on who the criminal was, the cause of the crime and the political implications for himself.

Most women didn't work outside the home, unless it was to wash clothes or sew for others. There was a large Catholic church and several non-Catholic ones, and the largest of these was the Methodist Church where I taught the course. Most of the women in the class were Methodists, though we did have a few Catholics, which made it a very interesting and unusual group. They were very different, yes, but they shared more things than were to the contrary. There was no ecumenism at all in the town and, in fact, it was a struggle to get the Catholic priest to attend our graduation. He did, and it was probably the first time a church program had both Protestant and Catholic clergy present and the first time a priest participated in a ceremony in a Protestant church. It was quite an accomplishment, and wonderful. The church was full.

****

Lurdinha was a member of this group:

My name is Maria Lurdinha. My childhood was one of suffering. My father and my oldest brother were alcoholics, while my mother went hungry with her nine children. My mother and my oldest sister were always ill.

In 1977, we moved from the state of Pernambuco in the northeast of Brazil to Itaguaí, a city in the state of Rio de Janeiro, where we were forced to live for a time in the homes of others, which was humiliating.

In 1982, at the age of thirteen, I began to date – in secret, of course. I wanted to marry, as I thought that there would then be one less mouth to feed in my family's house. I was thinking especially about my younger brothers and sisters.

At fourteen, I got pregnant. I married my boyfriend and my son, Bruno, was born. At nineteen, I once again gave birth, to my daughter, Karen.

I had begun school at the age of nine and studied until Bruno was born, but was then unable to continue because I had to care for my children and work to support them. I didn't feel I even had a right to dream of better things until that lucky day when I began Barbara's Community Health Educators Training Course.

Lurdinha

Before finding this course, I was sad and unmotivated to better my life in any way. But through this course, and Barbara's confidence in me, I began to believe that I was a capable person. After the first two months of the course, I went back and finished grammar school, then high school, and then went on to get a job. I've never stopped working since.

I was married for eighteen years to my children's father, but then we separated and I went on to take a dental hygienist course, which changed my life even more by giving me a certain status and self-esteem. I have three grandchildren, Karen's Gabriel and Bruno's Marcos and Anja. I am now married to Rogerio, who has a son, Roje, to add to our family. My father died and one of my brothers was stoned to death in my presence. My mother lives near me.

I am grateful to have had this opportunity to take this course because it changed my life and that of my family. Today I know how to fight for the things I want. I work in a family health clinic, where I use the methodology I learned in that course. I also work in an emergency center. I am a happy woman and proud of my participation as a citizen. I help all those I can, just as I was helped. I was an unhappy child and a mother in adolescence, but today I am so thrilled to lead groups of pregnant women and young people.

At present, I am taking a class in proper breastfeeding technique and its importance. This course adds to the knowledge I gained in the community health educators course. I am a member of IUBAAM – The Basic Health Initiative, Friends of Nursing Mothers – which operates public health clinics that support mothers in breastfeeding, which is so important to the healthy growth and development of infants.

I am now forty-five. I work as a health agent for the city of Seropedica, serve on the city's health advisory council and volunteer for other health-education activities because I realize the importance of education in becoming an active citizen. My children are thirty and twenty-six years old, and though they were brought up through a lot of hardship they are responsible adults and parents.

Lurdinha seemed so young when she entered my community health educators course, but that was partly because she was so tiny, probably barely five feet tall. She had a very young face, and it was hard for me to believe her when she said she had two children.

She was very quiet when the course began and always seemed discouraged. Twice in the first months, she came to me and said she was going to quit, that it was too difficult. She said she wasn't smart enough to get it all and that the work in the community would be much too difficult. She said she was too young, and she was, in fact, the youngest of the group.

The first time she came to tell me she was leaving, she had such a sad face. She had no self-esteem at all and was so very negative about everything. We talked about her life, her feelings of inadequacy and her difficulties keeping up, but I was able to persuade her to give it just a bit more time.

A month later, she came to me again and said she was leaving, that she had so much to do at home and was just not good enough to do all this. I told her I wanted to come to her house to talk to her alone. She said that she was embarrassed about her home and neighborhood, but I convinced her that this didn't matter.

So one day, Gus and I drove to her home. Her house was outside the city of Itaguaí on the banks of a small river filled with garbage. There was no real road, just dirt and stones. Her home was in a community of small houses, each built by the owner in various styles, some crude, others surrounded by vegetable gardens. There were no streetlights and no garbage collection.

191

Lurdinha's house was made of crude brick and was so close to the river's edge that when it rained a lot her yard flooded. The inside of the house was unfinished, with a very crude bathroom and with mold and signs of dampness everywhere. But the house was clean, the cement floor shining with the red wax coloring so common in these types of homes.

Her children were at school but her husband was at home. I now understood why she was so worn down. Her husband, Gildo, quite a bit older, had contracted polio as a child and had lost the use of his legs; he used handmade crutches to get around. He couldn't get a steady job but was handy with motors and electricity. He was a talker, very pleasant, but clearly controlled the household and Lurdinha's life.

We had a wonderful talk and Lurdinha's husband was supportive of her continuing with the course, recognizing that this knowledge was much needed in the family and community. When the children came home, their faces were happy; and though they were thin, they looked healthy.

My husband and I became quite friendly with the family and visited with them in their home many times. We had several cookouts there and became well acquainted with the children, especially Karen. Still, Lurdinha seemed so young to have children of this age.

As time went on and Lurdinha moved ahead with her schooling, we watched her change. She began to stick up for herself when her husband questioned her always being away from home – practicing what she was learning about health in the community – and her new friendships from school. We noticed the changes in his attitude toward her, and we began to be concerned.

Then one day as we turned into the dirt road leading to her home, we saw groups of people standing around near the house. We could see something was wrong. When we stepped into the house, Lurdinha came to us crying, almost uncontrollably. It seemed that because of rivalry or robbery, or a combination of both, some people in the community had taken the law into their own hands, tied her brother to a tree and beat him to death.

Lurdinha doesn't tell her brother's story in the story of her life that I translated above because she was ashamed and horrified, realizing that for the poor there is little justice. The police did nothing to investigate and no one who witnessed the crime spoke up. It ended there. But from then on, I saw a change in Lurdinha, a determination to move out of that place, to better her life, to give her children a better life. And she did it. She'd awakened, and would move mountains.

Neuza

Neuza was a farm woman who lived near the city garbage dump in a small house with no electricity or running water, eking out her family's sustenance doing primitive farming. Tiny, muscular, almost toothless and semiliterate, she was the main source of income for her alcoholic, rather cruel husband and their three children.

Neuza entered our health educators training course with no self-esteem at all, having been encouraged to do so by a former student. Perhaps she wanted to escape her routine and domestic problems, but she also wanted to learn more about how to prevent the many illnesses that plagued the wretchedly poor community in which she lived and help lower the infant mortality rate. After finishing the course, she was ready to work.

Neuza

With a new set of false teeth and a perpetual smile, Neuza began walking miles to visit with pregnant women in a rural area in which there was no doctor. She took blood pressures; measured abdominal swelling; did urine tests to detect pregnancy risks; and taught proper nutrition, hygiene, family planning and the benefits of breastfeeding. After births, she was there to monitor the weight of the infants and teach illness prevention to the mothers, all the while offering encouragement. With her broad smile and new haircut, she was on the road to liberation while helping liberate others. Empowered with health knowledge, she empowered others.

Neuza lived three miles off the main highway where there were no roads, just paths, and you had to climb over fallen trees to get to her hut. There was no electricity anywhere in the area. There was no water immediately available; it had to be hauled from wherever they were able to beg to fill their buckets, which were carried on their heads and shoulders and hauled through the woods.

All around her hut – which had but two rooms, a sink and a woodstove – were gardens in which the family grew most of what they ate and more to sell or trade. Meat was hardly ever eaten, though they did have a few chickens. It was very primitive farming, and then they would walk miles to sell the harvest. This was an isolated community of five huts and people depended on one other to survive. The men sold the roots and vegetables and chickens and eggs to earn money for what they needed to buy, or they traded them for necessities like milk.

Neuza made her children's school uniforms and walked with them each day to the main road to catch the bus, carrying the children's books and supplies. Then she walked back home to do her fieldwork. Her husband thought school was unnecessary and complained all the time that their son, who was about nine at the time I met Neuza, should be home helping out – that, in fact, even their daughter of seven should be helping.

All the children were born in these huts; there was no way to get to a hospital and the public health system in the town was very rudimentary. Neuza had assisted in several births, but in the past year three infants had died, and in one case the woman would have bled to death if the men had not carried her all the way to the road and begged for a ride to the hospital. Neuza wept over this near loss of a friend, and for the infants who had died.

She had always been interested in curing people and in caring for the sick. The family didn't go to church often because of the distance, but it was while Neuza was attending a wedding that she learned that a health educators training class was going to be offered the following month.

Initially, she was like a fish out of water. She had no self-esteem and little in common with the other women, who were from the town of Itaguaí. But from the beginning, her

195

determination made her stand out. She'd had no experience of much of what we discussed, had not finished grammar school, but she listened. And as the months went on, she began adding her home remedies to the course and became enthusiastic about the possibility of teaching others what she was learning.

She began with her own family, then her community. Claudia was one of her first patients, a twenty-three-year-old pregnant woman who had moved to the area from the northeast. She told Neuza that she had no children but had lost two due to what sounded to be eclampsia and another to dehydration.

When Neuza came to visit her, Claudia was a sad woman, quiet and resigned to her fate of never having children. She was pregnant again, in about her fourth month, certain that something would once again go wrong. Neuza examined her and gave her vitamins and encouragement. These were things Claudia hadn't received in her other pregnancies, and she looked forward to Neuza's visits and informative talks.

All seemed fine until Claudia's seventh month, when her legs began to swell and her blood pressure rose, signs that Neuza had learned about in the course and knew were serious. She first took Claudia to a public health clinic some distance away but couldn't get her in to see a doctor, then to an emergency room, where Claudia was instructed to take a diuretic and cut down on salt intake. Neuza visited her weekly for the next six weeks to ensure she was taking her medicine correctly and monitor her blood pressure.

One day in her eighth month, Claudia awoke with a severe headache and swollen legs. When Neuza arrived, she was shocked to see how swollen she was. And so began Neuza and Claudia's long, torturous, frustrating journey to find help for what Neuza knew was a situation in which if no help was found, Claudia would once again lose her baby and possibly her own life.

There were few doctors and nurses in this rural area and there were very few beds in the small city hospital. So when they got to the hospital, Claudia was given an injection and told to go home to wait out the remainder of her pregnancy.

But Neuza wouldn't accept this answer. She barged into the director's office, presented her health educator's badge and told him Claudia's health history. He told her that there were no free beds available in the hospital.

Still, Neuza wouldn't give up. She knew that Claudia's condition was too precarious to return her home. So hand in hand, off they went to the police station.

There, as Neuza tells it, she caused a ruckus. Though a tiny woman, Neuza had a commanding presence, and now she was in battle mode. A police car was summoned to take the women to a hospital in the next city.

By the time they arrived, Claudia's blood pressure was extremely high and she was feeling faint; a C-section was performed. Neuza's health care expertise, and her newly acquired self-esteem, saved this baby's life, and perhaps Claudia's too. Claudia gave birth to a healthy boy.

What a totally different woman Neuza was from that insecure, very rural woman who had come to my course two and a half years prior. This woman with the permanent smile, helping and educating others, is truly a marvel and a gift to me. Education in whatever form empowers, and with empowerment comes self-esteem. This I have witnessed over and again – sleeping women awakening and moving mountains.

Publishing the Health Manual

The second year after we arrived in Rio, a man, who I mentioned earlier, named Mark Boyd visited us. He had been given my name by a Global Ministries pastor and was interested in what we were doing. He was very enthusiastic about the work, visited several communities in Rio where I was giving the course and one day asked me if there was anything he could do to help. I told him that I had been trying to raise money to publish the health manual that I had written with my students in São Paulo. Right on the spot, he wrote me a check for what I estimated to be the full cost! It was unbelievable!

And so with the help of the women's group at ISER – most especially, Pastor Rosangela, who spent days entering the text in the computer and teaching me how to use it – we finally got it together. We knew that most of the women who would be taking the course didn't have much schooling, so we'd kept the writing simple and relied heavily on illustrations. I'd found a good editor at ISER, Jacinto Correa, and, through him, a cartoonist, Calicut. Heliana Soneghet Pacheco was our graphic designer. We were a great team, and though it was hard work we had a lot of fun. The men involved said they better understood women's issues after working on the project.

It had taken a long time to get the manual published, but now it was in use, and it was working!

****

One of the scenes that I will never forget from when we were putting the health educators training manual together is of Calicut asking about how to draw some of the procedures that were being taught, such as CPR. I tried to explain, but he just couldn't imagine how to draw it. So we decided to illustrate. Jacinto got down on the floor on his back and I climbed over him, bracing my knees on either side of his hips, and placed my hands on his chest to perform CPR.

There we were, when suddenly the door opened and in walked Rubem César, the coordinator of ISER, with two visitors. We were, after all, in his large office, so it was logical that he would bring visitors there.

You can imagine the faces on the three of them as they looked in on this scene. We all had a good laugh.

The Community Health Educators
Training Course manual

Egypt: The International Conference on Population and Development

In September 1994, I attended the United Nations-sponsored International Conference on Population and Development in Cairo. The conference brought together people from all over the world to exchange ideas on such topics as abortion, reproductive rights and sex education, with the objective of initiating a global plan of action. I was attending as a representative of the Institute for Religious Studies.

How exciting it was to be going to this conference. How would I have ever dreamed that one day I would go to Egypt! I was a bit scared – I'm not a traveler to begin with, and this was going to another world.

Then in the days leading up to the event, I received all sorts of instructions – or warnings, as I understood them – stating that shoulders, arms and legs had to be covered; hair must be covered or tied up. We were warned of street robbers and that we shouldn't go out alone.

There were also newspaper articles about fundamentalist groups who would be protesting the conference and might cause problems. But the organizers had arranged for extra police protection and we were assured that we'd be safe.

I would first be stopping off in London to see a woman who had worked with me in São Paulo and would then meet up with Cristina, a young Methodist minister, at the airport in Cairo. I say young because I was sixty-four and she was in her late thirties.

The day came, and off I went, all alone. Nowadays, with travel abroad so common, most people are used to this, but I was not. In my youth, such a trip was so rare it wasn't even imagined.

I arrived in Cairo and my friend and I looked for our bus among the many that were waiting at the airport for the participants. Each bus had the name of a hotel on it, but we couldn't find one with the name of ours.

There were quite a few Brazilian participants, but most of them were sponsored by larger institutions and were staying at the Hilton or a similar type hotel. Our sponsoring organization, the Institute for Religious Studies, couldn't afford such places, so we were registered in a hotel that was well off the beaten path and, as we learned, not registered with the conference, which was why there was no bus there to greet us. We were a bit frantic as we tried to communicate with the drivers. Eventually, one of them pointed us to the bus that would take us the closest to our hotel.

Most of the registered hotels were in a very Americanized area, and as we dropped people off at these luxurious hotels I was amazed at how much it looked like a tourist destination, in Florida, for example.

We rode and rode and then entered an area with hardly any lights. It was night, so we could see little from the bus,

International Conference on Population and Development,
1994, Cairo, Egypt

but we knew we were heading farther and farther away from the tourist district. We were the only ones on the bus and the driver had to stop to be sure he was going to the right hotel.

We finally arrived. The bus stopped in front of a small hotel, not at all like the ones at which we'd dropped the others. We entered a large room with a high ceiling, an extremely large chandelier and a huge winding stairway leading to the rooms. We walked to the registration desk. The man on duty spoke English.

The manager, seeing that I had an American passport but was registered as coming from Brazil, asked what my title was and what kind of work I did. I replied that I was a minister and that I worked in the field of health. He recorded all this and we were shown to our room, where we immediately collapsed into our beds.

****

The next morning, a Sunday, we had to be at the conference to register. We got up early and went downstairs to find out how we would get there. After a quick and simple breakfast, we found a cab and were off.

And, oh, my, now that it was daylight we could see where we were! Everything was sandy colored – the buildings, the roads, everything in sight; we were right in the midst of history. The buildings had balconies and rooftops where families were having breakfast. The streets were full of activity. It was truly another world.

And then there was the traffic! I had thought that traffic was bad in Rio and São Paulo, but this was so much worse – unimaginable. We had been told in our conference instruction manual that if a driver got into a traffic argument or accident, to get away from the scene as quickly as possible. As I looked at the traffic, I wondered if we could possibly get there without an accident. There were no traffic lights; it was first-come-first-go to make a turn.

There were battered cars and trucks on the roads and no dividing lines. There were whole families on bicycles – father, mother in her long-sleeved dress and as many as three children all on one bicycle. There were wagons pulled by horses and mules. And the noise! It seemed like everyone was screaming at everyone else, plus the honks of the cars. It was unbelievable. An adventure! But we arrived intact.

The conference center was huge, but my first impression wasn't of the size of the place – it was the people, all different colors and clothes of every type, representing so many countries and cultures.

It was like ECO 92 in Rio, and the colors and beauty of the women once again caught my attention. This was going to be exciting. The guides were all young people who could speak English and several other languages. I was a presenter at the conference and was shown the room where I would speak. We then ate lunch in a huge room, where all sorts of local foods were among the choices, along with fast-food machines. Then, tired but excited, we hailed a taxi and took a harrowing ride back home.

****

When we arrived back at the hotel, we saw three white-uniformed policemen, one of whom approached us and started chatting away in a worried voice. I had no idea what he was saying. But the manager, the one who had checked us in the night before, stepped in and told us that we should contact this policeman whenever we left the hotel, as he was responsible for us. This made no sense, but we agreed.

When we came back down for dinner, the manager led us to a table set off from the others, a private area, and we had our own, exclusive waiters. We thought this too was quite strange. We then returned to our rooms and prepared for the start of the conference.

The next morning, as we came down the stairs, we noted again the three men in white uniforms standing near the entrance. At the reception desk, a day manager greeted us, addressing me as "Minister Barbara de Souza."

He explained that this was a family hotel and that though no conference buses had been assigned to it, he had arranged transportation for us. He then pointed to the three men in white, explaining that they would be our special caretakers. Whenever we needed to go anywhere, we were to tell them where and they would arrange safe transportation, and that we shouldn't ever leave without notifying the desk, who would in turn notify the policemen.

One of the policemen then led us outside, saying something that we didn't understand, but indicating with hand signals that we were to wait there with him. Once again, the streets and balconies and roofs of the apartments were teaming with activity, though it was still early in the morning.

Soon, lo and behold, a bus arrived. The policemen signaled for us to get on. We did. The bus was empty; the door closed, and off we went, just the two of us on this large bus!

We then noted that there was a motorcycle in front of the bus and another behind. What kind of protection was this? When we arrived at the entrance to the conference center, some of our Brazilian colleagues saw us drive up and asked where we were staying and how we got a bus just for us – and with a motorcycle escort. We all laughed, but thought nothing more about it. There were too many other exciting things going on.

****

About forty people, mostly women, attended my presentation. Some were teachers, others medical professionals. Some were very young. I had the doll we used to teach sexual education and some items used to illustrate body systems. But the objective was to talk about the methodology of teaching women how their bodies function so that they might take more control of them; the focus was on sex education and family planning. After the talk, a number of people stayed to ask questions.

A few of the young conference guides then helped me pack my things, and I noticed that one of them was wiping what seemed to be tears from her face. I didn't think it was my place to approach her, but after she left I asked one of the others if she was not feeling well. No, I was told, she was just feeling so much emotion. First, because of the fact that girls and women in Brazil had the right to study and talk about sexuality and, second, because she had been circumcised as a young teenager – still a common practice in Egypt, especially in the rural areas – and had been promised in marriage, which she had come to Cairo to escape from.

I went after her, but when she saw me approaching she walked away. I had thought Brazilian woman were so far behind in terms of control of their own sexuality, but things were even worse here.

The women at this conference were from all over the world – of all colors, cultures and beliefs – but one thing they had in common was the struggle for equality in male-dominated countries; for the right to education, health care, especially maternal care; the right to make their own choices, to make their own marital choices, and to have a say in the size of their family.

Listening to these women talk, I was many times brought to tears, especially when female circumcision was discussed. These magnificent, courageous, though oppressed women stood up and spoke for themselves, even the ones whose bodies were completely covered, with only their eyes exposed, showing such courage. The feeling of solidarity, of the commonality of all women was so strong, it moved us all.

Yes, many of these women were waking up, and mountains would move, in spite of beatings and abandonment. It might take years, but I was confident it would happen.

****

When we arrived back at our hotel that night, we were told that two men from Russia had checked in who were participants of the conference. The manager told us that they spoke English and that he would sit them with us in our private area. We said yes, of course, though my companion was a bit nervous, as she didn't speak English.

During the meal, we talked about the conference and one of the men asked us if we were married. He said this while eyeing my young friend Cristina, a very attractive woman. She was not, but when I translated to her what the man had asked, she kicked me under the table to indicate that I should say she was.

The man then said, "Do your husbands allow you to travel alone?" When we said yes, he said that in Russia this would never be allowed, that their wives would never go far from home without them. From that point on, they looked upon us differently, and we had to discourage their "friendship."

The next morning, the bus was waiting. The two Russian men joined us, and I now learned why we were getting this special treatment. The manager of the hotel had told them the night before that they were invited to sit with a high-ranking member of the Brazilian government and her companion! He had translated the word we use for clergy, "minister," as a political title. And since I had said I worked in health, I had become the Brazilian minister of health!

Cristina and I determined it best to say nothing.

****

The third night there, we were invited to go to a luxurious hotel where other Brazilians were staying. I informed the manager where we were going and he had one of the policemen hail a taxi. The manager walked outside with us and spoke with the policeman and the taxi driver, and we saw what looked like money passed into the hands of the driver. We climbed in, a bit confused, and off we went on another wild ride – and wild it was! I was sure my life was going to end in Egypt at sixty-four!

We had a wonderful evening sharing all our experiences and it was well past midnight when we stepped out to return home. I said to Cristina, "Let's pick a taxi with an older driver," thinking that an older man would be less daring. I was wrong, terribly wrong; he set off like a bull with a fire under him.

As always, the streets were full of activity. We came to one of the many traffic circles, and as we swerved around amidst the circling cars the taxi gave a spurt or two and died. The driver let out some words that we knew were curses, turned to us and began chattering in a loud voice. We, of course, had no idea what he was saying, but by his gestures gathered that he was telling us to stay put, he would be right back.

He jumped out of the taxi as horns blared all around us, dodged his way to the sidewalk and disappeared. There we were at two in the morning, shut into a taxi in the middle of a traffic circle, cars jammed up behind us and on both sides, drivers shaking their fingers and shouting.

We sat there for about fifteen minutes, no sign of our driver, then decided to make a run for the sidewalk. It was a death-defying dash, dodging through cars traveling well over any speed limit, screeching brakes. But somehow we made it through this traffic war zone.

And so there we now were, a sea of cars whipping by. We held our hands out, hoping a taxi would stop. Finally, one slammed to a stop and a young man jumped out, gesturing for us to get in. He pointed to our old taxi, understanding why two foreign women were standing here amidst this chaos.

But it was not to be. Suddenly, our former driver reappeared, a gallon can of gasoline in his hand, and a fight between the old man and our young new driver commenced. A crowd began to gather; there was much screaming and shaking of fists, and I then remembered the warnings I had read in our manual – that if you get in a traffic accident or around one, get away fast.

We were scared. As we started to open the door, the new driver gave a yell, pushed the older man, startling him, jumped into the car, and we were once again on our way. And we were flying.

After a moment, the driver turned to us and told us, in English, that we had just escaped a very dangerous situation and that we should not be out alone at an hour such as this. We were surprised to hear him speak English, and I asked why he hadn't spoken to us immediately when we stopped him. He just laughed, and shared with us the story of his life.

We arrived safely, just held out our money and he took what he thought was appropriate. Whether it was or not, we'll never know – we were just grateful to be back where our faithful men in white were awaiting us.

****

Shopping in the local market was another reminder that we were in a totally different world. The corridors were narrow and colorful curtains separated the stores. It was full of people, a tide of humanity: men shouting or singing of their wares and women in beautifully colored dresses with veils and head clothes to match, equally adept at bargaining. The language barrier prevented us from actually negotiating the price, but the salesmen expected it and added more items to tempt us.

Suddenly, there was a lot of screaming and some young boys came running in our direction with men in uniform and a few others in pursuit. A woman told us in English that if we saw anyone, child or adult, with a finger or fingers missing, he was a petty thief who'd had his finger cut off as a warning; in other words, he was a marked thief. We were told we might even see one without a hand, and could be sure that he had stolen multiple times.

Though she had been warned to always cover her long hair, on this day Cristina hadn't, and was attracting a lot of attention. The salesmen made all sorts of gestures to her and, assuming I was her mother, indicated to me in broken English or sign language that we should join them behind the curtains of the crowded salesroom for tea. An elderly shop owner told us that it was assumed that a woman with uncovered hair and without male companionship was available, and that they were bargaining for her, in exchange for their wares.

So this was the value of a woman? Suddenly, by my reckoning, Brazilian women were way ahead in their rights!

Another afternoon, we visited the tomb of one of the pharaohs and learned that when they died their wives, servants and pets could be sacrificed and buried with them.

We next went to some sand dunes. There I saw a woman climbing dressed entirely in black, with nothing visible but her eyes. We were told that she must be a woman of means because her children and servants waited below while she climbed. We had seen other women dressed similarly, walking in dignity with their heads held high.

It was only the poorer women who walked with heads bowed, as they hurried to their destinations. What would it take to awaken these women, I wondered? Were they happy? Were they even aware of other possibilities – that women could have the freedom of choice? Marriages were still arranged, and they were in many regards owned by their fathers, then husbands.

We did as much sightseeing as we had time for and I felt lucky that we were in a lower-class family hotel, far from the touristy area. Walking one day, we came upon several camels whose owners were calling for riders. Would I? Dare I? I did, and what a memorable experience it was. As the camel lowered to his knees so I could climb aboard the saddle on his hump, I hesitated. But I saw a woman in the traditional dress climb on and be led away, and I was determined.

I felt as if I were on a roller coaster, rocking around, almost like a boat at sea. All the while, the owner of the camel was prompting him to go faster and faster. I called out for him to stop, I was dizzy, but he continued on. Soon it was over and Cristina had me pose for a picture for posterity, at which moment I was thrown to the grown as this giant animal grunted, dropping to his knees to dismount me.

****

Time was running out on our visit, and on all that special treatment. My plane for London was scheduled to leave at five in the morning, so I would need to leave the hotel around two. I informed the manager and was told that a cab would be ready. When I walked down the winding stairs to the lobby, there were the three policemen dressed in white. The manager and two of his office staff were also waiting, with a small bouquet, preparing to bid me goodbye.

As I stepped into the taxi, they all stood in a line and wished me well. And then, there I sat. No one moved, and neither did the taxi. I began to get nervous, and as more time passed my anxiety became apparent. Reassuring me, the manager told me that we were waiting for my escort to the airport. An escort? I certainly didn't want a stranger to climb into the taxi with me! Then the taxi driver turned on the engine and two motorcyclists appeared. We were off through the streets of Cairo at three in the morning, sirens screaming all the way to the airport, announcing the arrival of the health minister of Brazil!

****

As a postscript: Out of the conference came the Cairo Program of Action, signed by 179 nations. Initiatives were launched in the areas of population, equal rights, education, health, environment and the reduction of poverty through an approach centered on human development.

An important initiative was a focus on the sexual and reproductive health of young people, with the objective of reducing adolescent pregnancies and unsafe abortions and preventing sexually transmitted diseases. There was also an emphasis on the recognition of gender equality.

The contingent of Brazilian women at the conference generally supported the initiatives but emphasized that population control wasn't so much of a problem in Brazil because of the high rate of infant and maternal mortality at the time. A statistic was presented, indicating that one in twenty women in developing countries die from complications of giving birth, compared with one in ten thousand in industrialized countries.

To my mind, the conference was largely about the rights of women, the struggle for the end of a patriarchal society. From the beginning, the subject most discussed was women's reproductive rights. Women were the principal subject! The voices of half of the human population were crying out to be heard on issues of gender, poverty, education, health and family planning. Reproductive rights and abortion were the most polemic issues because of the stance of the Vatican and of fundamentalists of other religions, especially Islamic ones.

As Sandra Kabir of Bangladesh said, "No woman likes to have an abortion, but it is our responsibility that when she has one it is done safely and securely." But it was this that incited the Vatican's protests.

In spite of these protests, an accord was drafted that called upon the governing authorities of countries in which abortion isn't against the law to provide it as safely and securely as possible and to propose health services for women who had suffered the consequences of abortion.

Neither the Vatican nor the Islamics would agree with the idea of legal abortion, constantly registering their protests, and the accord was left out of the final document.

The women of Latin America held numerous meetings demanding their reproductive rights, contraception and safe abortions, despite the fact that the majority of them were Catholics and were contested by members of the Right to Life group and Islamic men. These women and those of other countries showed their courage in speaking out, as did those who spoke out against genital mutilation. The majority of Brazilian women supported Brazil's position of agreeing with the final document, despite the opposition of the Vatican.

Canal do Anil

Returning from Egypt to Rio my head was filled with the voices of women from all over the world claiming their rights to be heard, to own their own bodies, to make their own decisions. From the more modern countries to the most fundamentalist, the feeling was the same: "Why should men, governments or religion control our lives? We want the rights to education, to equality and to decide how many children to have."

I was even more certain that the way to empowerment, the way to claiming the rights these women demanded, was through education, including health education. And this I was determined to provide.

I had chosen to live in Jacarepagua, near my dear friend Lea, and I soon met a woman, Ione, who worked at ISER and attended a Catholic church, Capela do São Pedro, in the favela of Canal do Anil, a couple of blocks from where we were living. The priest of this community, Padre Alfonso, was a professor at the Catholic University in Rio, where Ione was also a professor. We became friends and she encouraged me to offer my health course at the church in the favela, aware of how much these women needed this type of education.

We began another course close to where we lived, in a vacant favela hut beside the canal. I was told that the canal was once clean enough to wash clothes in, but now it was polluted with garbage and sewage. The roads were all dirt and logs were used to cross over the canal, a precarious undertaking.

There was a tiny Catholic church in the community that became very much involved in our work. My first students helped me form the Association of Community Health Educators and construct the health clinic. All of the women were married with children except for two teenagers, Kelly, whose story I'll be telling you, and Adriana, the youngest of the group, who substituted for her mother who had to have surgery.

I'd like to tell a little about the history of Canal do Anil. The following is excerpted from a history written in 1999 by some leaders of the Catholic church and Isabel Maria Fernandes da Silva, one of our health educators, upon the inauguration of the Family Health Program in the community:

The community of Canal do Anil is located in one of the most noble regions of Rio de Janeiro, called Barra da Tijuca. It is a friendly community, where the large majority of dwellers were born where they now live or have lived there for sometime. During the last few years, this community has grown in an almost alarming way, which has in some respects changed its character. The population in 1999, according to the dweller's register done in November, is about 6,339 persons.

The history of Canal do Anil doesn't differ from many other favela communities' stories of struggle. It is a story filled with sadness as well as joy, of losses and gains; but above all, it was and is a struggle for the right to exercise our citizenship. The history of this community is alive in the memories of the men and women who took part in this adventurous story.

The favela Anil

213

A little more than a half-century ago, fishermen made their mud huts on the banks of the Canal do Anil, which at that time was clean and was close to areas where there were markets for the sale of fish. As the years went by, the community grew fast because of so many rural families, mostly from the northeast, fleeing to the big cities to find work. They were unskilled men and women whose small farms were unproductive or who were expulsed by rich landowners when rent for the farmland they used couldn't be paid.

When I began to work in Canal do Anil, there were somewhere around 10,000 people, the majority being women and children. A large portion of these families were headed by women – widows or women abandoned by their partners – who had to work outside the home, leaving their children alone for at least half the day.

Dona Esmeralda Conceicao dos Santos, now eighty-one years old and a resident of the community since she was twenty, remembers when there was no water and the street was just a cattle path surrounded by thick woods. Dona Esmeralda collected firewood, for cooking, some distance from her house.

Another longtime resident, Dona Dalvina, remembers that when she came to live in the community, there were land poachers who threatened them with expulsion, armed men wandering in the alleys.

Despite the difficulties, the community grew and living conditions improved some. But daily life remains a struggle. The canal is now too contaminated for fishing, and the salaries of at least half of these families are below or just barely at the minimum wage. Most of the women work as maids or selling homemade wares. The men work mainly in construction or at odd jobs.

There are many more schools today, though not nearly enough. When I came to Canal do Anil in 1993, the majority of young people had not even completed grammar school. When I left, almost all attended grammar school and three-quarters went on to high school, many of them going on to some kind of a technical school, and some, as you'll learn, attending a university.

The Floods of 1996

The health course that started in Canal do Anil in late 1994 was attended by twelve students who would become great examples of what awakened women (and one man) could do in a community. We were about halfway through the course when a tragedy occurred that, while disastrous for this community, paved the way for the future of the health clinic.

On February 13 and 14 of 1996, it rained continuously. I had never witnessed such destruction from rain. The favela was in a valley, and water came from everywhere, draining into the canal, which began overflowing the first day and continued to do so. Water flowed down the canal in frightening waves, destroying the many homes of this favela community. For those families who lived along the main road, aside the canal, it was total loss.

When the floodwater receded, I could do nothing but weep. What the water didn't take away or destroy, the mud did. Walls tumbled and mud filled homes; the ones on lower ground were buried almost completely. Rats were everywhere – as one woman told us, crawling over her grandchildren as they slept on makeshift boards above the waterline

Though we lived just a block from the canal, the roads were impassable, and Gus and I were unable to get into the favela for several days. When we arrived, we couldn't believe what we saw. We waded through the mud to get to the hut where we'd been holding our classes, but it was gone.

And such chaos! These poor families had lost what little they had. But I'll always remember what Flavia, one of my students, said as she spoke to me in front of what was left of her home on the edge of the canal: "Well, no one died, and for this we can be thankful."

Homes and possessions could be replaced, she said with a smile, but a life could not.

I asked myself: "Would I have felt the same if it had been my home and possessions that were lost?" I doubted it. I would have lamented all that I'd lost.

****

My students now sprung into action, prepared to practice what they had learned. Some wealthy members of the church brought food and clothing, which the women distributed, and tetanus shots were donated because of the rats.

"Now," I thought, "who will give these shots? We will: the members of my class." We hadn't even discussed how to give a shot, but I now taught them, using oranges, then each other.

I remember so well those days that we vaccinated. In what was left of one of the huts, we set up four stations and each of the students took turns administering the shots. At the outset, some cringed as they gave them; but they learned.

One line had few candidates at first. It was Adriana's. She was only fifteen, and not many people were comfortable having her give them a shot. But as time went on, and they saw that no one complained, her line grew longer.

Our efforts to save the community from further disaster caught the eye of the city health department, and a nurse, Marcia Cid, arrived with vaccines from the city's pharmacy. She was very impressed with our work, and an awareness of the importance of our health educators training course to a favela community began to spread. A newspaper headline read, "Community Group Acts in a Disaster to Aid the People."

Our students became famous, and donations in money and medicine arrived. Dona Teresa, Kelly's mother, offered us the roof of her home, a larger one and made of brick, to attend to the community. (The Catholic church also began using the roof to conduct masses while its old church was rebuilt.) Students were taking blood pressures and temperatures, looking down throats, cleaning wounds and educating families on hygiene and nutrition – in sum, being health educators.

216

And then came a real bonus. Dr. Ana Lipke, director of one of the hospitals in the area, read about us in the newspaper and began coming to our rooftop clinic several times a week to attend to patients. She brought with her a friend, and later another.

And the idea of a health clinic in this favela community was born. Dr. Ana suggested that we form an association and work toward legalizing our health-education program. She found us a lawyer, and in October 1996 my students and I became the legally recognized Association of Community Health Educators, a nonprofit, philanthropic organization.

****

We needed a real space to do our work. The women of the community sold donated clothing to raise money to buy medications, but where would they be kept? All we had to separate the doctor's "office" from the public was a curtain.

The answer came: A man from São Paulo who was an executive in a multinational pharmaceutical firm, one of two that gave us donations, came to visit us and was so impressed with our work that his company provided enough money for our association to buy the second floor of a bicycle shop on the other side of the canal.

In October 1996, we moved into our clinic at 128 Avenida Canal do Anil, an occasion that was honored in the community with a special celebration at the Catholic church. Both Father Alfonso and Sister Maria Carmen were, from the beginning, staunch supporters, encouraging in every way and working with us side by side. Father Alfonso and the local Methodist minister both blessed our new clinic.

We grew. More and more members of the community realized how valuable our work was and began to trust the work of their own people, the women of the favela. Once again, we needed more space. In 1998, we built our first addition. With donations from churches in the U.S., we closed in the cement roof of our building. It had three floors, two of which were ours, and there was no room for further growth.

Dr. Lipke, still volunteering at our clinic, was able to arrange a meeting for us with the health secretary of Rio de

Janeiro. We brought pictures and stories and convinced him that we deserved financial support for our health clinic.

In May 1999, as president of our newly formed Association of Community Health Educators, I signed a contract with the mayor of Rio de Janeiro, Dr. Luiz Paulo Conde, joining three other community programs to form the initial Family Health Programs in the city of Rio de Janeiro. The city health department then contracted two doctors, two nurses and two nurse's assistants for our now-legalized clinic, and twelve of my students, who were now called health agents, were hired.

A newspaper article titled "Canal do Anil turns tragedy into victory" read in part:

> February, 1996, a tragic flood which hit the city of Rio left hundreds of people homeless in the community of Canal do Anil (a favela). In the midst of this chaos, a group of students of a health educators program, dwellers of this community, distributed donated medicines and vaccinated the population against tetanus. Thus was formed the embryo of the Community Educators Association, an NGO that today victoriously signed an agreement with the City of Rio de Janeiro's health program....

> Yes, this community turned a tragedy into a victory not only for the health workers but the population.

Signing the contract with Dr. Luiz Paulo Conde, mayor of Rio de Janeiro

The Formation of the Family Health Program

Signing this contract with the city meant that our methodology was recognized as the best means of reaching the favela community: using the health educators of the community to teach their neighbors all they had learned about illness prevention. And at last, everyone would receive a salary.

Our first program began with two health teams. Each team was composed of a doctor, a nurse, a nurse's assistant and six health educators.

The favela, then much smaller than it is today, was divided into two parts and each team was responsible for one. Each health agent had from 150 to 180 families in her care. Her job was to visit each family once a month to check on health and sanitary conditions and bring these reports to the doctor and nurses on her team. Each health agent had a record card for each family with the number of adults in the family, the children's health records, living conditions, all to be recorded in her team's file.

While visiting each family, blood pressures were taken and questions asked about the health of each member. The medications they were taking were discussed. If a child was ill or missing school, temperatures were taken and symptoms examined. These were reported to the team, and if necessary a doctor's appointment was made. After the appointment, the family was visited daily until the person was recovered. The health agents also talked with the families they visited about illnesses and how to prevent them; they discussed sanitation issues and reported when the water used for drinking was not being filtered. Rain damage was also reported.

In addition, of course, the health agent became a friend, a confidant, someone counted on for help and advice. These were their neighbors. When questions arose about health issues, they were sought out as they walked through the alleys with their health packs and first aid kits. They stopped on the streets to chat, to hug a child or to be told of some family that should be looked in on.

****

For several years, medical universities would send their students to watch how our Family Health Program operated. Men and women studying to be doctors or nurses would come to our staff meetings then go out with the health agents on their visits throughout the favelas. They were mostly from middle- or upper-middle-class families.

We received the following note of gratitude from a student who had just spent some time with us:

It was a distinct pleasure to spend this month with you! I think the best way to thank you is to tell you how much I learned during this time.

I have never seen a specialty presented with such perfection! I have never seen a specialty that fits so well into the most poetic definition of medicine. I learned that a thousand patients could show absolutely the same illness yet require different treatments. No matter what he or she has, each patient is different, and must be treated as an individual. I learned to analyze a patient with an understanding of his or her social and emotional context. Knowing this is important in selecting the most effective treatment.

It's incredible how we can live so close to poverty and yet not understand it at all. And the worst part is, we think we know so much. At least that's what I thought. But after this experience, I realize I had no idea of the reality of real poverty, not until I entered the houses, those tiny cubicles, where an unfinished rough brick wall is a luxury. Children playing in piles of garbage and in alleyways with stagnant water left from the rain, and with rats as companions.

But I also met strong women with such courage and determination as to make me envious; women who are not doctors, the majority of them with limited formal education, but with a very special talent: the ability to care for people in a very special way! They are medical professionals who treat people in a most affectionate and caring way in spite of their limitations and offer medical advice in simple language.

220

Each of these women is indispensable to this program. No matter what their task might be, they are truly remarkable women!

I thank you, dear teachers and all the wonderful people I met in Canal do Anil, for the impact this experience with you has had on me and for how important this month has been in my life.

Paulinha Vargas, fourth-year medical student

****

Our new clinic

Soon we were out of space to do all the work necessary. So in 2002, once again with donations from churches in the U.S., our association bought an adjacent house and added another building to our favela clinic. From the roof of a favela house, we had grown into a three-building Family Health Clinic. From my group of twelve students, we had become a professional group in a Family Health Program that would soon also include a physical therapy program.

****

221

Health agents at work

But there's one final story I'd like to tell about the floods of 1996. During one of the torrential storms, a mother, worried about her daughter coming home alone from school, put her two-month-old baby down on the bed and instructed her five-year-old to watch him and her younger brother and sister while she went after her older daughter.

The river by which the favela was located was overflowing and water began to enter the house. Within a short time, it had almost reached the level of the bed where the three children and the baby were huddled.

The five-year-old, though terrified, began to sing. The only songs she knew by heart were those she had learned in church school, and now she loudly repeated them. As the water rose, she sang even louder, above the noise of the wind and rain.

Suddenly, the door flew open. Help had arrived to take the children to the church, where their desperate mother now awaited them. She and the older child had been unable to get through the rising river to their hut.

"You were so smart to be making so much noise," the mother told her daughter as she hugged her, "so that people would know there was someone in that hut who needed help."

The little girl smiled and said, "We were singing so that Jesus would hear us and send help. That's why we sang."

And, she added, smiling, "He did hear us, didn't he?"

Luiza

I was born on December 18, 1958 in the interior state of Espirito Santo, in a small city called Apiacá, where I lived with my family and was taught to respect others, be humble and, above all, be honest and content with the little we had – to be loving and kind.

When I was thirteen, I went to Rio de Janeiro with my family, arriving with only the clothes I was wearing. We stayed first with an aunt, but soon rented a wooden hut in a favela. To help my parents, I began to work as a maid, dividing my time between working, studying and taking care of my brothers. I managed to complete eight years of schooling. My father was finally able to buy us a hut in a favela, and as the years went on, with a little money coming in from each of my brothers, things got gradually better for us.

When I was twenty-six, I married. My husband was an alcoholic, and our relationship fell apart. Then he got sick and died of tuberculosis, and I became a widow at twenty-nine. His death made me sad in spite of our poor relationship, but I found that by studying I was able to gain the strength I needed, and I earned my high school diploma.

I then became one of Barbara's students in the first health educators training course offered in our favela. While I was taking the course, the community experienced the tragic floods of '96, and I lost my home completely. I got a job cleaning up the mess, a difficult and unrewarding job with little pay and risky health conditions. I worked as a street cleaner for ten years, until Barbara invited me to work in the now-established family health clinic as a health educator. I jumped at the opportunity.

After a while, I was encouraged to further my studies and completed a nurse's assistant course. I then took this position at the clinic, a job I still hold today.

All my life, I attempted to take advantage of all the opportunities that came my way, like my studies, which satisfied my hunger for more knowledge, the most important thing in life for anyone, especially women. I was lucky to have marvelous people around me who recognized the potential of others and encouraged them to take advantage of opportunities to grow, not only professionally but as people.

Each day that passes, and with the experience I've been gaining, I think about how women can and should work to improve their lives, but also about the hard work that's required to achieve your dreams. One day though, they'll be rewarded for believing in themselves.

Luiza was a student in the first course I taught in Canal do Anil. She was a shy woman with no self-esteem whatsoever. I think she suffered a lot more in her life than she writes of; she's not one to complain. But in talking to her over the many years I've known her, her suffering has become apparent.

She had never had time to think or do for herself. She was quiet and studious in the health course, always worried that she wouldn't

Luiza

do well enough in the assignments. She also seemed to tire easily and often didn't feel well. When we studied TB, she had tests done that indicated she was positive and received prophylactic treatment, maybe saving her life. If she hadn't, with her many years working as a street cleaner, handling garbage and wading in sewer water, she would have been at very high risk.

I watched her during her years as a street cleaner in the community, admiring her dedication to the job, though she didn't like it. It was hard work, with long hours and little sanitation or protection. For years, no gloves or boots were provided; only in her last years on the job did these improvements come.

The woman who received the money from the city government to pay the street workers kept for herself, each week, a share of their meager salaries. They all knew this was happening, but those who confronted her were fired, and Luiza desperately needed the job. I fussed at her for accepting these conditions, but she could say nothing.

I watched her all those years, remembering what a good student she had been and how her self-esteem had improved. I wanted to hire her, but we couldn't afford to pay for another position. When a spot finally came open, I told Luiza, and she literally jumped for joy, but was afraid to tell her boss.

And she was right to be afraid: The woman said she couldn't leave, that she was contracted. She knew that Luiza was a graduate of the health educators course and trained to work in the clinic, and that she was desperate to work there, and she was determined to make it difficult for her. She told Luiza that if she left she would receive no severance pay, which is required by law, because she was quitting without notice.

But Luiza, with her ideas of how to treat people, her honesty and respect, taught from childhood, was now a different person. She knew she could do the job at the clinic, and, with her friends cheering her on, she upped and quit, ignoring the threats. She was determined now.

She became a health educator, a job she had wanted for so long. And she was a wonderful worker, soft spoken, affectionate, patient and very accurate in her analyses of people's health problems. She was also a wonderful teacher, good at providing simple explanations to the patients she visited on her rounds. She had never liked to speak up in class, but now she spoke out in staff meetings with her ideas for improvement. When the chance came for her to take a course for furthering her career, she did so, studying nights.

When I remember her as she was when I met her, all her years of suffering, the delight that shines in her eyes now as she interacts with her patients gives me so much pleasure. Another victorious woman, surmounting difficulties of class, race, illness and poverty to become what she is today. I remember her gleaming face when she was handed her diploma. She had moved mountains.

****

There's one other story I'd like to tell about Luiza.

226

There are many things we discuss in the health educators training course that won't necessarily be put into practice but that are subjects a health educator should know, like the signs of pregnancy or the kind of prenatal care necessary for the birth of a healthy baby.

These are things that, perhaps, we take for granted here in the States, but in the rural areas of Brazil babies are delivered at home. Only when families move into the big cities is hospital birth the norm. And there are still some rural people who are afraid of hospitals and treatment, and who shun prenatal care. After all, they say, our mothers and grandmothers had their children at home, there was always someone who knew what to do, and so on. They don't speak of the complications that developed and the loss of babies at birth or soon after, or of maternal deaths from the loss of blood or infection.

Throughout our course, all this is discussed, as is how to assist a woman giving birth in an emergency or what to do before help arrives. But who would imagine that this knowledge would ever have to be put to use? Certainly not Luiza.

Then one rainy afternoon when she was visiting the homes of her assigned patients, she learned otherwise.

When Luiza arrived at Maria's home, her ten-year-old daughter came crying to greet her, saying that her mother was sick. Luiza knew that it was near the time for Maria's baby to be born and had come to check on her, take her blood pressure and listen as best she could to the heartbeat of the fetus – a task Luiza sometimes had problems with, though she never ceased to try to improve, and if she had doubts she would call on the nurse on her health team.

But when she entered the tiny room and looked at Maria, she knew the time for the baby to be born had come; the bed was soaked, Maria's water had broken. At first, Luiza panicked. What to do? The daughter was crying and wringing her hands, which prompted Luiza to gather herself.

"Boil some water quickly and send your brother to get help at the clinic," she said.

227

As the water boiled and Luiza sterilized the scissors, the mother screamed, "It's coming." And sure enough, Luiza saw the head.

"Has your brother gone to get help?" she asked the daughter.

"I never found him" the frightened child said.

But now it was too late anyway. With the daughter's help, a clean towel was put under her mother and, as Luiza now recalls, she put aside her fears, leaned forward and held the baby's head as it pushed its way into the world.

A little girl! Luiza, remembering what she had to do, called out to the daughter to find some string to tie the umbilical chord. At the moment the baby let out its first wail, the brother arrived on the scene and his sister told him in no uncertain terms to get help and fast.

Luiza now said a prayer of gratitude that the baby had made a sound. As she had learned, she measured out the distance to where she should later cut the chord. Then she hesitated, filled with emotion to the point of crying.

"I have to wait," she thought. "I can't do this."

And at that moment, the doctor and nurse from the clinic arrived and took over.

To this day, Luiza remembers the thrill, as well as the fear, of delivering a baby, of helping to bring a new life into the world.

Kelly

I met Kelly in 1995 when she became my student in that first Canal do Anil course. My work in São Paulo had proved that education is the key to women's empowerment and liberation, that women could be awakened and mountains moved. Lives could be changed using a very basic course of learning about how the body functions and the illnesses that affect it and then challenging the students to go out and teach others. Kelly would be an example of this.

As I've said, most of the women I met in the favelas didn't have a complete grammar school education. Their mothers and grandmothers were brought up to believe that their place was in the home as housekeepers and mothers and that a school education wasn't necessary for that.

At sixteen, Kelly was one of two teenagers who enrolled in the class; the rest were mothers and grandmothers. Her mother was a cleaning woman and semi-literate; her father, a recovering alcoholic without a steady job. Her older brother and sister worked only intermittently.

From the outset of the course, Kelly was an excellent student and showed great interest in learning. Then came the floods of 1996. I watched Kelly as her enthusiasm for medicine grew. But could she, a favela girl with only a grammar school education, ever realize her dream of entering the medical profession?

I encouraged her to begin by finishing high school. Though she had to work to help support her family, she could go to school at night, and with the help of more donations from churches in the States she did just that.

She had dreamed of going to college. And though it had once seemed impossible, now it was going to happen. It took a year or so to find a school that wasn't too terribly expensive, and Kelly was accepted. Through the generosity of my seminary friend Lois Kitto and Jean and Ken Letterman, who I had met many years before when I had spoken at their church and who were now enthusiastic followers of our program, we got the money together for the tuition. To pay for books and supplies, Kelly taught our health educators course in several nearby communities; our association paid her a small stipend, as we did all of our teachers.

Kelly earned honors in college. In January 2006, I attended her thesis presentation. It was on understanding women's health needs in a male-dominated medical field and was very well received. As I watched, I swelled with pride. Who could have imagined that that sixteen-year-old girl, learning simple things about the body, health and sickness prevention, would stand before an audience of her peers, college professors and visitors with such poise and self-confidence?

I attended her graduation and was invited to stand with her proud parents beside her on the stage as she was handed her diploma. A true victory, mountains had been moved and still more would be in the future.

In May 2006, Kelly was hired as a nurse to work in the Family Health Program in the clinic that she had helped launch. Her dream had come true. She serves her own community in gratitude for all the help she has received to fulfill her dream.

Kelly

Mariazinha

I was twenty-two years old in 1992 when I arrived in Rio de Janeiro with nothing and no one to help me. I went to live and work as a maid with a family I didn't know. After a while, I decided to go back to school at night, and a year later left this family and went to live in the favela of Rio das Pedras.

At the end of 1995, I became friendly with a young man who was new to Rio, and, lonely as I was, I became pregnant with my first child, Vinicius. I was desperate, but didn't give up. When my labor pains began, I was terrified, with no money and nothing prepared for this birth. I went to the street and hailed a bus. I told the driver I had no money but had to get to the hospital to have my baby. I guess he felt sorry for me, because he not only let me ride the bus without paying but, seeing my pains increasing, drove directly to the public hospital, a full bus and all.

After my son was born, I wondered what I would take him home in, as I had nothing. When the time came, the nurses and aides brought me beautiful clothes to take my baby home in and a bag of diapers and clothes they collected. Plus, the nurse supervisor sent me home in a taxi! I thought, "How can I ever thank them for such a show of love?"

In February 1996, there was a terrible flood in Rio and I lost my home to the floodwaters, as did so many others. Pregnant and homeless, I went to live in a temporary shelter in a school in Rio das Pedras and waited for the mayor to give me and the others in the same predicament a place to live.

In May 1996, my daughter Larisse was born. When she was six months old, I got pregnant again and, still alone, I met Isabel Maria, a student of Barbara's who was bringing the Community Health Educators Training Course to my community. I decided then that this was my opportunity to better my life, and so in 1997 I resolved to take it, throwing myself, body and soul, into learning.

The following year, my second son, Renan, was born and in May I received the keys to my own house, one of many provided by the city government to families who had lost theirs in the floods. Once again, I decided to go back to school. I finished the community health course and with Barbara and Isabel's encouragement, I went to work with them in the family health clinic in Canal do Anil. I also finished high school.

Then the following year, my daughter Lais was born. Renan and Lais' father is with me off and on. He is addicted to drugs and is in and out of treatment, so I don't depend on him. I'm now independently raising my children.

I took a nurse's technician course with financial help from the Association of Community Health Educators, graduating in 2013. I thank God first, then these women who believed in me. I am the mother of four beautiful children and the grandmother of Larisse's daughter.

I met Mariazinha while visiting Isabel's class. I was struck immediately by Larissa, seemingly happy but emaciated. Vinicius was not much better, but he was too small to attract much attention. Larissa's tiny frame was strikingly thin and her skin was a yellowish color.

But Mariazinha was smiling and positive as she learned how to better care for her children and help others. She was bright and eager and her colleagues helped her as much as they could – the poor aiding the poorer, giving and sharing what little they had.

Then Mariazinha's life took a turn for the better when she was given her home, and she graduated from the community health course a different woman.

I really came to know her after she asked if she could volunteer to work in our budding clinic on her day off. She began to work at my side. She wanted a chance to practice what she had learned in the course; a seed had been planted. And later, when our clinic was legalized, she became a paid health educator.

Right from the start, Mariazinha wins your heart and admiration; she's always smiling and eager to learn and she has a quick, intelligent mind. She was a natural to become a nurse, and she was an inspiration to me.

Mariazinha proved that a seed planted from a basic health education course can sprout into self-esteem. Knowledge does that. Education empowers. Mariazinha has learned, most of all, to love herself, to be proud of who she is, of what she is capable of, and this drives her on. She has risen above her humble and difficult beginning, and has moved her mountains.

Mariazinha

$\sim$

Story of Beta

My name is Elizabeth, better known by my nickname, Beta. I have one child, a daughter, who is now fourteen. My parents were semi-literate people from the northeast of Brazil. They taught me what was of most value in life: to have good character in all my life's relationships.

Though my parents were uneducated, they encouraged my brother, Israel, and me to reach the highest level of education possible. In our family, no one yet had a university education. My brother was the first to finish college, eight years ago, with a degree in administration from the excellent Catholic University. And soon I will graduate from one of the best schools of higher education, the University of the State of Rio de Janeiro, with a degree in social work.

I cannot tell my life story without citing the importance of the church community of São Pedro do Canal do Anil. From birth to age thirty, I was a member of this community and had the privilege of knowing people who gave of their time for the betterment of the lives of others, without any self-interest.

These were people who helped youth in numerous educational projects and in gaining an understanding of politics – that is, a political know-how that would give us a critical vision of the cowardly politics that exist in my country. They helped guide us through a program called the Community College Preparatory Initiative for Blacks and the Underprivileged and through the Community Health Educators Training Course. I was a participant in both courses in the São Pedro community.

The Community Health Educators Training Course provided critical health information but was also a great incentive for women to exercise their citizenship, recognizing that women must be the owners of their own bodies and their own life stories. A group of students, led by Barbara de Souza, founded an NGO, the Association of Community Health Educators, which later entered into contract with the city health department to bring to the community of Canal do Anil the Family

Health Program. This provided employment to numerous women like myself who had never worked before.

This work brought so much happiness to me and my family. The same year this contract was signed, 1999, my daughter was born, and this allowed me to dream of being able to buy things I never had been able to have because of my family's financial situation.

In 2007, just before the Pan American Games [in Rio de Janeiro], the community of Canal do Anil was invaded by city officials claiming that because of very unhealthy conditions our area was uninhabitable. The authorities felt they had the right to remove families without any understanding of the social ties formed over decades.

The community reacted, and with the help and knowledge of friends of the church we began a legal struggle for the rights to our homes. Our community organizations had prepared us with the know-how and strength for the fight. As a result, the mayor was prevented from removing the families from the community. But the struggle to keep our homes in our community continues.

Beta

I am thankful to God for placing along my path such formidable people who didn't just hand me things but made me understand that I was fighting for my rights. I love these people and will be grateful to them for the rest of my life and will always carry them in my heart.

I would like to say that I am grateful for the many people who have struggled to empower me and hundreds of other women.

I hope I can find the words to describe this woman who became a representative of the disenfranchised, the political voice of her community. Though after finishing the health training course she became an employee of the Family Health Program, she didn't feel the call to work in health care. But in her work as a health agent, she witnessed the poverty of the families in her community and how they were treated by the authorities as inferior because they lived in a favela.

235

I don't know if this was all part of her awakening. When I met her, none of this "fight" for social justice was apparent. She was pregnant when she took the community health educators course. As I recall, she had lived with the father of the child in a stormy relationship, but he had been murdered. It's worth noting that in telling her story, she doesn't even mention this relationship. I believe this is because it wasn't of significance to her. She did though realize that the father of her child was a victim of poverty and an unjust social and educational system.

Through the organization for blacks and the under-privileged, Beta was able to prepare for college-entry exams. This initiative enabled participants to make up for the poor education they received in public high schools. However, as Beta tells it, when she entered college at Santa Ursala she was the only black and the only favela dweller. She sometimes went to her classmates' homes for group studies, but she would never invite them to her own home. I believe this strengthened her awareness of the unfairness of life for the poor and the uneducated. Her brother, also being very political, urged her on.

But her mother, Dona Damiana, in her quiet and determined way, is the real strength behind this remarkable young woman. Beta's father had died long before I met her. Though semi-literate, Dona Damiana was, in my estimation, far more knowledgeable in the ways of life than most people I've known. She truly made the most of what she had.

Their home was in a less developed area of the favela, built with no foundation on a muddy piece of land beside the canal. After the birth of her daughter, Beta lived in the basement of the house in one tiny room, the floor of which was always damp because of the mud beneath it. But Beta never complained because she was too busy struggling for the right of the favela dwellers to remain on the land their homes were built upon, no matter what the conditions were.

After a year at Santa Ursala, she dropped out because she didn't feel she belonged there or in the program they had assigned to her. She wanted to be a social worker. She wanted to help others straighten out their lives and fight for their rights. She had found her field, and I felt it was the right thing to choose.

I didn't always agree with some of the decisions Beta made, but I admired her struggle and determination. She did get into another college and into the program she wanted. She and her brother are constantly involved in community political activities.

I take my hat off to Beta. She is truly an awakened woman who has already moved mountains, and will move more, I'm certain!

Jupiara

To describe Jupiara, a beautiful, biracial woman, is not easy. She is a woman never to be forgotten – exceptional in her personality and determination to "be somebody." She's going to tell her own story here, but I'd first like to share a few of my impressions of her.

Jupiara has dark skin but otherwise indigenous features. She would frequently say that her ancestors were "Indians," and if you questioned this she would grow annoyed, denying her black heritage, though it was apparent in her parents and her children. She always had a story intended to prove her racial heritage. And though it wasn't really important to anyone, she was insistent.

Jupiara was another student in my very first community health course in Canal do Anil. From the beginning, it was clear that she'd had little formal education and that she wasn't very quick to learn. Much of what was taught in the class was beyond her. But she was always cheerful and laughed at herself and her errors without ever admitting that she didn't understand. Many times she was laughed at, but she remained firm in what she said and did and never gave up.

An example of how she was that no one in that class will ever forget was her cardboard doll. Each student was given the material and patterns to make a life-size doll and was instructed to draw onto separate pieces of cardboard the genitalia. We would then discuss how the menstrual cycle worked and how pregnancy occurred and could be prevented.

I told the women the doll's body and facial characteristics could be anything they wished – black, white or whatever. It was their doll but it would be later used to teach other women and thus should be recognizable as a woman. I reiterated that the doll would be presented to numerous groups and to keep that in mind when designing the doll's features.

The women were given a couple of weeks to make their dolls, and when they were completed they reflected the many races that make up the Brazilian people. Most of the women made dolls that roughly resembled themselves, though one had Asian features.

Jupiara

Then came Jupiara's doll – the woman of many colors. Each body part was a different color: one arm blue, the other green; legs, red and yellow; the face, a mixture, as was the torso.

We all laughed, but she didn't care; she had drawn attention to herself. Perhaps a psychologist would find some meaning in this. We just accepted Jupiara the way she was. She was accepted.

****

Jupiara claimed she had a high school education, but didn't have a diploma to show for it, which caused some problems when the city took over the clinic. She also claimed that she spoke English. So when a friend of my oldest daughter came to visit from the States, we paired them together.

I watched as Don and Jupiara danced together and seemed to hit it off, and I thought that perhaps this time Jupiara had been telling the truth. But when we returned home, Don asked me why I thought she spoke English. All she could say was hello and her name, he said. We smiled – Jupiara and another of her stories.

Around the same time, several of the girls working in the clinic decided they would like to learn English. They found someone who could come to the favela one afternoon a week to teach basic English – which Jupiara still insisted she knew. But as the girls told me later, not only did she not know any English, she couldn't seem to learn it, and because she couldn't the teacher had to keep repeating things, which held up the others. Soon after, they convinced her to leave the course and gave her the task of making posters.

Jupiara really enjoyed taking blood pressure readings, and as soon as she received her own kit she was off and running. We had to rein her in a bit, because she did make errors, which she wouldn't own up to until she got into trouble with a wrong reading. She had a hard time accepting her error, trying to make excuses. But we told her that a teacher would need to check all her readings until we were sure she was doing it correctly.

I think that what really appealed to Jupiara was the attention she received as she went around doing the readings. She would tell wild stories as she worked. She once told a woman that she could tell by her blood pressure that she was pregnant. This caused some worry among a few women; her classmates just laughed. This was just Jupiara – or Jupi, as she was called – always smiling and ready to go to work in the community. When the floods came, she worked even on weekends as a faithful health agent.

****

Jupiara was quite a vain woman. Messy as all get out in every way, when dressed up she did it up right; gaudy and showy, she would never be missed in a crowd.

Often when I was asked to speak about health issues, I would bring along a few women from the course. I would sometimes ask Jupi to come because she loved to do it and, being such a warm and friendly person, she made people feel at ease. But of course we had to closely monitor what advice she might give.

I was called to a meeting in the city to talk about grassroots organizations and what they could accomplish, as ours, by this time, had a solid reputation. It was in the heat of summer, well into the nineties, and as we prepared to leave we all were fanning ourselves and complaining,

240

praying that the room where the meeting was to be held would be air-conditioned.

Then Jupiara appeared. She was dressed in a thick leather jacket and long matching leggings, plus a hat and her usual long, dangling earrings. She was already perspiring as she walked to the car. We all just stared!

"Jupi, where did you get that outfit, and how could you bear to put it on today?" one of the girls asked.

She proudly raised her chin and said, "My sister got it at an international church fair and thought of me because I'm taking English classes."

"But Jupi," we said, "it's not for this weather."

She didn't bat an eye as she climbed into the car.

It was now too late for her to go home and change, and, believe me, she drew lots of attention at the meeting. But she never showed any concern, and though soaked, with perspiration running down her face, she spoke and read blood pressures, smiling all the time.

That's our Jupi, we all agreed on the ride home. Even then she didn't shed her jacket!

****

In the floods of February 1996, the area of the favela where Jupiara's home was situated was totally destroyed. Water entered everywhere and what little furniture she had was ruined, as were the walls.

During the months it took to rebuild, she, her husband and two children lived amidst mud and chaos. Watching this, I wondered how she could live as she did. The only money the family had to live on was what she made working at the clinic. Beyond occasionally collecting birds and selling them, her illiterate husband never worked. But in spite of the life she was living, Jupi was always an enthusiastic health worker, never missing a day and never complaining.

And, in fact, she raised two remarkable children. Her daughter, Rose, was a star athlete and finished high school with excellent grades. She married young and has two children who are the light of their grandmother's life. Her son, Paulo Roberto, is tall and gangly, very quiet, but a thinker. He finished high school, doing well, but didn't have much luck finding a job. When our children's program began, Jupi suggested that he help out. He did, and was wonderful; the children loved him. He proved to have a talent that neither he nor his mother knew he had: He was a born teacher.

Then, through this work, another talent emerged: He was an artist. At first, this talent was used strictly to teach the children, but later he worked with stone and tile and also made furniture, which he sold. Recognizing his valuable work with the children, our association found a way to pay him a meager salary. But even if he had earned none, his dedication would have kept him there. He painted a fantastic mural in the hall of one of our buildings.

Jupi had always spoken for her son, and it took a lot of work to get him to speak up for himself. In time though, he told me how much he wanted to go to college, to be an art teacher, a dream he felt was impossible. But with his mother's prodding, he got himself into an art program. He then met a young woman to whom he is now married. They moved away, and, though it was difficult for us to lose him, and worse for Jupi, we all felt it was best for him to be on his own.

Jupiara is a treasure just for the way she is. She finally did finish high school and continues in the clinic as a faithful health worker and, even more so, faithful to the association in all our battles with the politics that affect health programs in Brazil.

She is an unforgettable personality whose life has been changed by gaining the self-esteem so necessary for growth. She has moved her own mountains of poverty and ignorance, and has made a name for herself.

****

Now here is a short essay Jupiara wrote, describing what the health educators course meant to her:

I began to work at the age of nine, taking care of my brothers and sisters so that my mother could go to work after she separated from my dear father.

My father went to his encounter with God soon after Barb arrived. I struggled with this loss and then Barb proposed a new life that didn't seem possible, but it was a beginning. I had only lived to take care of my children, the only value in my life. With difficulty, I finished the basic school requirements, and I was proud of this, thinking that this was all I was capable of.

Then the sun shone through the clouds and the flowers bloomed with the Community Health Educators Training Course. In 1995, I saw how important it was to work towards a better future. The São Pedro Church was always open to us, and I cannot forget Father Alfonso, who was our supporter.

Then came the worst moment for all of us, the floods of February 13, 1996 that destroyed everything except our desire to work to help the community recover. It was a difficult time for all of us, but we pulled together to turn this disaster into a victory. Father Alfonso and Dr. Ana Lipke did volunteer work in our makeshift clinic on top of Dona Teresa's house. We showed the city health department what we were capable of.

And it wasn't just a few things, although I have to confess I was a bit scared. We gave vaccines, visited the sick, observed the destruction and called attention to the health issues, which brought us in contact with the health director and the eventual founding of our clinic in the favela. With the help of U.S. churches, we built the first part of a health clinic. I proudly worked as a health worker and, as the years went on and our clinic grew in size and the city health department continued to sign contracts with us, I studied to become a nurse's assistant. This was very difficult, but I had the support of so many. I was growing, and so was the fame of our clinic.

And as is so typical of Jupiara, she ends her story (which was very difficult to translate and put in some order) by apologizing for her Portuguese, and writes:

Please correct what I have written, for I have had a very hard day at work and am out of gas at home. Don't forget to write of my multi-colored doll, because for me it signifies the freedom of expression and the joy of living!

That's our Jupi, moving mountains in her own way.

Lea

Lea was an important part of my life and work, a true sister of the heart. Our lives have been entangled from the moment we met in late 1967.

First, her story in her own words:

My father's name was Sebastiao and my mother's was Zelina. I have two brothers, Antonio and Nelson. I was born in the state of Rio de Janeiro in a small city called Saint Sebastiao de Caico. When I was two months old, my family moved to the state of Quanabara and we found a place to live in the community of Tavares Bastos, a favela on a mountainside overlooking the ocean with its beautiful beaches.

We had a very difficult life growing up. We suffered a lot because my father drank so much, and when he arrived home drunk we were so frightened and tried to hide. We had no childhood, nor adolescence. My mother had to work so much to support us, washing clothes for others.

At the age of fourteen, I received working papers and got my first job, helping my mother. My brother Antonio got a job as a mechanic's assistant. It was necessary that we both work because my father spent any money earned on his drinking habit.

At seventeen, I decided I wanted to leave home to live on my own. I told my father that if he didn't stop drinking I would take my mother and my brothers with me and he would never hear from us again. As a result, he began to drink less and less and life began to get better, thank God.

I continued to live in this community, got married and had my first son when I was eighteen. Sadly though, he lived only forty-five days. I suffered so with this loss, but my faith in God comforted me.

Five months later, I became pregnant again and on September 14, 1963 my son, Rogerio, was born. I was so happy. Two years later, on August 26, 1965, my daughter, Rosane, was born. I had always wanted to have a little girl, and I thanked God for my two perfect children.

244

My life continued in Tavares Bastos, and then, in 1967, a star and a sister of the heart appeared, when Barbara and Agostinho came to live and work in the community. In 1981, they returned to the U.S. for a few years, then in 1985 went to São Paulo to work. Finally, in 1993, they returned to Rio to live in Jacarepagua, in our condominium complex.

Barbara began to train community health educators and I became a student. In 1996, I was encouraged to take a course to become a physical therapist's assistant and in 1998 I began to work with Barbara in the community of Canal do Anil, first working with patients in their homes and later in our clinic. In 2008, I received a gift: I became a grandmother to Valentina, daughter of Rogerio and his wife, Marcia.

On July 12, 2011, Barbara returned with Agostinho to the United States to live. And though a great distance separates us, her legacy lives on and we miss her.

Lea was so much a part of my life in Brazil, and all those years living far from each other has done nothing to change our friendship.

When I met Lea in 1967, we were both young, but in different places in our life journeys. She was a young mother of two and her husband worked in a hotel in Copacabana. Though they lived in a favela hut, her home was spotless and her children were polite and well cared for. She ruled them with an iron hand, and the results would be borne out in their bright futures.

Lea is a woman of little formal education but with a vision of a better life. She managed every

Lea

aspect of the family's life; she was a born leader. In those first years, 1967 to 1981, that I knew her, I watched her take on a leadership role in the community and saw her capacity to care for others. She was my assistant in our free pharmacy, which was beside her hut, watching over it when we were away. Her home was across from Dona Sebastiana's, near that of Dona Joaquina's, and she was a neighbor of Dona Maria Emilia. My beloved Dona Maria Gorda was her godmother.

I was well aware of Lea's ongoing issues with her father and observed her mother's heroic efforts to watch over her children and grandchildren. I watched her mother suffer over her youngest son's rather foolish life choices, marrying while still in his teens and soon becoming a father. Lea was always there, taking over when needed and always in charge.

In the late 1970s, Lea talked her husband, Bide, into moving out of the favela. Against his wishes, they moved to an area outside the city of Rio, to Jacarepagua, buying a small home in a housing project. It was a risk, but the visionary in Lea knew it would work. Her husband's commute to work would be a long one, but they were out of the favela and their children were in better schools. They sold their hut to us, allowing us to open our first health clinic.

When I returned to Rio in 1993, Lea had become very skilled at remodeling homes. Here again, she was a visionary. During the time I was away from her, she had redesigned her tiny home, making it unrecognizable from what it had been. She also had become a leader in her housing complex, helping to pull the community together to remodel a community center, where she then planned parties. She also became a professional cake maker. And she then launched a clothing business, going to neighboring countries where clothing was cheaper and bringing it back for resale.

****

We kept in touch throughout our years apart, maintaining our "sisterhood." I was with her in spirit when her father died and the family had to care for Dona Zelina. Thus when we were called to return to Rio to work, the only place I could imagine living was near her. And thus we once again became neighbors.

But we would soon again become collaborators as well. The favela of Canal do Anil was near where we lived, and when I began teaching there Lea wanted to get involved. She was already taking a course in physical therapy, and with her children now grown Lea was ready for a new challenge. She became my student in the eighteen-month health educators training program and began practicing what she was learning, incorporating it into her physical therapy course.

In 1998, she was introduced to Maria do Rosario, who had become paralyzed after several strokes. Maria lived in a small hut, cared for by her nine-year-old daughter, Odette. This child bathed and carried her mother wherever she needed to go. She left her alone only to go to school for four hours each day, then rushed home to change, bathe and feed her mother. She did this in the very worst of conditions: one room with no running water or toilet. Odette slept on a mat on the floor beside her mother. She had no childhood.

Lea was shocked, and went to work. She began physical therapy on this severely disabled woman and took measures to alleviate Odette's suffering. She found people to donate food and clothing and even found workers who laid water pipes into the home. Until Dona Maria died when Odette was a teenager, Lea was there for her. Though Odette was extremely sad to lose her mother, she was, finally, at sixteen, on her own, free to live her life. When she turned eighteen, Lea encouraged her to take a job as a health educator in the Family Health Clinic.

In 1997, we made space for Lea to practice physical therapy in the Family Health Clinic building, allowing her to offer her services to people who couldn't possibly have otherwise received such treatment. Lea was doing this as a volunteer, with donations from U.S. churches paying for equipment and supplies.

But as our program grew, we needed more space, and Lea set out to find herself a new location. In 2002, she found a shack for rent and, with her talent for remodeling, turned it into a charming one-room physical therapy office, a sanctuary of cleanliness and order.

Then when, later that year, we received funding to expand again, Lea moved her practice back in with us. She now had a large well-equipped physical therapy clinic and was again a part of our practice.

But physical therapy was not considered a necessary treatment by the health department and wasn't funded by the city. So in order to help finance it, we once again asked for donations from churches in the U.S., and brought in enough to hire two assistants for Lea.

In 2010, when the city created what they called social organizations to take over the administration of all the Family Health Clinics (to put a stop to the corruption they'd found with other associations), we arranged for the city to pay our association rent for the use of our buildings for the clinic. This money is used to pay Lea and her two assistants, Vanessa and Renata.

Lea has created such a pleasant atmosphere for her patients that often they're sad when their treatment is over.

Lea has come a long way from that little hut in Tavares Bastos where we met in 1967 – two young women from such different worlds – to where she is today. When I left Brazil, she took over some of my responsibilities as advisor to the clinic's employees. She's moved many mountains, and will yet move many more.

Pan American Threat

In 2007, the community of Canal do Anil became neighbors of the Pan American Games Village. The favela residents had overcome sufficient obstacles to deserve their own medals, and we at the family health clinic were witnesses to this. We had struggled with them to improve their lives as they survived the poor infrastructure of the area – the absence of sewers, paved roads and electricity and the poor health care system.

But since this community was near the apartment buildings that would house the athletes during the games, more than five hundred families were now threatened with immediate removal. Favelas are eyesores, evidence of the social and economic injustice that the city wanted to hide.

No one, however, was informed officially that there would be an expulsion of these families. Everyone was surprised when, in January, city employees representing the housing department arrived in a bus and began marking numbers on these houses with blue paint and taking pictures inside and outside of the homes. They forced those who were at home to fill out forms and sign them, with threats that if they didn't they would be penalized.

As a local fisherman who had lived in this community for thirty-two years said, "They came here, didn't speak with the community leader, the president of the association, as they should have when it concerns the whole community; didn't tell us anything. They just invaded our houses without permission."

This frightened man told the person who entered the home in which he lives with his wife and three children that his children attended school nearby and that his wife worked in a neighboring shopping center, and that it was necessary that they live here. At no time did these city employees say why they were marking numbers on these homes.

Then one day, again without warning, a bus and cars arrived filled with men who jumped out and began destroying homes with crowbars and hammers.

The startled community sprang to action. Men leapt upon the intruders, as women and children were pulled to safety. Our health workers treated the frightened and hysterical families. Others laid all sorts of barricades in the road so that no more of these people could enter. A warning shot or two was heard. Someone called the police, and soon the action was over, but not before five homes had been destroyed – five homes built through the sacrifice of poor families in search of a community in which to live and raise a family.

****

A meeting was held outside the office of the Association of Community Dwellers next to our clinic. This favela had changed, gained self-esteem, with the development and construction of its own health clinic, staffed by members of the community, and wasn't going to take this lying down.

Supporters arrived from outside the community – priests, ministers, the head of the state's human rights department, a retired judge, representatives of numerous NGOs – all in resistance to the arbitrary removal of favela dwellers.

Also present was a group of lawyers, plus members of the Catholic Church's workers' ministry and members of the Federation of Favela Dwellers.

The lawyers informed the community that there were laws to protect them from this kind of action. These laws included informing leaders of the community of the proposed action; participation of the community in the discussion of alternate plans, such as the purchase of land no farther than ten kilometers from the area; and reimbursement or the construction of other homes for the families. None of the above had been done, and there was no way it could be done successfully in the four months left before the start of the games.

When our clinic's social worker tried to speak with the person in charge of the house markings, she was told that this was none of her business. When we objected, we were threatened.

The women of the health clinic were ready for action. Once again: "When sleeping women awake, mountains will move." With the help of lawyers and others, the community began legal action against the city for ignoring laws and for the manner in which these representatives of the city government had acted when they had come to destroy homes that in some cases people had lived in for more than forty years. We then received notification from a judge prohibiting any removals or other action during Carnival, which was about to begin.

Time was now running out, and the removal plans were terminated. Other favelas weren't so lucky. But in Canal do Anil, the people had organized, and it had made the difference.

Anniversary Stories

At the ten-year anniversary of the association, Bel, now a teacher and leader of the community health education course, recruited some of the women to tell of their experiences in the health program. I'd like to share some of these stories.

My name is Lena. I was born in the impoverished interior of the state of Minais Gerais on a very hot afternoon, December 27, 1955. When I was two, my father died, and my mother, a poor widow with no way to take care of either myself or our home, abandoned me. I was raised by a neighbor and went to school until the age of twelve in a rural one-room schoolhouse. I then left home and moved to the big city alone, married and had four sons.

During the next twenty years, my routine was cleaning, cooking and caring for the children and our small garden. I saw myself as the poorest of human beings, had no self-esteem, felt betrayed and humiliated. I felt like it was the end of me! But all was not lost.

I was invited to spend a few days in Rio de Janeiro with my friend, the daughter of the woman who raised me. It was like a total explosion! This is the only word I can find to adequately describe what happened to me. While there, I was invited by Barbara to take a training course for community health educators, which opened my eyes to myself and the society I lived in.

Soon after, I received another invitation to become part of a theater group called the Theater of the Oppressed. I was excited to accept the invitation, for the name hit home: Oppressed was how I felt at this time in my life. My interest in this project and my desire to fulfill my ambitions grew stronger every day. I finished grammar school, took a nurse's assistant course and then finished high school, all at night. I then worked as a health educator in our Family Health Program. These opportunities were all made possible because of the community health educators course.

I was promoted to nurse's assistant in the Family Health Program and a leader in the Theater of the Oppressed, where I created pieces of work that I was able to use in the children's health program. And I continued to dream my greatest dream: to attend a university to become a full-fledged nurse!

Lena did realize her dream, and graduated in 2010 from the Castelo Branco University with a nursing degree and now works in the Family Health Program as a nurse.

As she said, she had been brought to the course by the daughter of the woman who raised her, Nara. Nara had decided to take the course but had to miss the first class and sent her daughter Adriana instead. Enthused by what Adriana had learned, she brought Lena with her to the second class.

Lena

Nara was shy and quiet, but not Lena. She spoke up and performed every task with enthusiasm. Her creative talents were obvious, as was her ability to express herself. She was just a born caregiver.

Lena was everywhere in the community. Her husband remained in the interior on a little farm and came to visit when he could; Lena was able to work and study as she wished. Her boys encouraged their mother during her studies and work. Her participation in the Theater of the Oppressed gave her the opportunity to meet new people and express her creative talents. As the group became more popular and traveled to other areas, Lena's world grew.

As Lena was helped by the association to pay her college tuition, she now contributes a bit of her nurse's salary each month to our association to help others gain an education. She is an outstanding person in every way. It was a privilege to know her and to watch her come to truly exemplify the title of this book.

In a poem, she wrote: "The years go by, knowledge endures./I want to be reborn." For Lena, knowledge is rebirth.

****

My name is Garcia. I came from a very poor family of six children, brought up in the impoverished interior state of Minas Gerais. In spite of it being a very difficult life, my childhood was for the most part a happy one. But my parents made it clear to me that girls didn't need to go to school to learn to read and write because their future was to marry and take care of the home and children.

I am married and have two daughters and one granddaughter. I worked in the Family Health Clinic, first as a health educator, then as a nurse's assistant. But to get to this point was a long, hard struggle. I was a housewife, mother and cleaning woman with many dreams that seemed impossible to become realities, as I had only four years of a grammar school education and no possibility of going back to school.

Garcia

Then in 1995, Barbara invited me to the health educators training course. And with this course, my whole life changed! I discovered self-esteem; belief in myself returned. These, we were told, were the objectives of the course, and that nothing was impossible as long as we knew what we wanted.

With these thoughts, I was awakened and began to value myself and seek more opportunities. I returned to my grammar school studies through a TV course that took nine months, and I was reborn. Yes, this was happening to me. I was born a new woman!

After I finished the grammar school course, I took an assistant nurse's course and then went to night school and finished high school. None of this was easy, because I had many roles to fill. But I finally succeeded in reaching my goals. It seemed like a dream come true!

But I continue to dream. I don't want to wake up until all my dreams come true because I now know that to realize one's dreams in life the desire has to come from me and my own efforts. I believe that there are ways to overcome the obstacles that appear in the paths of life.

Garcia didn't start the health educators course until the third class, but her leadership abilities were immediately

254

apparent. She was a questioner, always wanting to know more. Whatever work group she was assigned to, she was the organizer, and though she had limited school education she wrote well. She was creative and was an outstanding student. She had discovered her capacity to study and learn and she wanted more. She discovered she wanted to enter the health field and not be a cleaning woman any longer.

When our association was formed and we opened our clinic, Garcia was hired and, as she said, she knew then what she wanted to do. She and Lena soon were in night school. They finished grammar school together while continuing to work in the clinic and out in the community as health educators. Each educator had about a hundred and fifty to two hundred families to visit each month, and Garcia would get very involved in this work.

She also became a multiplier as a teacher of the course and earned extra money by taking on students of her own. With the new health manual in hand, she led groups in the course. Their graduations were victories for her as well.

Garcia did realize her dream and graduated from the Castelo Branco University in 2010 with a nursing degree. She is presently employed in the city's Family Health Program in Rio.

****

My name is Lilliam. The Community Health Educators Training Course brought about so many changes in my life. When this course came to my community in 1998, I had just been released from the detention house where I had spent four years. You can imagine how I was feeling, psychologically, economically and socially.

When we began to study sexuality, I discovered that I had an illness for which there was no cure: AIDS. It was horrible. I knew I would be discriminated against. As the course continued, I learned things that would help me help myself and other women to improve the quality of our lives and increase our self-esteem.

I finished the course and then became a multiplier, a teacher of this course in my community. I am now teaching my fourth group and am involved in various health projects in the area. Because of the course, I learned how to recover my dignity, my family and community and, I can say, my social life.

255

When Liliam first came to the class, she made it apparent that she was in control. She was a large woman, dressed very informally, with a loud, rather gruff voice. I knew nothing of where she came from or her background, only that she was a leader.

I was even more certain of this as I watched her in the working groups. She immediately took over, and the other women generally bowed to her. She was always asking questions in class and often challenged me. Many of the other women already knew each other or soon became friends, but not Liliam. She stood alone.

The sexuality part of the course doesn't come until a bit more than halfway through, when, hopefully, the women have gotten comfortable enough to open up on this very private, taboo subject. The conversation is essential to gaining self-esteem and empowerment. Women need to share their experiences of sexuality to be liberated, to own their own bodies.

Liliam, however, seemed to close up. She had begun to mix a little better and to be a bit friendlier. But when we got into the subject of sexuality, she seemed to withdraw, while continuing to ask a lot of questions.

I asked all the women to get Pap smears, mammograms and blood tests, and it was then that Liliam discovered she had AIDS. She first began to miss class, which she had never done before, and when she was present she talked loudly, controlling the discussion. When the women were asked to make posters or perform dramatizations, she dominated. She was full of ideas, which the group had to accept. She was beginning to annoy the other women. There were other women in the class who had serious health problems in their families, and they wanted more time for their issues. So I felt I needed to talk to Liliam.

It was then that she told me she'd learned she had AIDS. She asked that I keep it a secret. Of course, I agreed, but made her promise to get the proper treatment, though there wasn't much available at the time. There were rumors that you could catch AIDS in the bathroom, on the bus, shaking the hand of a contaminated person and so on. It was a time of fear and ignorance. Though the women in the course now knew none of this was true, Liliam was afraid of their reaction. She then told me that she had been in a detention home for drug use and that her former life had been quite sordid.

But she became a changed woman. She not only took what treatment was then available but began to give talks about the virus. She was such a good speaker that we suggested she start a health education class of her own. She was very bright and had done so well in the course.

Liliam went on to teach the course four times. Her first course was so popular that she had to find a larger space for the second one. The local school offered her a room.

I went to the graduations of two of her groups, and I saw the respect and love her students had for her. I was thrilled! She had truly overcome her past. She decided to finish high school and try to get into college to be a teacher. Though I lost track of her, I have no doubts that she is succeeding. She had moved many mountains in her own life and others', and would move many more.

****

My name is Isabel Maria Fernandes da Silva. I come from a family of nine children, from the northeast of Brazil, and was brought up in a very humble home, but one of respect for our mother and father.

As I remember my childhood, I remember that though I was part of a very poor and large family with so many financial difficulties – not enough food on the table for so many, used clothes that often didn't fit – I was nonetheless allowed to really be a child. And in spite of these hardships, I have

Isabel and her
daughter, Barbara

no bitterness. When I think of those times, I remember the best, the good times, and very little of the times that were not so good.

As for my adolescence, even though I had little freedom, because I was a female, to express myself, I had many dreams. I told everyone that I didn't want to marry, that I wanted to study and join the Marines.

But my plans changed when, at sixteen, I met the man who was to become the father of my daughter Thamyres, now twenty-one. I was so very young, just seventeen, when I married in 1985. What did I know of life? Though my parents also thought I was too young to marry, they agreed to it. The best that parents who were poor could wish for their daughters was to marry well.

After marrying, we moved to Rio de Janeiro. Like most women at the time, I thought that my vocation was to be a housewife and mother. But when in 1994 I began participating in my church's women's group, I was awakened to other possibilities. I went back to school and found a vocation.

Through the community health educators course, I discovered that I had a talent for health work. Encouraged by my teacher, I took a test for a nurse's assistant course at the Brazilian Red Cross college, passed and entered in January 1998. The course took a year; I then joined the health team at the Family Health Program in my community, Canal do Anil.

I just couldn't believe that my life could change so radically in such a short time! Right out of school, I was doing important work. I was also then invited by Barbara to become a teacher of her health educators course in the Rio das Pedras favela. For me, this was quite a challenge, but I succeeded.

My husband and I remained married for fourteen years and are now divorced, but I certainly don't regret marrying him. I might never have moved to Rio de Janeiro and met some of the most important people in my life.

I continue to teach the course and to work as a nurse's assistant in the Family Health Program. I love what I do. I finished high school and am taking computer courses and intend to go to college to earn a degree in teaching. This all began with a tiny seed: the Community Health Educators Training Course.

Bel did go to college – a dream she couldn't have imagined would come true – and graduated in 2014. But there's so much more to tell about her.

Bel was a student of the first community health course in Canal do Anil. She came to the course already a leader in her church community. She was married to a much older man and had a two-year-old daughter. She lived in her mother-in-law's favela hut, which she kept exceptionally clean and organized, and also cared for her husband's aunt, who was developmentally disabled.

Bel wasn't shy; she spoke out and soon demonstrated not only intelligence but leadership skills. When the time came to send the students out into the community to begin to put into practice what they'd learned, she proved to be both talented and creative. She organized projects and oversaw them. When the floods came and our group went into action, Bel was the leader. She was a force both within the clinic and out among the people.

She then took up the challenge to be a multiplier of the course, becoming a teacher. She came to me and said she wanted to offer the course in another favela that had also been hit hard by the floods. She began teaching it under the worst of circumstances, because so many of the huts had been destroyed and many of her students were living in a shelter house that the city had set up, with terrible sanitary conditions.

Despite these difficulties, Bel, with her ingenuity and creativeness, graduated her first class after two years of study and practice. And she did it all while continuing to work as a nurse's assistant and maintaining all her duties at home.

As time went on, I became more and more involved in the administration and growth of the clinic and no longer had the time to teach, and Bel took over my classes, as well as a leadership role among the teachers. She was now my assistant.

When the city health department took over the administration of our program, it made changes and demands that Bel couldn't accept. She decided to leave and devote her time to teaching the course independently.

At about this time, she and her husband separated due to his inability to accept Bel's long hours away from home and her desire to pursue further education. Though she kept her daughter with her when the child wasn't in school, he accused Bel of being a poor mother and wife. She had to leave her home, since the house was her mother-in law's, and for a while she found refuge in various places. Luckily for her, it was at the time when the houses the city had built for flood victims were completed, and so she moved into her own little home in the new community on the other side of the canal.

Our social worker had started a program for children who arrived home from school to an empty house and those who were having trouble in school and needed tutoring. The program was an immediate success and was developing wonderfully when the health department eliminated the social worker position. The children's much-needed program looked lost.

But, once again, Bel stepped in. With money the association raised from church donations, she took it over. She used her creativity to develop new learning-skill activities. She arranged for the kids to broaden their horizons by visiting museums and art shows and she started a community garden.

During these years, she found a new relationship and had another little girl, but never stopped her teaching, which she loved. And as she presided at the graduations of courses taught by former graduates, she always spoke of her desire to earn a teaching degree.

****

In closing Bel's story, I'd like to tell of a young boy whose life was deeply affected by her work in our community.

Pedro was a problem at school. Not only was he not learning but was disruptive in class. He was such a disciplinary problem that by age nine he'd been expelled from three schools. He was disliked by the other boys, causing him to be even more angry and troublesome.

One day, his mother came to us and begged Bel to take him into the children's program. The problem was that we had space for only twenty-five children in the morning and twenty-five in the afternoon, and there was a waiting list. There was no room for Pedro. His mother broke into tears; she didn't know what to do.

So Bel agreed to take him in. That semester, she had a young man volunteering to help her. He worked in the theater and as a clown, and he agreed to give Pedro some special attention.

At first, Pedro was the problem he had always been, and the other children didn't like him. But things began to gradually change; the attention he was receiving was paying off. On the day of the class Christmas party, each child in the group was asked to tell what this program had meant to him or her. Who would be first?

Pedro, standing quietly with the others around the Christmas tree, raised his hand. "I just want to thank you," he said to Bel and her young assistant, "for all you have done for me. I would like to thank my friends," turning to a couple of the boys, "for being my friends and helping me to be part of the group."

All the children clapped, and among the visitors, including his mother, there wasn't a dry eye. The American poet Ella Wheeler Wilcox wrote, "With every deed you are sowing a seed, though the harvest you may not see."

Bel may not see all that Pedro will become, but the seed has been planted. Empowered people empower others.

Bel says today, "I've acquired confidence in myself and have my dignity. I'm happy."

She has taken my place, and I see her as I was when I was young and first arrived in Brazil. She is truly moving mountains, and will move more in her lifetime.

Marinalva's Story

I could hear her singing those old northeast Brazilian country folk songs or whistling through the corridor near the pharmacy where I worked. She would smile as she went by, broom and dust rag in hand.

"Need anything, Dona Baba?" she would ask in her rural accent, smiling as she passed.

This good-humored woman is Marinalva, one of the three cleaning women we had in our clinic.

Marinalva was responsible for the part of the building where the pharmacy was. It's difficult to believe that she could maintain such an upbeat disposition given the difficulties with which she lived and of her earlier life. Marinalva was an inspiration for me and for many. Her story is a great example of how knowledge creates self-esteem and what this can mean in the life of an impoverished woman.

She was born in the rural northeast of Brazil into an extremely poor family some thirty-four years before she came to work with us in 2006. She had no childhood, beginning work at the age of ten cleaning houses for city folk. She was always eager to learn, and in spite of her hard life she kept at her schooling when she could, in a rural, poorly equipped school.

Marinalva

Marinalva married at nineteen and soon became pregnant. She lived in one small rural town, worked in another and attended the only school in the area in yet another. As the birth of her first child approached, this life became too much for her, and three months shy of completing grammar school she quit.

When her oldest child was four and her second just two, the family migrated to Rio de Janeiro to the favela where we

262

had established our health clinic. She had two brothers who had come earlier. Marinalva's husband's work experience was as a waiter and he soon found a job. But in the next few years, two more children were born and life became so difficult that they decided to return to the northeast. This back and forth is common in Brazil, from the poor areas of the northeast to the big cities in search of job opportunities, then back, homesick.

But like so many others, Marinalva and her husband found that life in the northeast was even more difficult than they remembered – no schools nearby, no public health facilities like they'd had in Rio – and after a few months, they returned to Rio. Marinalva worked as a cleaning woman or in factories before she came to work in our clinic.

She had been with us for about six months when her husband became very ill and lost his job as a waiter. Things became very difficult for Marinalva, but her disposition never changed. One day, I was told that one of her children had passed out in school from hunger. I went then for the first time to where she lived in the favela, and what I saw shocked me.

Her "house" consisted of one small windowless room with bunk beds where she, her husband and her four children lived. The children shared the beds, while Marinalva and her husband slept on mats on the cold cement floor. In the corridor leading to this room was her kitchen with an old stove and a small table with a dishpan for washing. Water came from a spigot in the wall and a crude bathroom was shared with the other families in the building.

They paid rent of about a third of their combined salaries to the owner of this shabbily built three-story building. Her husband, still feverish, was lying on the bottom bunk. I thought to myself, "How can we allow one of our employees to live like this and not do something to help?"

With the help of our faithful U.S. donors and Marinalva's coworkers, we were able to see her through these difficulties, until her husband recovered and found a new job. Marinalva never stopped working cheerfully as she cleaned the clinic and her gratitude showed in many ways.

For some time, she had been a student of our community health course. As one of the outstanding students of the group, she was chosen at graduation to read the dedication and the educators' final vows. And we had a special award for her. She was to be hired as one of the educators in the Family Health Program. No longer would she clean the building, but would be out in the community teaching others about health care.

But when I asked her for the documents required by the city health department, which included a grammar school diploma, we had a problem. We took her papers to a local private night school and were told that if she passed a test she could receive her diploma, but must continue on in the program to high school.

She passed the test, and when she arrived on November 5 of that year in her health educator's uniform, her smile was one of triumph. And though she would no longer be where I could hear her singing or whistling, she was out in the community singing that victory.

Marinalva finished high school and later took a nurse's assistant/technician course and today works in that profession. Who knows what she'll be motivated to do in the future?

Epilogue

As I look back on those women I met when I first came to Brazil whose stories I shared, I am once again amazed at the power women have, most unaware of it; but when they are, mountains move.

Remembering these stories brings back such wonderful memories. But it brings sadness too, realizing that this time of my life – a time in which every day was a challenge and an adventure, when life was full and I would often wake up in the morning feeling gratitude for the day, that I was alive and life was wonderful – is over. Yes, there were struggles, some causing stress and tears, frustration, but a battle was on and I was in it. That's all over, and the grieving process continues. I must recognize that I'm older now, and telling it all reminds me of that. It was wonderful, and I was victorious through the victories of others, the wonderful women who graced my life and made me feel worthwhile, made me know for sure that when sleeping women awoke, as so many did, mountains had moved.

I awoke to the fact that all women are marvelous, fantastic, stronger than men in so many ways; that financial poverty, poor living conditions, do not and will not stop women from changing their lives, rising above this by living with it, moving their mountains, and that I was intertwined in it all.

My mission work was in health education because I believe that the teaching of health education is a form of evangelism as we train health educators who will be going out in their favela communities to teach and train others. I would tell them that they were evangelizing. They were spreading the "Good News" of the love of Christ in the form of health education so that diseases can be prevented and people can live longer and healthier lives, so that children won't die unnecessarily and the old won't die before their time.

A conversion experience would occur as people were converted from ignorance about their bodies and their body's needs and were empowered to better care for themselves, their families and their communities. This is the Good News, especially in third-world countries where the public health and educational systems are inadequate.

Jesus cared about people's physical health as well as their spiritual health. He went about healing, preaching, empowering others with his love. These women do the same as they teach others; they empower others to better care for their own health and that of their families. They discover in the power this knowledge gives them the love of Christ. The care of one's body is a celebration of creation.

These women go on to do marvelous things as they are empowered. An example is in the health education clinic in a favela. As we told our graduating students, "Now go forth and spread the Good News of how to care for the greatest gift of all, our bodies; go forth in love and evangelize, teaching others what you have learned, converting ignorance into knowledge."

Before closing, I'd like to add something that means a great deal to me and surely makes my life worthwhile, my dreams realized, my mission accomplished.

On September 27, 2014, my husband and I had the pleasure of being at Bel's college graduation. She graduated valedictorian of her class. What a story of victory, not just for Bel, a favela woman and mother of two daughters, but a victory for me too, and for

Isabel's graduation

266

the other woman who can look to her as an example of what they can do once they are awakened. As Bel finally realized her dream of a college education, so too can they.

Bel received all the honors that could be given and a scholarship for the three years it will take her to get her master's degree in pedagogy. As I watched her standing beside the rector of the college and the professors, I was reminded of the young mother from the impoverished northeast of Brazil who had migrated to Rio in search of a better life.

Bel has moved mountains and so have others that I had the privilege of knowing, and there will be many more. Because the seed has been planted and as it grew to fruition in Bel, so it will in others.

****

How could I ever have known that my life would have such an effect on others, and these lives on me, when I was just me – no intellectual, just someone who loved these women; who had questioned injustice but had been unaware of the depth of the injustice dealt out to women in so many countries; who grew with each group; who learned how women, in spite of the poverty and of being female in a macho culture, could become aware of their power, their strength, their independence. "I can do it. I did it."

We would talk about power, that it can be used wrongly when it's not shared or it's used to lord over another. I used myself as an example. I said, "When we began this course, I had all the power because I had the knowledge; I knew the subject matter. Then as time went on and you learned all that I knew, I no longer had power. We were equal."

And, I added, they too would have the same experience as they taught other women what they had learned. With each group I taught, I was awakened to what is possible, to what I could do. I too was awakened to my own capabilities, my own talents. And as I saw the changes in these women and the mountains they moved once awakened to their own capabilities, I was able to move mountains of my own.

There is just no way I can put into words accurately my feelings about these forty years living and working with these women who became community leaders, demanding better health care, building a clinic. We became well known in the area and were able to walk among the health authorities and be heard. We were called to make political talks and demands in front of many, and when the favela was to be wiped out we were asked to stand up and speak and be heard.

But it was not my person or power alone: It was these women behind me. We were together in this battle.

Appendix 1

Women's Rights in the Home, the Community and Society (written in the late 1980s by the São Paulo course groups):

1. The right to be respected as men are at all levels of their professional lives and society
2. The right to be heard
3. The right to the same jobs as men
4. The right to the same salary as a man when the professions are the same
5. The right to marry whomever they wish
6. The right to choose their own religion
7. The right to be respected physically
8. The right to good health care
9. The right to study family planning
10. The right to schooling (study) at any age
11. The right to participate in social actions
12. The right to choose their clothes, cut their hair, use makeup
13. The right to plan the number of children they want and to choose the method of contraception
14. The right to advise in a family matter and to educate their children
15. The right to work in the community and church
16. The right to independence, to decide for themselves, to not be dominated by husbands; in other words, the freedom to act separately from husband, father, brother
17. The right to have their own opinions, choose their political party and to vote for whom they wish
18. The right to have sex when they feel like it and to know about their own bodies' function

19. The right to work outside the home and decide how to use the money they earn
20. THE RIGHT TO BE THE SUBJECTS OF THEIR OWN HISTORIES and not the objects
21. The right to vindication; that is, to make a denunciation if they are beaten, abused verbally or humiliated
22. The right to be responsible for their actions
23. The right to say no whenever they wish and be respected for this
24. The right to a place where they can receive help solving problems
25. The right to the freedom to be correct or to err
26. The right to complain when they feel things are going wrong
27. The right to be a single mother and not be discriminated against; that is, to have the same rights as a married mother
28. The right to go to the doctor alone if they wish
29. The right to make decisions for the family, even financial ones
30. The right to give their children permission to go out without asking the father
31. The right to decide their own futures
32. The right to be free in every way, and the right to know their rights.

Donas das suas proprias vidas!

Appendix 2

Durvalina was a student in one of my health education courses. At the end of the course, I asked the students to write or draw something about how this course might have changed their lives. Durvalina's story symbolizes the acquiring of the self-esteem necessary for the empowerment process.

First she shows how she had seen herself: a prisoner in her own home unable to become involved outside the home, for home is where women are supposed to stay.

Then she shows herself leaving her house and, over the disapproval of her husband, she says, "I'm going [to the health education class]."

The third picture shows her going into the church where she learned about the course.

The fourth picture shows her going to the health education classes.

The fifth picture shows her becoming a multiplier: a teacher of the course herself.

And, finally, she sees herself empowered to do more things as she learns to drive. She has gained the self-esteem necessary to follow her dreams.

271

CPSIA information can be obtained
at www.ICGtesting.com
Printed in the USA
FSOW03n0446270117
30004FS